A SOCIAL HISTORY OF THE ENGLISH COUNTRYSIDE

A SOCIAL HISTORY OF
THE ENGLISH
COUNTRYSIDE

G. E. Mingay

ROUTLEDGE
London and New York

First published 1990
by Routledge
11 New Fetter Lane, London EC4P 4EE

Simultaneously published in the USA and Canada by Routledge
a division of Routledge, Chapman and Hall, Inc. 29 West 35th Street, New York,
NY 10001

© 1990 G. E. Mingay
Typeset in 11/12 Bodoni by
Butler & Tanner Ltd, Frome, Somerset
Printed and bound in Great Britain
by Butler & Tanner Ltd

British Library Cataloguing in Publication Data
Mingay, G. E. (Gordon Edmund)
A social history of the English countryside.
1. England. Rural regions. Social life, history
I. Title
942′.009′734

Library of Congress Cataloging in Publication Data
Mingay, G. E.
A social history of the English countryside/G. E. Mingay.
p.   cm.
Includes bibliographical references.
1. England – Rural conditions. I. Title.
HN398.E5M57   1990
307.72′0942 – dc20   89-70221

ISBN 0 415 03408 6

CONTENTS

ILLUSTRATIONS

ACKNOWLEDGEMENTS

Thanks are due to the following for permission given to reproduce the illustrations specified: Aerofilm Ltd (figure 1); The Institute of Agricultural History and the Museum of English Rural Life, University of Reading (figures 2–6, 12, 13, 15–20, 23, 25, 26 and 28); British Museum (figures 11 and 14); *Country Life* (figure 21); Mr J. Styles, University of Kent at Canterbury (figures 22 and 24); and C. P. Davies Collection, University of Kent at Canterbury (figure 27).

INTRODUCTION

This study of the rural past is essentially a group of essays dealing with some of the major aspects of rural society as it developed through the centuries, and with the economic and agricultural setting in which that society moved. In some degree the choice of the topics is a personal one, reflecting the interests and knowledge of the writer; but in some degree also the material has been chosen with the purpose of providing the reader with a rounded picture, and, so far as is possible, a realistic and informed one. That picture can be only an interim view, and the conclusions drawn from it must be provisional in nature, for there can never be a final word in history. Research continually produces new material which in time modifies established views, and the interests of historians themselves change over time, influenced in part by fashion and by the issues which affect their own immediate society. This book would have been written very differently when the author was himself a student, and no doubt it will be very different again if attempted after the lapse of another thirty or forty years.

The emphasis of the volume is on the changes of the eighteenth and nineteenth centuries, with which the author is most familiar, but which also are the more relevant for understanding the transformation to the industrial and commercial urbanized society of our own times. It was in these centuries that agriculture began its long decline from being the predominant occupation of the people to becoming only one of a number of equally important sources of employment; it was consequently the period in which typical English people ceased to get their income directly or indirectly from the soil and became town-dwellers.

*   *   *

We begin, however, back in early times with the formation of village communities. Immediately we run up against one of the great problems of trying to create a broad picture of the past: that of regional and local variations. England is a small country, but it is rich in the variety of its topography, its natural conditions, and its ethnic and cultural origins and traditions. The regional historian, even more the local historian, can explore such variety in depth, and indeed the history of each individual hamlet, village or country town has a strong element of the unique. The historian who seeks to draw the national picture cannot hope to do justice to this diversity, though he or she cannot ignore it, and awareness of it will temper any observations and attempts at generalization.

Because of local influences the pace and nature of change in medieval England were themselves extremely varied. Nevertheless, there were some long-term factors of a more general kind, which we believe to have exerted widespread, though not uniform, effects throughout the country. Among these pride of place must be given to the growth and waning of population, and the consequences that greater or fewer numbers had for markets and prices, and for labour supply and the demand for land. The period from Domesday to the fifteenth century was not, of course, one of a slow steady advance in population numbers, nor in production methods and living standards. Though scholars differ in their analysis of cause and effect, and particularly in the ways in which they present differences in regional experience, the accepted general picture is one of mounting population pressure leading up to a crisis in the early fourteenth century, the crisis then followed by a severe decline in numbers and subsequently a gradual recovery. Population was not the only factor, but its rise and fall played a major role in loosening the ties of duties and obligations which circumscribed rural life in the early middle ages, so that the society which entered on the sixteenth century was in many ways radically different from that which was dominant two or three centuries earlier.

Disease, together with famine, had a devastating influence in the crisis of the fourteenth century, reducing the population, and even in some cases threatening the very existence of rural communities. Yet in subsequent periods, with the prime exception of the Great Plague and Fire of London of 1665–6, natural disasters and their effects largely sink from view. There were, of course, many causes of sickness, incapacity and premature death, but it is somewhat strange that relatively few historians, apart from demographers, have concerned themselves with the consequences of disease for the growth of population and the state of the people's health, to say nothing of the effects on the supply and efficiency of the labour force. Only a very little examination of private correspondence in past centuries reveals how preoccupied people were with their health and that of their families, their dread of vagrants who might be carriers of some noxious malady, their alarmed reports of outbreaks of smallpox or typhus in nearby towns and villages, and their anxious collecting of information on remedies and treatment. So pervasive were the common dangers to health in the current of daily life that we have gathered together some material on the subject in the third chapter of this book.

As population increased and declined, as techniques developed and production expanded, so living standards changed over time. Fundamentally, living standards depended on the current balance between population and production, tending to rise when the second exceeded the first. But the situation of individual families was more closely influenced by the distribution of income and wealth, and by the large gap which existed between the means of the rich and the poor. 'The poor', a common description of the labouring class, were always numerous, though differences between them depended on such factors as occupation (or combination of occupations), on access to land or lack of it, and on the nature and fortunes of the local economy. The rural labourer's standard of life depended on the value of his earnings in relation to the prices of food and other necessities (though payments were commonly made partly in kind), the contribution which might be made from a possible right to graze the common and grow his own produce, the nature of his housing, the availability of fuel, his customary diet, and many other conditions which varied locally in great degree. In particular, the life of many of the poor was influenced by institutional changes in the system of poor relief and the Settlement Law, by legislation against poaching, and by the enclosure of open fields, commons and waste lands. The last, after a hundred years of research and discussion, remains a matter of controversy, not least because of local variations in its nature and effects and the paucity of hard evidence as against assertion.

At the apex of rural society stood the landowners, whose incomes ranged upwards in the eighteenth century from as little as £50 a year to many thousands, equivalent at the highest levels to those of multimillionaires living in a tax haven today. They controlled much of the country's land and commanded wide-ranging influence on farming, on politics, and on local government and village society. Their concerns were naturally with property and the means by which it might be acquired and preserved, while the great country houses, frequently much expanded in size and opulence in the course of the eighteenth and nineteenth centuries, might be influential centres of political discussion, county administration and, not least, sport. Their personal control of a large proportion of the countryside's inhabitants was reinforced by a connection (often a family one) with both the parish and the higher clergy.

In common with the landowners themselves, the country parsons differed in the priority they were prepared to give to the sustaining of conventional morality and amelioration of the conditions of village life. There were many whose love of society and enthusiasm for sport involved a near-total disregard of their parochial duties, the services taken by a wretchedly paid curate, the church and parsonage allowed to fall into decay. Again, not a few parsons were chosen to serve as magistrates, and indeed were often among the more active in the pursuit and punishment of wrongdoers. This office, combined with aristocratic connections and a superior education and lifestyle, alienated them from the ordinary villager, who saw in the parson only an extension and close ally of the squirearchy. There were others, however, who resided constantly in their parishes and sought funds to repair the fabric of the church and rebuild the parsonage house, who introduced schools, benefit clubs and allotments for the poor, who did what they could to relieve illness and poverty, improve cottages and remove dangers to public health, and who tried generally to leave the village a better place than they found it. In time, with the rise of Nonconformity, many villages saw a political, religious and social division form between church and chapel, with the parson and preacher ever at loggerheads, the one associating with the squire, larger farmers and wealthier tradesmen and craftsmen, the other with the smallholders, petty tradesmen and labourers.

Up to the latter part of the nineteenth century the countryside was often far from being the haven of uninterrupted peace and pleasure that is sometimes supposed. True, there were village feasts and celebrations and occasions for sport and merriment, while bucolic somnolence was dispelled by visits of troupes of travelling players, by the rounds of carriers, hawkers, cheapjacks and owners of performing animals, by vendors of patent medicines and tracts, and many others. But there were also highwaymen, footpads, housebreakers and armed gangs of robbers, smugglers and poachers. Some villages were notorious for being the homes of lawbreakers, and for their drunkenness, brawling and drug-taking. In times of scarcity there were numerous food riots, attacks on corn merchants and millers, and seizures of supplies on their way to market. After 1815, with higher unemployment, inadequate wages and tighter restrictions on poor relief, the grievances of the poor exploded into rioting on a more threatening scale. Mobs of angry, hungry people attacked merchants, shops and inns in East Anglia in 1816, again in 1822, and most alarmingly in the much more widespread Swing riots of 1830–1, when demands for higher wages were accompanied by attacks on labour-saving threshing machines. In Wales, on the border of Pembrokeshire and Carmarthenshire in the 1840s, the consequences of rather different grievances were the Rebecca riots, which also had to be suppressed by use of troops. And every year until about mid-century there were local outbreaks of arson, maiming of animals, destruction of machinery, and attacks on the homes and property of unpopular farmers, magistrates, parsons and Poor Law overseers.

Many of the upper classes viewed unrest primarily as being a result of ignorance, and saw an answer in the provision of schools and the preaching of self-help. In fact, however, the decline of rural unrest owed more to the new opportunities of employment provided by the railways, the rise of industrial towns and the possibilities of a better life there or abroad. Migration from the countryside increased, and by the late nineteenth century had become so extensive as to give rise to much concern about the 'flight from the land' and its consequences for agricultural production, for urban overcrowding and employment, and for the nation's reserves of able-bodied countrymen of good physique to supply recruits to the army and the police force.

The flight from the land coincided with a prolonged downturn in the prosperity of farming which had far-reaching effects on the stability of landowners and farmers alike. Old-established landed families gave way to newcomers from industry and commerce, and many found it increasingly difficult to maintain country mansions and keep up their traditional way of life. As the old-style farmers gave way in the face of low prices and bad seasons, to be replaced by newcomers who farmed more economically, so the relations between owner and farmer, the old landlord–tenant partnership, deteriorated. The decline was accelerated by the gradual erosion of the political power of land. The extension of the franchise to a wider, largely urban, electorate, the secret ballot, the supremacy of the town consumers' concern with cheap food over the protection of agriculture, all signified the approaching eclipse of the landed interest. And at the local level, many of the old powers and functions of the magistrate-squire had come to be lost to elected Boards of Poor Law Guardians, Watch and Highway Committees, School Boards, County Councils, Rural District Councils and even Parish Councils. In this welter of change the squire clung on to some declining degree of influence, often becoming prominent on the new elected bodies, for example, but the old days of undisputed power and authority had gone.

By 1914, although farming conditions were somewhat improved, the political and economic decline of land had been made only too evident by the new taxes of the Liberal government, by the enforced impotence of the House of Lords, and by radical assaults on the competence of landowners and farmers. They were accused of failing to keep farmland in production, of failing to house farmworkers properly, and of failing to pay them adequate wages. The farmworkers, though still very poorly paid and often badly housed, it is true, were nevertheless considerably better off in terms of real income and home comforts than perhaps ever before, and certainly since the deprivation experienced in the early nineteenth century. With this partial exception, the countryside as a whole was in decay, with landowners obliged, or even anxious, to sell off estates, with farmers forced by foreign competition to resort more to grass or turn to fruit, vegetables and poultry while still finding it hard to make ends meet. Old family houses were shut up or sold and converted to other uses, the shooting let out to wealthy businessmen. Villages near major cities saw an irruption of villas built by well-to-do middle-class commuters, and many country towns faded into torpor as their accustomed trades and crafts became increasingly obsolete. The changes produced by the shift to a new industrial and commercial society, based in swollen cities and expanding new towns, were now painfully obvious. In 1914 the shift had been developing for well over a century, but its consequences were not at first immediately damaging to agriculture, and indeed much of the early expansion of industry occurred in the countryside. Only after the coming of free trade, and the rapid growth of the world economy from about 1870, did the change prove disastrous to the rural community. By the eve of the First World War nearly half a century of more rapid transition had enmeshed that community in continual response to external forces which it could not control. And though the effects were still not yet fully worked out, it was very clear that a great transformation had occurred: the rural population, and the occupation which supported it, once the mainspring of both government and economy, had wound down to become a disregarded appendage of the industrial state.

1

LORD AND PEASANT

Twentieth-century English people have lived through an age of rapid change when ancient country towns have sprouted industrial estates and 'enterprise zones', their high streets have become cluttered with cars and vans, traffic lights, 'street furniture' and pedestrian crossings, and their old-established road patterns disrupted by motorways and by-passes. The villages, similarly, have been strangely altered by an alien rash of commuters' villas and unimaginative rows of drab council houses, while mellowed Tudor and Georgian cottages have been disfigured by the intrusion of modern shop-fronts and ice-cream signs. Such changes make one more prone to believe in a past which was unchanging, or at least more reassuringly stable. But, as Christopher Taylor has remarked, 'all we have today is the latest phase of change, more violent perhaps than before, certainly faster than that in previous centuries, but a direct descendant of it, and merely part of the same ebb and flow of the tide of human occupation'.[1]

Indeed, the pattern of rural settlement in the past was much more fluid than may be commonly supposed. Some hamlets grew into large villages, while others declined to a solitary house or two; some villages grew only to fall away again, and many settlements, usually the smaller ones, disappeared completely, their existence known only by some chance mention in the records or by telltale signs of former foundations and enclosures which may best be seen from a low-flying aircraft in the evening light. Strangely enough, numbers of settlements did not disappear completely but changed their site for another, often one nearby, perhaps a mile or two away, leaving stranded in the fields a lonely church with perhaps the traces of a former manor house or castle.

The factors in this 'settlement drift', and in village growth and decline, were various, and at this distance in time it is often impossible to do more than guess at what they may have been. We know from modern instances that the decisions, sometimes eccentric, of an individual or of government, may bring about changes which would otherwise be inexplicable, and no doubt there were many examples in

1

the past which, if we knew the facts, could be put down to the same irrational sources. Lacking such knowledge of individual motives, historians have singled out certain physical influences, such as intractable or infertile soils, situations too exposed to the elements, or even gradual changes in climate, which reinforced other reasons for change. Forces of undoubted long-term significance were the movements in population: the considerable growth in numbers in the early middle ages, when the population of Domesday, probably between 1.75 and 2.25 million, grew to reach perhaps as many as 4.5, 5 or even 6 million in the middle fourteenth century – a level not to be exceeded until the seventeenth or eighteenth century. This period of expansion was followed by a subsequent decline to a figure of only some 2.5–3 million in the later fourteenth and fifteenth centuries.

With changes in population went changes in the availability of land and labour and in the demand for food, with consequent effects on land use. When the population was growing, arable or mixed farming concerned primarily with the production of bread grains expanded, with cultivation spreading into former forest and waste lands, encroachments on village greens and extensions of village housing, sometimes in an organized or planned manner. The increased demand for land meant that some new settlements grew up in formerly unattractive upland areas, on bleak heaths and moors, even 1,200 feet up on the eastern edge of Dartmoor. When the population fell, however, and economic conditions were reversed, there was a retreat of cultivation. Farms in marginal areas, where soils, altitude and climate were not well suited to grain production, went out of arable and might be converted to pasture for sheep or cattle, or perhaps abandoned altogether. The shifts in village locations and the advance and retreat of the limits of settlement, associated with the surge and subsequent decline in population, indicate that the country people of medieval England were a good deal more mobile than was once thought. In law the unfree cultivators (as distinct from the freeholders) were strictly bound to their manors, but in practice many obtained the lord's permission to move away (which might be readily granted when the population was rising and labour was plentiful). Others simply thumbed their noses at the law and ran away to seek a better life in sparsely populated districts where land was available, or to find other kinds of work in the expanding towns. There was, furthermore, a measure of seasonal migration of workers round the countryside in the busy seasons.

Local studies have revealed that deserted village sites are very numerous, and some 3,000 of them have been pinpointed. As just noted, some of these disappearances were due to population decline and the reduced profitability of grain production in the later middle ages, but many villages were abandoned for quite other reasons and in earlier times, even well before the medieval period. Farming on marginal lands was made more hazardous by climatic change from the late thirteenth century, when the weather became colder and wetter and crop failures became more numerous. Conversion to grazing for sheep or cattle was then perhaps the only way of giving many families a livelihood and, since less labour was required, met the conditions of reduced availability of workers in the later middle ages. The fortunes of some villages, undoubtedly, were adversely affected by the famines and epidemics of the fourteenth century. Disastrous seasons, as in 1315, when torrential rains ruined crops and flooded pastures from May until the autumn, led to starvation among the human population and heavy losses of livestock. The decline of flocks and herds was intensified by a murrain which followed among the cattle, leaving pastures empty and ploughs bereft of their teams of oxen.[2]

The Black Death, though commonly blamed for the decline of villages and the phenomenon of isolated or ruined churches, was not generally a major factor: for example, of eighty deserted sites in Northamptonshire only two can definitely be ascribed to the great pestilence. Some villages were indeed devastated by plague, but subsequently recovered, or were re-established nearby. Usually the Black Death helped further to weaken settlements that were already in decline, or began a process of destruction that other forces completed.[3] This is not to say that the plague was not gravely damaging. Even in a sparsely populated district like medieval Swaledale it is thought possible that colonies of rats in outlying farmsteads served to transmit the disease from one settlement to another, and certainly eight of the eleven Yorkshire churchyards specially dedicated for the burial of plague victims were in the very north of the county.[4] In Nidderdale about half of the land held on customary forest tenure was vacated through deaths in the year 1349–50, and the work of clearing new land for cultivation was brought to a halt. In this same terrible year 45 per cent of the beneficed clergy in the Archdeaconry of the West Riding, the rectors and vicars, met their end.[5]

Throughout the medieval period, and indeed earlier, a number of other factors operated to create new settlements or to cause the decline or migration of old ones. Ancient fortresses were abandoned, leading to the migration of the farmers and craftsmen who had formerly found shelter and profit close to their walls, while newly built castles encouraged a movement of people to their sites. Changes in road patterns and the building of bridges attracted people who came to cater for the needs of travellers. Some small settlements, especially in northern upland areas, were displaced to make way for religious houses, as in the wastes of Yorkshire, where the Cistercians brought sheep

3

and cultivation to their abbeys of Rievaulx, Byland, Fountains and Jervaulx. Some other villages were lost through the inroads of the sea – such as Dunwich on the Suffolk coast (which, however, long continued to return members to Parliament). French raiders, crossing the Channel, periodically ravaged Sussex ports such as Rye and Winchelsea, the Welsh made incursions into neighbouring parts of England, and in the northern border counties the marauding Scots spread destruction over a large area already laid waste by William the Conqueror. Even the North Riding of Yorkshire was not spared the attention of the Scots when the English defeat at Bannockburn in 1314 left the roads south open to the invaders. Homes were burned, their inhabitants taken prisoner, cattle driven off, and those who resisted put to the sword. In 1318 the Scots penetrated so far south as to plunder and burn such towns as Northallerton, Boroughbridge, Ripon, Knaresborough and Skipton. The wealthier inhabitants of these places were able to save themselves by paying tribute, or by flying to some place of safety, such as Richmond Castle, but so general was the destruction that 128 villages in the North Riding were relieved of having to pay a subsidy to help fight the marauders, 'because of Scots damage'.[6]

In the west midlands, where deserted villages were numerous in both low-lying river valleys and clayland plains, and also on the Cotswold hills, the abandonment of settlements had a long history, going back – as throughout England – to the Anglo Saxon period. Later desertions were especially numerous in the hundred years after the Black Death, though again the plague seems mainly to have had the contrasting effects of both weakening settlements and creating opportunities for survivors to take up vacant holdings elsewhere. The process of decline was protracted, most villages that were destined eventually to disappear not succumbing immediately after the plague: many still held some inhabitants a generation later, as we know from the poll taxes levied in 1377–81. The key factor in decline was not so much the direct effects of the plague and the fall in population as the indirect influences on migration as holdings on better land were left vacant and landlords relaxed their attempts to restrain mobility. Even relatively stable villages, we are told, experienced a turnover of families as high as 75 per cent over a space of some fifty years, while declining villages saw a much higher level of movement. The reduced demand for grain in this period made more attractive the areas where grazing, or some more flexible form of mixed farming, could be carried on, in contrast to the greater rigidity of farming committed to common-field arable. Although generalizations are difficult, common characteristics of deserted villages included the inherent weaknesses that they were seldom large and were often secondary settlements, not the chief villages of a parish. They were also generally very close to neighbouring settlements, so that as many as four-fifths of deserted villages in Worcestershire lay within a mile of another village. Indeed, desertion may be seen 'as the thinning-out of a countryside over-stocked with villages'. Finally, they were predominantly agricultural settlements: villages that were much engaged in industry, such as in cloth-making districts in Gloucestershire or metal-working ones in south Staffordshire, did not feature in the list of deserted settlements.[7]

*   *   *

Settlements took many forms, and the nucleated type of village which is often thought of as typical of England, was in fact rare in the south-west of the country and over large parts of East Anglia and the south-east. The nucleated village appeared around the beginning of the eleventh century, and came to dominate about a half or a little more of the countryside: it was closely associated with the development of the common-field system of arable farming, particularly on the midland plain, though even there many hamlets and isolated farmsteads were to be found. Elsewhere, in the highland zone, in the extensive forested areas and on heaths and moorlands, scattered hamlets and solitary farms were the common elements of a very old dispersed pattern of settlement, the sites of numbers of them being under continuous occupation since Anglo-Saxon times. As the population expanded in the early middle ages lowland areas became more densely peopled, while further dispersed settlements were established by the 'assarting', or clearing, of waste land and forest carried out by individual farmers and small groups of settlers. The new placenames – Southwaite ('damp, sour clearing') and Roundthwaite ('clearing of the mountain ash') in the fells of Westmorland, for example – commemorated the work of the pioneers. The use of moors and heaths to graze sheep, as undertaken by the Cistercian abbeys, saw isolated homes built to house the shepherds, just as extensive rabbit warrens required dwellings for the warreners. The concept of the parish as an ecclesiastical and administrative entity preceded the middle ages, going back to the estate of Roman times, and long pre-dated the building of Christian churches. The coming of Christianity, late in the sixth century, led however to the imposition of tithes to maintain the village priest, and, since the value of the tithes depended on the yield of the parish, this created the need carefully to establish and maintain the boundaries of the village lands, though it might be many years before all the land in the parish was in constant use for some form of production.[8] Generally, as the numbers of villages and hamlets grew, the very large original parishes were divided up, the new boundaries often becoming identical with those of the village.

Detailed investigation has shown that a surprisingly large number of medieval villages were laid out on some kind of plan, set out systematically along a road for example, or round a village green. The planning of a site was often associated with new settlements, especially in the northern counties when they were re-established after the harrying of the north by the Conqueror. Planning was also involved in new sites elsewhere, and there is evidence from earthworks, building debris and unearthed fragments of pottery of some degree of planning in old villages, perhaps when for some reason the centre of the village or alignment of the houses was changed, or an extension made to accommodate a larger population.[9]

Some planning, or at least a large degree of communal agreement, was involved in the creation of the common-field system of farming. The gradual clearance of land for cultivation would normally proceed outwards from the original nucleus of settlement, with each successive new intake of cleared land forming a private enclosure if the work of one family, or added to the common fields if cleared communally, and then called a 'furlong', though this term did not connote a precisely measured area of ground. Furlongs were frequently of between 5 and 15 acres, but could be smaller or, indeed, very much bigger. The villagers would expand their fields as needed, but not without some measure of organization. Natural obstacles, as well as soils and aspect, determined the location and limited the freedom of choice of new intakes, and the best-watered fertile land, as that by a stream, was reserved as a communal meadow for making the invaluable hay. Surplus land was kept as a common pasture for the village livestock to graze in summer, heavily timbered areas were reserved for the benefit of the building timber, firewood, the making of poles and hurdles and the beechmast for the pigs, while the poorest land was left as 'waste' to be used for cutting turf, quarrying sand or stone, snaring rabbits, and as additional rough grazing as needed. Some of this waste land might never be reclaimed for cultivation if the population remained small or if the land was so poor as to be not worth the effort of clearing. Indeed, some waste lands were not exploited until the near-famine conditions of the Revolutionary and Napoleonic Wars at the end of the eighteenth century made enclosure highly profitable and drove the plough on to bleak moorlands and up steep hillsides.

The 'classical' three-field system – two crops and a fallow – was neither uniform nor ubiquitous. There might be two, three or more fields, and the number of fields might be increased when circumstances made this desirable. In any event, the crop rotation was not necessarily connected closely with the number of fields, but rather with the furlong. Groups of furlongs formed the basis for the pattern of cropping and fallowing. In some parts of the country, in northern England, East Anglia and the south-east especially, the field 'system' was in fact highly irregular, and further, where the cultivated lands consisted of assarts from woodland, as in the Kent and Sussex Weald and the midland forests of Sherwood, Charnwood and Rockingham, the holdings were made up of enclosures, and common fields were absent. And again, in those forested and upland areas where the soils were thin and infertile any common arable fields were small and served only to supplement a livelihood which came mainly from the grazing of stock, the manufacture of wooden articles such as barrels, tubs, staves and poles, or some branch of the textile industry or of iron-making. In such areas, too, an 'infield–outfield' type of farming was pursued, where only the best land, usually that near the homestead – the infield – was cultivated regularly, supplemented as required by temporary intakes further off – the outfield – which were cropped for a few years and then allowed to revert to waste.

Climate and relief, of course, largely determined the division between the more pastoral north and west and the more arable south and east. But this division, though fundamental, was never hard and fast, as considerable arable districts were established in the predominantly pastoral west (such as the Vale of Glamorgan and the Vale of Taunton Dean), while in the predominantly arable east there were also large pastoral areas (such as the meadows along the Trent Valley, a large part of Suffolk, the Weald of Kent, and the sheep grazings on chalk and limestone hills and wolds). A sheep–corn form of husbandry flourished on the upland wolds of Yorkshire and Lincolnshire, and on the downs of the Chilterns and Cotswolds, where the shallow soils were made to bear good crops by the night-time dunging of the large flocks of sheep kept during the day on the hill pastures. The arable heart of England, the broad midland plain, came to be covered by large common fields supported by their accompanying meadows, commons and wastes, by which the cattle and sheep were maintained during the summer months. On the western borders of the midlands, however, common-field arable gave way to pastoral vales where livestock predominated over the plough, and indeed over much of the midlands the farmers had some degree of choice between leaning more towards arable or more towards fattening and dairying.

Specialized fattening and dairying came to be established on the rich grass of marshland areas, such as the Romney Marsh in Kent and Sussex, and the Thames-side marshes of Essex. Extensive heathlands, with their thin sands and gravels, as in East Anglia, carried great flocks of sheep to fertilize and consolidate with their treading the arable fields; while elsewhere small patches of heathland supported smaller flocks used to support the farmers' main activities of fattening or dairying on the better soils nearby. In the forest districts, such as Nottinghamshire's Sherwood, Leicestershire's Charnwood and Hampshire's New Forest, the sheep, together with small intakes of cropland, were used to supplement woodland and industrial occupations, or the keeping of pigs and ponies. The fells and moors of the Pennines and northern border country, the North York moors and the south-western wastes of Dartmoor, Exmoor and Bodmin, were necessarily pastoral, with cattle on the lower slopes and sheep on the exposed hills, though sheltered valleys could be made to produce hay and some crops of oats, barley or rye, perhaps on an infield–outfield system or in small common fields. Lastly, the inhabitants of the extensive fenlands around the Wash, the estuary of the Humber and the Somerset Levels, employed their rich river-borne silts to fatten cattle and produce dairy products, with some limited ploughlands used for subsistence, supplemented by fish, wildfowl, osiers and willows for making baskets, reeds for thatch, and peat for fuel.[10]

It is very evident that natural conditions make English farming highly diversified, and this was true even in the middle ages, when limitations on movement and high costs of transport forced most country people to practise some degree of subsistence farming, so that even areas best suited to grazing had their patches of arable, while many arable farmers relied heavily on sheep for their manure (and the secondary considerations of their wool and mutton), and kept a cow or two in the dairy. It is therefore quite inappropriate to see the countryside as entirely dominated by the common arable fields, which in many districts were unknown, or existed only in a limited or modified form.

Nevertheless, common fields dominated the midlands, and in the middle ages and for long after, could be widely found elsewhere. The basis of the system was the existence of common rights. Each farmer had the right to pasture stock on the common (though the right frequently came to be regulated and restricted as livestock grew in number and the common was in danger of being eaten bare). In addition, each farmer had the right to depasture his stock on the common fields once the harvesting was completed, the beasts gaining some nourishment from the stubbles and at the same time enriching the fields with their manure. The communal basis of the farming was to be seen also in the sharing of the valuable meadowland (which might be periodically reallocated among the farmers), and in the sharing of plough-teams and the village bull, few farmers being able to support a whole plough-team or to keep their own bull. Furthermore, the farmers' individual flocks were joined together into one large flock, under the care of a full-time communal shepherd, so that in autumn and winter all the sheep could be systematically folded on the fields, penned in by hurdles which were moved every day to ensure that all the land was as thoroughly dunged as was possible. Lastly, the senior farmers made up a 'jury' which periodically perambulated the fields to see that no one had encroached on to neighbouring land, that drains and watercourses

Figure 1 An aerial photograph of former open fields at Byfield Hill, near Woodford Halse, Northamptonshire. The patterns of old furlongs and strips are still clearly visible long after the subdivision into enclosed fields, marked off by trees and hedgerows.

were kept cleared, and that stock pastured on the pieces of grass used as access-ways to the strips were properly tethered and were not trampling down the growing corn. Defaulters were presented to the manorial court, and were fined if proved guilty of an offence.

In the common fields themselves, however, the 'selions', or long strips of land which made up a farmer's holding, were individually occupied. The field was divided into furlongs, often highly unequal in size, and not separated from neighbouring furlongs by any permanent fence or hedge. A large common field, containing many furlongs, might stretch to well over 100, or even to 1,000 acres (in modern measurement), and its surface was completely unbroken by any permanent barrier. The subdivision of furlongs into selions, or strips, to use the modern term, was associated with a scattered pattern of ownership and occupation, suggesting that each strip represented an allocation of newly cleared land to the families which had played a part in the original clearing and cultivation. In the course of time it was inevitable that strips would be sold, exchanged or surrendered to the lord where there was a failure of heirs or whole families succumbed to disease, or where, as after the pestilences of the fourteenth century, inhabitants moved away to occupy vacant holdings on better land elsewhere. Strips might also be consolidated for the sake of convenience and for more economical working where farmers agreed to exchanges for the purpose, or when a successful farmer was able to expand his holding by acquiring neighbouring strips. The move towards consolidation was encouraged by the fall in population in the later middle ages, which gave the farmers greater bargaining power and forced the lords to make concessions.

Some maps of late sixteenth-century date suggest by the regularity of allocation they show, that the inconvenient, irregular scatter of occupation typical of an earlier period had been replaced by a more orderly organization of the strips. This may reflect systematic communal assarting, perhaps directed by the lord; although where assarting was continued by individuals, the holdings in the new furlongs were bound to be both scattered and irregular, or the new assarts might form enclosures on the periphery of the fields. Indeed, Dr Joan Thirsk has argued that regularity of distribution of strips within furlongs represents not a survival of the original distribution to families clearing the land but rather wholesale reallocations which were undertaken by landlords, probably in the heyday of medieval farming, the fourteenth century. Possibly, too, the pattern of furlongs and strips revealed by the oldest maps and by modern aerial photography may not record the original character of the common fields but a modified and modernized version of the middle or later middle ages.[11] What is interesting is that the pattern of allocation, whether irregular or reorganized into a systematic scheme, remained basically a scattered one, and one which survived, indeed, until the era of parliamentary enclosures in the later eighteenth and early nineteenth centuries. Whether the scattering of the strips was designed to share out fairly both good and bad land, or to give farmers a range of situations and aspects suitable for a variety of crops, or to provide an insurance against failure of a crop in one field, or merely represented the strength of custom, are questions which still fascinate historians.[12]

The usual size of a common-field selion, or strip, was 220 yards long by perhaps only $5\frac{1}{2}$ yards wide (though it could be wider), giving an area of about a rood, or a quarter of an acre. (The original use of the term 'acre' seems to have been as an alternative for 'selion', and was not intended to convey any accurate idea of area. Later there were both statute acres of 4,840 square yards and larger 'customary acres', just as there were statute miles 1,760 yards long and 'long miles', which might be as much as twice the distance or more.) It has been suggested that the selion length of 220 yards was the optimum distance over which an ox-team could pull a plough without tiring, and which did not involve frequent turns and wasted time and effort. Similarly the common width of some $5\frac{1}{2}$ yards may have been a convenient one for the turning of the plough-team at the end of each furrow. There has been some controversy over how strips were divided from one another: ditches and stone markers were in use, and there were certainly grass access-ways so that farmers could reach their strips without treading on growing crops, but whether the grass 'balks' were confined to divisions between furlongs or also ran between individual owners' strips is subject to question.[13]

Detailed studies have examined the great variations which existed in field systems. Even in the 'classical' midland system there were marked differences in the frequency with which land was fallowed, and often within the confines of a single village: the supposedly rigid two crops and a fallow was by no means invariable, and the better land might be rested only every fourth year, while the poorer parts lay in fallow every other year. It is possible that a two-field rotation was widely practised in the early middle ages, with half the arable land always in fallow, and that this gave way over time to more sophisticated and less wasteful rotations as population pressure increased or the means of maintaining fertility became more readily available. Traditional rotations including wheat, barley, oats and rye were modified by the inclusion from the mid-fourteenth century onwards of peas, beans and vetches. Sometimes these crops replaced spring corn, sometimes the fallow. Since they put nitrogen back into the soil and helped supplement the supply of fodder, and thus manure, they facilitated less frequent fallowing as well as making it possible to keep more livestock.

Another means of restoring fertility and also of keeping more stock was provided by the practice of putting some arable strips down to temporary grass – leys – known to have been adopted at Wymeswold in Leicestershire at least as early as 1425. Again, the taking in of small closes from the common fields for such purposes as fattening, stock-rearing or the growing of special crops was in use from before the fifteenth century, while lords and communities frequently permitted an individual farmer to take in a piece of land from the waste to be used as the farmer wished. Lastly, the fields themselves were not sacrosanct: their boundaries could be changed as assarts were added or enclosures subtracted, and the number of fields might be increased (by dividing the existing fields if necessary) in order to allow for more varied rotations. And within a field, as we have seen, the furlongs could be treated as separate units for cropping purposes, so that wheat and rye, or spring grains and peas and beans, could be grown within a single field.[14]

Field systems varied in detail from parish to parish, but there were also marked regional differences. In East Anglia, for instance, there was much early piecemeal enclosure, and a more irregular and complex field system made for considerable flexibility in the proportion of land that could be devoted to particular crops. In this region turnips were being grown as a field crop as early as 1674, while at Linton in south-eastern Cambridgeshire in 1695 nearly 24 acres of carrots, peas, turnips and parsnips occupied forty strips in fourteen furlongs distributed in seven of the nine common fields of this parish. Another peculiarity of East Anglia was the fold-course, or sheepwalk, which enabled large farmers to keep extensive flocks. This arose from the custom whereby the whole grazing of a village's lands was in the hands of the manorial lord or his lessee, irrespective of who occupied the land. This was in contrast to the situation in the midlands where pasturage rights belonged to the community as a whole and were jointly exercised. Because there was usually more than one manor in each East Anglian township there was frequently more than one demesne flock, so that each fold-course was confined to clearly defined areas, which might, however, take no cognizance of field divisions or even township boundaries. Even more confusing was the position in a county such as Kent, where it is known that some common fields existed among a landscape dominated by enclosed fields. Common meadows and common pastures also existed, and were carefully regulated, but it appears that the common fields were not in fact farmed in common, and since they were not the basis of a communally agreed rotation of crops their number, indeed their very survival, was of little consequence.[15] This was no doubt the reason why common fields disappeared in Kent without their leaving any record of formal enclosure.

*   *   *

The complexity of field systems arose as a result of varying natural factors such as the abundance or shortage of cultivable land, the availability of pasture, the relative unimportance of the arable in forest or upland areas, the natural fertility of the soil and the supply of manure, the importance of the sheep flock, and the lack or presence of occupations that could be combined with farming – to mention only the more obvious ones. The old view that differences in field systems reflected ethnic differences in the origins of the settlers of the regions – the East Anglian field system springing from the Scandinavian settlers, the Kentish one from Roman farming – has now been considerably discounted in favour of the influence of differing physical conditions, though it must be said that such conditions do not always explain the many variations that have been found within regions.

As the farming system varied, so too did the nature of the village community, its size, its degree of dependence on agriculture and its degree of subjection to the control of manorial lords. Generally speaking, large villages were more common in the south and east of the country, small villages and hamlets in the north and west. The manor represented the territory over which a lord exercised certain rights over the inhabitants. This territory, however, varied considerably in extent, and especially outside the midlands was by no means coincident with the area of a parish. A parish or township might be divided among a number of manors; by contrast, a large manor might stretch over a number of parishes. Neither were the lands of the manor always concentrated in one place; some Kentish manors, for example, had highly scattered holdings. The manor, further, was not an 'estate' in which the lord owned or controlled all the land, since the manor often contained a substantial minority of freeholders who were in large degree independent of the lord, and in particular could bequeath or sell their land as they wished. Rather, the manor might better be described as a unit of estate administration, in which the lord usually had certain powers over the bulk of the land and the majority of its inhabitants.

The single manor represented the lowest step in the structure known as the feudal system. The Norman Conquest had resulted in the establishment of a new military aristocracy in England, one which displaced the Saxon thanes and introduced a more thoroughgoing form of feudalism, where service in war was strictly bound to the tenure of land. The Conquest further entailed the legal principle that all land must have a lord, who granted it upon terms of suit and service. Thus many of the peasantry were thrust into a state of deeper dependence on the more powerful, and the term 'villein', originally villager, came to imply servitude – the servitude of a serf tied to the lord's soil. However, the proportion of unfree households, although constituting over 70 per cent of the Domesday population, declined substantially as time went by and the military basis of the feudalism introduced by the Normans tended to wane.

The greater lords, the king and his bishops and barons, possessed rights over a score or perhaps many scores of manors. Below them came the wealthiest knights, some of them holding as many as six manors and not very far removed from baronial status, and after them the lesser knights, esquires and other retainers who held smaller numbers. These lesser vassals owed numerous financial obligations to their lord, which he used in part for meeting the expenses of his swollen household and for paying the fighting men required to garrison his castle and help make up the feudal array when called upon by the king in time of war. The rule of primogeniture, which had become fully established by the later thirteenth century, was associated with the need of the lord to ensure that the obligations of his tenants were duly fulfilled when their lands changed hands. Under strict feudal tenure the lands so held had to go to the eldest son, though in Kent, where the custom of 'gavelkind', or division among heirs, ruled, a tenant could bequeath his land to younger sons or daughters. In due course, however, 'uses' developed by which the strict rule of primogeniture was overcome, and by 1327 all feudal tenants had achieved a degree of freedom of alienation over their lands so that if there were no son to succeed, the inheritance was shared between the daughters.

The passing of land to daughters and widows made marriage the simplest and quickest way of acquiring wealth, and lords were careful to maintain rights of consent over the marriage of a tenant's daughter and the remarriage of his widow. Particularly valuable was the lord's power of controlling the fiefs, or grants of land, of those vassals who died leaving an unmarried daughter as heiress or a son who was still a minor. Such rights over 'wardships', established from the twelfth century, enabled many lords to augment their incomes by exploiting the property of their wards and by arranging profitable matches for them in return for a fee.

The vassal's fief was usually his principal or only means of income, though he might hold land of several lords. The unfree peasants, or villeins – the majority of farmers over much of the country – worked the lord's land, or demesne, for him. They needed land for their own support, and so they had a share, usually the major share, of the village lands set aside for them. In return for their holdings the peasants were under obligation to work on the lord's demesne for a number of days each week, and to perform additional 'boon' tasks at harvest. The number of days' work required by the lord varied from place to place over the country, but was roughly related to the size of the peasant's holding, which itself varied greatly and could be very small. Two days' work a week was a fairly common obligation, and four days in harvest. In addition to these labour services, the villein had to pay tallage, a form of taxation, and the lord demanded also the best beast or some other fee in return for permission for the farmer's son to succeed to the holding or for the marriage of the farmer's daughter. Other payments, originally exacted in kind, included 'larder silver' at Christmas, eggs and capons at Easter, and payments for grazing swine and gathering timber on the waste.

The lord's privileges extended beyond the waste to authority over forests and game, powers over the use of rivers for water transport and mills, demands on the peasants' teams and carts for carriage services, and sometimes the prerogative of putting hunting dogs out to board with the farmers – this last persisting over the centuries to feature in some leases of the eighteenth and nineteenth centuries. Extensive though these rights were, they were often less oppressive than those obtaining on the Continent: only rarely in England, for example, did the lord attempt to maintain an exclusive monopoly of the local flour mill, bread ovens or dovecotes. Moreover, the custom of the manor had the effect of protecting unfree peasants from the full force of possible exactions. By the thirteenth century the cost to the unfree peasant of obtaining the lord's permission to marry, to migrate, to buy or sell property, and to use non-manorial mills, breweries or ovens, was expressed in financial terms, and the financial cost was duly limited by the tradition or custom of the manor.[16]

Following the Conquest, William I distributed the lands of his chief barons across the country so that none of them owned a predominance of territory in any area which might form the base of a rival power and become a potential source of insurrections. Only in the wild and remote borderlands nearest to Wales and Scotland did the local magnates, or 'marcher lords', assume a large degree of independent power, and this owed much to the security their castles provided against the incursions of marauders and the prevailing sense of danger and insecurity. However, there was much social mobility among the lords, both upwards and downwards, and many lords managed to build up a significant, if still scattered, holding in a particular county or district with which they became closely associated, as the Percys, for example, were associated with Northumberland, the Nevilles with Westmorland and the Stanleys with south-west Lancashire.

Between the lords and their unfree tenants stood a middle group of free peasants. Their numbers varied considerably from place to place, but generally they formed a minority of the cultivators. Very frequently they had less land than many of the villeins, but they did not owe the onerous services imposed on the unfree peasants. They might, in fact, have to meet some small obligations, but unlike the unfree cultivators they were able to leave the manor and reside elsewhere without obtaining the lord's permission, and they could inherit and dispose of their land and property as they wished. The position of the villeins, on the other hand, was that, in law, their land and goods belonged to their lord. Above all, the freeholders had access to the king's courts – the main distinguishing mark of their free status – while the remaining unfree villagers could take their grievances only to the lord's court, the court baron or court leet, which had local police powers.

The lords punished offences such as minor assaults and petty nuisances, but they could go so far as to hang a thief if he were caught with stolen goods on him; in the west midlands there were numerous private gallows at the end of the thirteenth century.[17] These local courts also regulated weights and measures, particularly those relating to the sale of bread and ale, where fraudulent measures were a frequent cause of protest. In addition, markets and fairs, and the activities of pedlars and chapmen, were controlled, while the courts of more powerful lordships took the 'view of frankpledge', the presentation of tithings, or

15

groups of ten, into which adult males were collected for purposes of 'telling tales' or reporting crimes. Through his manorial court every lord exercised some powers of justice and administration, and the fines and dues levied there could form a significant source of income. The courts were also valuable for keeping a check on the tenants of scattered properties, to ensure that labour services were performed, and customary dues were paid. Disputes arising over titles to land, boundaries of holdings, use of commons and performance of labour services were heard by the lord or his representative, and a judgement handed down in accordance with the custom of that particular manor. In time the force of custom became so strong that it created a considerable curb on the lord's powers over his tenants.

*   *   *

The military ties that originally bound the vassal to his overlord weakened as the middle ages advanced. By the thirteenth century, if not earlier, vassals usually discharged their military obligations by paying a sum of money rather than by appearing in person, expensively equipped for war. The magnates, too, came to pay the king in money or by producing a band of hired knights to make up the feudal array. Considerations of private profit took precedence over military obligations. Many lords concentrated on managing their lands to the best advantage, and demesnes were extended and run in a commercial way, using the latest farming knowledge, as production became more specialized in response to the growth of markets. Consequently some lords found it convenient to commute the labour services of their unfree tenants into money rents, and to resort to hired labour for the working of their demesnes. Others found it more profitable to abandon altogether direct management of their lands, which involved much administration and the maintaining of bodies of officials, and instead leased out their lands to tenant farmers.

Whether commutation was the rule, or demesnes continued to be cultivated by labour services, depended on the nature of the demesne and on prices and market conditions. In the thirteenth century, an age of economic expansion and rising prices, commutation of labour services was often brought to a halt, and on some estates reversed, when lords found inflation eating into their money income and conditions favoured demesne production of grain or wool. Already by 1300, however, a large proportion of the lords were *rentiers* rather than agricultural producers. For a variety of reasons they preferred a more certain income from the rents paid by the lessees of the demesne to the uncertainty and trouble of farming the demesne themselves and risking the chances of harvests and markets. Further, with the growing pressure of population having the effect of increasing the demand for land, rents were inevitably tending upwards. In the villages the former villein holdings were often converted into tenancies at will or leaseholds, the occupiers paying a money rent instead of the former labour services. In this process some villeins' lands came to be regarded as hereditary, and the lords' strict control over their estates was considerably weakened. In Leicestershire, for example, it has been shown that at the beginning of the fourteenth century wage labour was being used to cultivate manorial demesnes, while many peasants paid money rents for their holdings and, though still attending seigneurial courts, were otherwise completely independent of the lords.[18]

In the later middle ages, with pasture generally more profitable than arable, the commuting of services and leasing of demesnes proceeded further until they became general on larger estates. Some minor services lingered on into modern times as obsolescent appendages to farm leases, but at least by the eighteenth century, and usually much earlier, such irksome obligations as the performing of carriage services and the making of gifts of produce at Christmas and Easter were normally commuted into money payments. Commutation of personal services, abolition of unfree status, and the alienation of demesnes did much in the later middle ages to improve the conditions of peasant farmers. Villein tenure was transformed wholesale into copyhold with money rents, and from at least the middle fifteenth century the protection of the equity courts, and even of the common law, was extended to copyholders. (A copyholder was so called because his right to the holding was entered in the roll of the manorial court, and he kept a copy of this entry.) Many demesnes, indeed, were leased on terms which gave the copyholder permanent rights of tenancy almost equivalent to a freehold interest in the land. Other tenants were less secure, however, holding leases which might not automatically be renewed, or were renewable only on paying a fine, the amount of which could be varied. When, as in the sixteenth century, farming conditions became more attractive, some lords reverted to farming their demesnes themselves; in turn they often leased them out again when times proved less favourable. By the later seventeenth century most landlords, except the smallest, had adopted a policy of permanently renting out for money rents the major part of their land, retaining in their hands only the home farm, and that principally as a convenient source of fresh food for the household.

The extension of commutation and the wider leasing out of demesnes in the later middle ages owed much to the secular deterioration in economic conditions which affected most of Europe in the fourteenth and early fifteenth centuries. According to the established view, this general economic decline was preceded by a period of population growth and a great expansion of the cultivated area, involving a resort to poorer soils. By the thirteenth century mounting pressure on the land had resulted in declining yields, both on the marginal lands and, probably, on some old cultivated areas. A more precarious margin now existed between food supplies and the demands of the enlarged population. The medieval economy came to be balanced on a knife edge. Already in the later thirteenth century there were difficult years of harvest failure such as that which caused the dearth of 1258. Even in more normal years yields varied greatly but were generally low, giving returns of less than a third of those obtained today. Plough beasts seem often to have been insufficient, and disease periodically decimated livestock while veterinary methods were primitive: witness the reliance placed on a mass and readings from the gospels to curb the murrain among sheep. Many peasant holdings were under 3 acres – far too small to provide a family with subsistence – and many country-dwellers, as well as townspeople, had no land at all. Supplementary earnings, from a craft or part-time industrial work, from the sale of wood, peat, wildfowl or eels, were often too small to compensate for the lack of land. A crisis of subsistence arose, stemming basically from an 'unfavourable balance of land and people'.[19]

More recent opinion takes a less gloomy view of the situation. It has been pointed out that in northern France and the Low Countries the pressures arising from an expanding population led to improvements in farming which raised the levels of productivity and output; and some evidence of demesne farming in England suggests that similar developments may have occurred here. However, if the true position regarding the balance between population and agricultural output in the later thirteenth century was less threatening than was once thought, a crisis certainly developed in the fourteenth century when the fine equilibrium of supply and demand was disastrously overturned by a series of exceptionally severe weather conditions and catastrophic harvests. A population weakened by hunger and hardship fell prey to the ravages of disease. The harvest of 1315, ruined by rain, was a disaster, and followed on a poor one in the previous year. Another terrible harvest followed in 1316, and the dearth was not alleviated until better harvests returned in 1317 and 1318. But then the murrains which had accompanied the harvest failures were followed by a fearful loss of cattle and oxen in 1319 and 1321, and again in 1320 and 1321 the harvests failed and grain prices soared to the unprecedented famine levels of 1315–17.

The terrifying Black Death, which struck the country in 1348, was in fact only one, if the worst, of a number of destructive epidemics. The effects, however, were uneven, with some areas, such as the Winchester estates in southern England, suffering little: there vacant holdings were rapidly filled up by new tenants (suggesting extensive land-hunger prior to the plague), and revenues were swelled by the increase in entry fines. Similarly, on the Duchy of Cornwall's lands most vacant farms were quickly reoccupied within a year or two of the Black Death, despite the plague's ravages in that county. Local people looking for land, newcomers from other areas, and existing farmers extending their holdings with land obtained at lower rents, soon made up the gaps in the rentals.[20] Elsewhere many of the peasants died or fled away, and it became difficult or impossible to continue cultivation. Some landowners found they could not keep up their demesnes and fell into financial difficulties. In such areas pasture gained at the expense of arable, and the poorest land reverted to waste. In the long run a further impetus was given to the commutation of labour services and the introduction of demesne leases for lives or for terms of years.

Owing to labour scarcity wages eventually moved upwards, while prices of farm produce tended downwards because of reduced demand. Increasingly, the shortage of labour enabled peasants to obtain commutation and personal freedom on easy terms, and, for their part, many landlords, faced by low prices and dear labour, were obliged sooner or later to offer attractive leases to such tenants as were willing to occupy their land. But the alienation of the demesnes was seldom abrupt: it had already gone some considerable way before the end of the thirteenth century, and it proceeded only rather gradually and often uncertainly on many ecclesiastical and lay estates after the disasters of the fourteenth century. However, it is an oversimplification to suppose that demesne tenants were mere peasants who were just beginning to rise in the world. Many demesne lessees were already substantial farmers, well on their way to becoming gentry. On the Abbot of Westminster's estates some of the lessees were manorial officials, reeves or foremen, rent collectors and bailiffs, whose offices provided them with some farming expertise as well as a little capital and a close knowledge of the lands in question. Others were already members of the gentry, small landlords, a knight of the shire for Worcestershire, and a merchant of Gloucester.[21] How far such relatively superior tenants worked the newly acquired lands themselves, and how far they merely added them to existing holdings and sublet them, remains uncertain. At the lower levels of landownership there was possibly more direct farming by gentry landlords in the fifteenth century than has sometimes been supposed.

At this time, too, the destruction of many of the old feudal nobles in the Wars of the Roses led to the establishment of the Tudors as a more stable monarchy, one that was able to curb and diminish the powers of the surviving magnates. Under the influence of a strong monarch the king's council became an instrument for keeping the nobles in their place, suppressing their numerous bands of liveried retainers,

19

and crushing their penchant for intimidation and violence. Estates were diminished by forfeitures and fines, and the great lords themselves began to find their traditional way of life too expensive as well as obsolete, a costly display of magnificence without real advantage or justification. Castles were abandoned and allowed to fall into ruin, or were converted to less defensible but more comfortable mansions. As the magnates declined in power and independence so the lesser landowners became less reliant on their patronage and rose in wealth and importance, climbing upwards through marriage, through successful exploitation of their demesnes, through the expanding political role of the House of Commons, and through royal office or local administration as Justices of the Peace.

While the lay nobility declined relative to the Crown and the gentry, the Reformation gave the Crown mastery also over the great lords of the church. The lands of the bishops and monasteries covered perhaps a sixth or a seventh, or even more, of the country, and in 1536 and the years that followed the monasteries were dissolved and ownership of their properties assumed by the Crown. The Crown, however, did not long retain them: sales and grants began immediately, and by 1558 three-quarters had gone. Some were given to courtiers and statesmen, but most of the seized lands were sold in the open market, with many of them ending up in the hands of rising new men, younger sons of landowners, lawyers, merchants and successful farmers. Some of the purchasers had been stewards, bailiffs or auditors of monastic lands before the Dissolution, and in general the fall of the monasteries gave gentry landowners a new opportunity of augmenting and consolidating their estates.

Such men were not likely to lend support to the short-lived rebellions of the period – such as the Pilgrimage of Grace, which sprang up in October 1536 in Lincolnshire and Yorkshire, partly in opposition to increases in rents, partly in protest against the threat to the church and its treasures, and partly against the extension of the power of the Crown. Even if they had some sympathy with the rebels' cause, the local gentry were wise enough for the most part to know which way the matter would end, and in preservation of their lives and estates cleaved to the king's side. Probably few gentry estates were built up largely or entirely by purchases of monastic lands, but the long-term effect of the Dissolution was to increase the middling landowners' share of the whole country to something approaching a half. The great losers were the church and the Crown, whose combined share fell from over a quarter to probably under a tenth. The great lords, too, experienced losses as their attempts to maintain their status and traditional lifestyle involved them in financial difficulties. Their share in the country fell to about a fifth or less, leaving the freeholder farmers with perhaps as much as a quarter or more. In Norfolk the gentry's share of the 1,527 manors in the county was increased from 977 to 1,094 by 1545; by 1565 the figure had risen further to 1,181. At the later date the Crown had 67 manors in the county, the nobility 159, the church 91, and colleges, hospitals and other institutions 30.[22] The proportion of manors owned by the gentry, though only a very rough guide to their share of the land, thus rose to over three-quarters. Norfolk, however, may well not have been typical, and whatever the actual figures for the division of the whole country were, there is no doubt that with the Dissolution, the profits to be made from successful demesne farming, and in some cases the salaries and perquisites of royal offices, the gentry landowners were able significantly to increase their stake in the country and to rise in wealth and status in relation to those groups which lost ground — the church, the Crown and the magnates.

*   *   *

Few country houses have survived from the middle ages and not a great number of fortified houses or castles. By Elizabeth's time castles had given way to much more comfortable country houses, though some of these might retain such castle-like features as towers and battlements as decoration. Most castles were unsuited to conversion, or too far gone in decay, and were left to decline into ruins, reminders of the march of military progress and a departed era of baronial independence and rivalry. Where they were still at least partially habitable they might serve for holding the Assizes, and as prisons and for storage of archives, and some descended to such mundane uses as providing housing for looms or a wireworks; where they were too far gone in ruin they served only as quarries for useful building stone.[23]

A major reason for the decline of castles was the sheer cost of maintaining them. Only a small number of landowners were sufficiently wealthy to build and maintain a really substantial mansion, much less a great stone castle. It has to be remembered that most local lords were possessed of only modest estates. In fourteenth-century Leicestershire, for instance, the four largest owners in the county had only between three and six manors apiece, and most of the manors could boast no more than 100 acres of arable.[24]

Medieval manor houses, therefore, began as modest affairs, and were rebuilt and extended if and when their owners improved in means and status. They were sometimes fortified with a moat and drawbridge, or with a wall and watchtower, and the house was surrounded by orchards, gardens and perhaps dovecotes, fishponds and a deer park. The earliest houses developed round the hall, which served as the communal living-room and meeting-place of the household. Originally wooden in con-struction, later brick, half-timbered or stone, the larger halls were divided into a number of bays by means of arched trusses known as crucks, a feature which also appears in surviving medieval barns. The importance of the hall derived in part from its role in the life of the village: the justice of the manor court was dispensed there, and there also the lord gave instructions to officials running the demesne. 'The Hall' was consequently the familiar name by which many a manor house came to be known, and it has come down to us as the name still used for the principal house of the village, as well as in town halls, guildhalls and the halls of schools and colleges.

The hall originally went up to the rafters and occupied two-thirds of the space on the upper floor of the manor house, the remainder being taken up by the private chamber, or 'bower'. Access was by an outer staircase, and the ground floor was devoted to storage and possibly kitchens and other domestic purposes. Later the ground floor became part of the hall, while the bower, cellar and kitchens were placed in adjacent buildings, and thus the house developed on a quadrangular or single-block plan. A popular design was to flank the hall by two wings, a private wing containing bedchambers and possibly a chapel, and a servants' wing which included the kitchen, buttery and pantry. The external door was placed at one end of the hall, under a porch, and opened into a passage screened from the hall which gave access to a minstrels' gallery above and the domestic offices on the ground floor. At the opposite end of the hall, on a dais, was placed the high table for the lord, his family and guests, with tables for the officials and other inferior members of the household set lengthways down the body of the hall. A door behind or to the side of the high table led to the private chambers, consisting of the withdrawing-room or parlour below, and the solar or bedchamber above. A stone hearth was built in the centre of the hall, and a louvre or turret covering a hole in the roof directly above allowed the smoke to escape, an arrangement which may still be seen in the great medieval hall at Penshurst Place in Kent. By the fourteenth and fifteenth centuries, however, fireplaces set in the walls with chimneys had become general.[25]

The wealthier landowners might perhaps be able to afford expensive glass in their windows, but more commonly the window space was filled by a lattice of wood or metal and covered by shutters in bad weather. The walls of the hall and private chambers were plastered and painted in bright colours or covered with murals depicting scenes from biblical stories or popular romances. In the fifteenth century those of greater wealth draped their walls with costly tapestries and Eastern embroideries. Vessels of gold and silver were displayed on the tables of the hall or on the cupboard, a term later applied to the chest in which the plate was locked away when not in use. By this time pewter tableware was replacing the wooden platters and 'trenchers', thick slices of bread on which meat was served. Both trenchers and bones were flung among the rushes on the floor for the dogs, and as the rushes were changed only infrequently the English hall might be unpleasantly noisome and unsavoury.[26]

From Tudor times onwards the space taken by the hall was commonly divided into two or three storeys. Houses increased in size and improved in appointments, and some impressive residences were fashioned out of converted monastic buildings after the Dissolution. The architecture became more extrovert and eye-catching, with elaborate wreathed chimney stacks, intricately carved high-pitched gables, mullioned and transomed windows piled up to form façades of glass, heraldic devices over doorways, and contrasting patterns of blue bricks to relieve the plainness of red-brick houses. The quadrangular plan maintained its popularity, which was one reason for the easy conversion of monastic buildings. Elizabethan times saw a gradual move towards the H-shaped house, where the cross wings overlapped both ends of the main or hall block, with the entrance projecting from the middle of the hallrange front. For new houses a north-eastern aspect was preferred, since it was believed that the south wind brought evil 'vapours' which a north wind purged, while a breeze from the east was 'fresh and fragrant'.

The early medieval village could well be described as made up of 'old hovels, decayed beams and half-destroyed walls'.[27] But peasant houses made the same kind of progress as the lords' mansions, from small impermanent structures of wicker or cob surmounted by a conical roof of crude thatch – not unlike the huts to be seen in Third World parts of Africa today – to simple one-storey structures of mud and stud, or ones of timber, timber-framed with brick infilling, or entirely of brick or stone in the case of the later homes of the wealthier inhabitants. The better-off yeomen and lesser gentry came by the end of the middle ages to have houses of two storeys, with a hall, parlour, bedchambers and kitchen on the ground floor, and chambers above used for storage of produce such as grain, wool, hemp, cheese and apples, and also as additional sleeping space for the farm servants. Outhouses were built for larder, brewhouse and milkhouse, probably situated at the rear of the kitchen. At some time after 1500 a brick fireplace and chimney would be installed to replace the open fire of the hall, together with a framed staircase and glazed windows.

In more modest houses there was rarely more than one upper chamber, if any at all, and the bedroom was on the ground floor alongside the hall. In some western and northern districts the tradition of the byre house, with humans and animals living under one roof, persisted even in new houses of the sixteenth and seventeenth centuries. The hall was a multi-purpose room used for cooking, eating, sitting and sleeping, and had a small storeroom or dairy beyond, while the byre part of the building, housing the oxen, cattle and other beasts, was at least as long as the residential part of the house. In time the storeroom or dairy might be converted into a bedchamber or parlour (the terms were frequently used interchangeably), and new service rooms added in an outshoot at the rear. Further sleeping room might be found by inserting a chamber over the hall, possibly reached by a ladder instead of a staircase. Improvements in building materials, accommodation, comfort and convenience came earliest in the south of England and later in the north, where the rebuilding of timber houses in stone began only around 1600 or even later.[28]

*　　　*　　　*

The established medieval community, with its manor house and hierarchy of manorial officials, farmers and cottagers, was typical only of lowland England, and even there many villages lacked a resident lord. Elsewhere there were extensive areas of forest and upland moors and wastes, populated only by scattered hamlets and isolated farmsteads, and by great flocks of sheep producing wool for distant markets, and occasional 'vaccaries', or large herds of cattle. Here the land might be controlled by an abbey, but often the manor house and manorial organization were lacking, and an unregulated community was free to look after its own affairs. Forested regions were the home of a variety of woodland crafts, and of mining and iron-making, the latter dependent on supplies of charcoal from the woods. Many of the craftsmen and iron-workers were seasonal or part-time, spending part of their labour on their trade, the remainder on their land – little intakes from the forest for grain, often combined with grazing in the woodland pastures, and the keeping of cattle or sheep on the moors and fells. Usually the farming was subsidiary to some branch of the textile trades, to forestry, coal, lead and ore-mining, iron-working, or the making of items such as poles, hurdles, tubs and barrel staves from the local wood.

Such districts, unpoliced and remote, were also the haunts of criminals and outlaws, who might live for years in the vastness of the forest with little fear of disturbance – in extensive wooded areas such as the Weald of Kent and Sussex, the New Forest, Waltham Forest, the Forests of Bere, of Dean, Epping, Charnwood, Rockingham, Salcey, Whittlewood, Sherwood, Clun, Bowland, Lune and Rothbury, to mention but the better known. Not all outlaws were of lowly origins: a number apparently came from the ranks of the yeomen or lesser gentry, and their exploits were elaborated, and no doubt romanticized, in the ballads with which, over many generations, the households of the gentry were entertained. Historical evidence substantiates the careers of some outlaws who took to the woods to escape the vengeance of the authorities, or to wreak their revenge on those who had given them offence. They might be depicted in ballads as robbing only those who had themselves waxed fat by squeezing the poor, a just retribution which carried with it the glamour of the 'gentleman bandit'. Most famous, of course, was Robin Hood, accounts of whom go far back, possibly as far as the end of the fourteenth century. In the telling, his exploits appear to have been transferred from his native scene of Barnesdale, north of Doncaster, to the more southerly location of Sherwood Forest, and his story intertwined in the ballads with that of the infamous Sheriff of Nottingham. It is now accepted that there was little or no connection between folk-heroes like Robin Hood and the real grievances of the peasantry which, under a leader like Wat Tyler, might well up into frightening outbursts such as the Peasants' Revolt of 1381.[29]

The disasters of the fourteenth century intensified by acute hunger and dread disease the hardships of the peasantry. In due time, however, the fall of population had the effect of easing the land-hunger of the previous age; and with more land, higher wages, commutation and manumission, the common people entered into the so-called golden age of the fifteenth century. The experience of individuals, of course, even of whole communities, might well not conform to the broad pattern of economic trends. Local and personal factors were always of significance. And at any time in the medieval period life for many was inevitably nasty, brutish and short. Progress in living standards, in general well-being, was slow and uncertain, and was at times reversed. But overall, in the long run, there was progress. The age was certainly not the static, unchanging era that is sometimes supposed. Population rose, declined and recovered; agricultural production and organization, industrial output and technology, the composition, direction and volume of trade, all shifted in line with changing economic circumstances. The England of 1500 was certainly much different from that of 1100, and so far as rural society is concerned, the shape of future patterns, future problems, may be detected in the developments of the medieval age.

2

THE PROGRESS OF THE PLOUGH

The medieval farming scene was both remarkably extensive and remarkably varied. Light loams, because of their advantages of fertility and greater ease of cultivation, were preferred by medieval farmers, but the limited areas of such soils, and the pressure of demand for land, forced many to resort to much less favourable land. If possible, however, they shunned intractable heavy soils that demanded large plough-teams and were difficult to work except in ideal weather conditions, electing rather for the lighter boulder clays that, if founded on permeable rock, gave adequate drainage. Thin, sandy soils were avoided, too, because nutrients leached out, and farmers rarely had sufficient dung to keep such 'hungry' soils fertile. Nevertheless, in the centuries before 1300 the demand for land was such as to force farmers to accept surprisingly bleak and unfavourable situations, taking the plough to some land which, after the fourteenth century, was destined never to see it again: to the brecklands of the Suffolk–Norfolk border, the Cotswold plateau and even the windswept wastes of Dartmoor. Not a few undertook the back-breaking work of clearing an intake of forest merely to obtain a little grazing and some meagre returns of grain from the poor soils that generally made up forest lands. Large parts of the forested areas, however, were strictly reserved for hunting, and medieval people lacked the means for dealing very effectively with swamps such as Sedgemoor and Otmoor, much less the vast inundation of the fenlands.

The pressure on land of the early middle ages, though varying locally in intensity, sprang essentially from a combination of mounting numbers of people seeking food and occupation, and an output from the farmland that was severely limited by the prevailing state of technology. Although yields of wheat as high as 10–12 bushels could be obtained on the better land, the average yield was much lower, possibly as little as some 6–8 bushels (compared with some 30–40 bushels per acre at the end of the nineteenth century), and from which $1\frac{1}{2}$–2 bushels had to be reserved for seed. Furthermore, although there

26

is evidence of more productive farming on some demesne lands, it may be that overall the average yield was declining as population grew, as resort was made to poorer and poorer soils, and as supplies of manure became increasingly inadequate. It must not be supposed, however, that medieval farmers had no kind of answer to their problems. Farming technology, though primitive in many respects, was not stationary; and the great local variety and complexity of farming systems and methods bear witness to the efforts made to develop the means of dealing with particular characteristics of soils and climate, and show that the farmers were continually seeking to put land to its most advantageous use. Moreover, in the later middle ages, as population pressure and demesne farming both declined, there was greater scope for flexibility of production and some greater degree of specialization, with regional differences becoming more marked. Land more suited for pasture was reserved for grazing, and some poor marginal areas were abandoned completely; on the arable land attempts were made to raise yields by methods first advocated in the thirteenth-century period of population pressure – by increasing the numbers of livestock and hence the supply of manure, by applying fertilizers such as lime, chalk or marl, by introducing new varieties of corn and more complex rotations, by keeping down weeds and reducing the losses through pests and plant diseases (this achieved in part through the lengthier rotations of crops).

The eventual decline of demesne farming by landlords was accompanied by a larger scale of tenant farming, and by the commutation of labour services and manumission, the easing, and the eventual ending, of serfdom. Farmers became free to develop their farming along more profitable lines, take on larger acreages or move to areas of better soils and easier access to markets. But how restrictive, in fact, were the conditions of serfdom in an earlier period, in the century before the Black Death served as a catalyst of more rapid change? Earlier still, the conditions of the villeins, the servile tenants, could be truly burdensome: they might often be obliged to pay services and dues that were in excess of the value of their lands, and their mobility, although it was possible to move with the lord's permission, might be restricted so as to prevent them from seeking more attractive conditions elsewhere. By the thirteenth century, however, the farmer's obligations were regulated, and restricted, by the custom of the manor, custom which hardened into local law. By this time, too, most obligations were usually expressed in money terms, and the wealthier villeins, at least, were able to hire people to perform the labour services they owed to the lord. As the population was increasing and labour was cheap the lords themselves came to prefer hired labour for working the demesne, and increasingly labour services were commuted into money payments. After another century had passed, labour services of two or more days a week had come to be performed by only a relatively small minority of unfree tenants.

The lord's earlier dependence on labour services sprang from a situation where land was plentiful but workers were scarce. As the population grew, so the managers of demesne lands found it easier and more efficient to employ surplus village labour than to extract unwilling labour services, the hired workers being paid for from the cash rents collected from the villeins. After the Black Death, however, the situation reverted to that of the early middle ages, with land again plentiful and labour once more relatively scarce. In these circumstances some landlords did attempt to restore labour services and to enforce those which had grown lax, but this reaction failed against the combined forces of custom, scarce and more mobile labour, and peasant assertiveness.[1]

Of course, unfree villein farmers made up only a part of the peasant community. Though the numbers varied widely, there were perhaps on average as many as two freemen to every three villeins, the former having always been able to buy and sell land freely, to move away from the manor if they wished, and to marry off their daughters as they desired. Usually they owed the lord no kind of labour service – paying suit at the lord's court and labour services being marks of servile status – but they were subject to the exactions of wardship. When a freeholder died leaving heirs under the age of 21 the lord had the right to take temporary control over the freeholder's estate and to arrange the marriages of the heirs, a right which could be highly profitable. Below both freemen and villeins in the village hierarchy stood the landless or near-landless peasants, who lacked even the security of having customary land of their own to farm.[2] Numbers of these poor peasants worked for the wealthier freeholders and villeins, and were hired by the lord to work his demesne; in many districts, particularly where manorial organization was weak, they worked not only as village craftspeople but also at some other occupation, in the textile trades, mining, or making iron.

There were considerable geographical differences, both in the numbers of freemen and sokemen (or semi-free tenants) in the village, and consequently in the type of society that emerged. Associated with this in some degree were differences in farming systems. Communities relying heavily on arable common fields frequently had large numbers of unfree tenants, and were found in the midlands and in the more heavily populated south and east. Communities dependent more on wood-pasture or open hill pastures, supported by small enclosures for either arable or pasture, relied heavily on their livestock and tended to have a large proportion of free cultivators. Some woodland pasture districts, such as the Forest of Dean and the Weald, were noted for their numbers of charcoal-burners and ironsmiths, while rather remote and hilly areas had their miners, such as the tin-miners of Cornwall and the lead-miners of the Mendips, the High Peak and 'Hexhamshire'. The distribution of enclosed lands and of infield–outfield types of farming was also associated with areas where arable was less profitable than pasture, as in the extreme north, the Yorkshire wolds, parts of East Anglia and Kent, the south-west, and parts of Wales.

Feudalism and the manorial system long pre-dated the Norman Conquest, though both were influenced by the change of rulers. Under manorial arrangements in the arable midlands and the east and south, the lord's share of the village land – his demesne – was at first cultivated by labour services, and then increasingly by hired labour paid for from money rents. The lord (who might be a baron or knight, or bishop or abbot) relied on the produce of the demesne, originally in kind, to feed his household and to meet the dues that he owed to a superior lord (for there was a complex structure of sub-infeudation, and several persons might stand between the man who actually ran the demesne and the ultimate tenant-in-chief). Whether the demesne was worked by labour services or by hired labour, or later was leased out, the lord was dependent on the village community for obtaining his share of the produce of the land. The villeins, and cottars and bordars (as the lesser peasants were described), depended in turn on the lord for their land or employment, and for the protection he might be able to afford them in time of war or unrest. Over the centuries the balance between the two was affected by changes in the availability of land and labour, tipping the scale first in the lord's favour and then back towards the advantage of the peasant. A complicating factor was that the demesne itself might vary from a very few acres to many; in the north of the country especially, the whole manor might be farmed by the tenants, while elsewhere the whole of the village lands might be in the lord's hands. It is inappropriate to offer an average of such diversity, but perhaps it might be suggested that a quarter or a third was the proportion which commonly made up the lord's demesne. And, of course, there were both large and small manors. Royal or ecclesiastical manors might constitute a large continuous estate, while it was not uncommon for the lands of a single village to be parcelled up among several manors: in Suffolk, noted for the minuteness of some of its manors, there was one of only 12 acres, tilled by the lord of the manor himself.

The largest group of unfree tenants, the villeins, held what became eventually hereditary lands, which descended indivisibly (where the lord was concerned to safeguard his dues) to the next heir. A villein's holding was commonly a virgate of some 30 acres, or a half-virgate, but might be much more or often much less. In some areas the holder of a whole virgate was distinctly scarce. To each holding were attached the labour services which the lord required for working his demesne. The basic service was the labour of one, two, three or more days a week spent in ploughing, carting or other work for the lord. However, the 'day' was really a long morning which ended at 2 p.m. or earlier, so that there were still some hours left in which the villein could work his own land. Further, as has been noted, the services need not be performed in person but could be delegated to a member of the villein's family or hired labourer.

In addition, there were the boon-works, supposedly voluntary services at pressing times like haymaking and harvest, which were rewarded by one or two meals a day. In this custom lies the origin of the traditional fare provided by farmers for workers hired for the harvest in later centuries. The medieval meals became fixed by custom, and could be expensive for the lord, for at haymaking at one place twenty-six mowers and eight haymakers were entitled to the bread made of four bushels of wheat, a live sheep, a fivepenny cheese, and a cheese-mould full first of salt and then of oatmeal. In another instance two men received a meal of bean and pea porridge, one wheaten and one maslin (mixed grain) loaf, meat and beer, and a second meal of bread and cheese. On some manors labour services might be quite specific, detailing the work to be done on a certain crop, and even including a requirement of three days a year to be spent in gathering nuts.[3] Further, there were the contributions in kind or in cash which the unfree farmer was obliged to make for the lord's permission to succeed to the holding, to absent himself temporarily or permanently from the manor, to marry off his daughter and to mark the festivals of Easter and Christmas.

Though originally subject to the arbitrary decisions of the lord, these exactions became subject in practice to the limitation imposed by the custom of the manor, which, as in other instances, gave greater certainty to the extent of the burdens on the servile tenant. Moreover, lords became unwilling, or even unable, to break the force of custom when, after the early fourteenth century, the risk loomed large of the tenant running away and leaving the lord without sufficient labour for his demesne. Below the villeins, the numerous class of petty husbandmen, cottars and bordars had occupation of only a little land, possibly only an acre or two, though perhaps as many as ten, and their labour services were correspondingly less than those of the virgater. They lived partly, or in the case of the landless entirely, by some craft or trade, and by working on the demesne or for the larger farmers. And lastly there were the squatters, who had settled on the waste or had cleared a patch of woodland for which they paid the lord a money rent, and who, having no land in the common fields or rights of common pasture, existed on the very fringe of manorial society.

Figure 2 The preparation of a seed bed required not only the ploughing and harrowing of the field, but also, on heavy soils, the crushing of the large clods of earth by men and women swinging mallets, a slow and backbreaking business.

Figure 3 Sowing broadcast from a wattle basket strung roung the neck, a method which prevailed in its essentials until well into the nineteenth century, when the seed drill at last came to be widely used.

31

Medieval farming manuals, dating from the thirteenth century, give us an idea of what were considered the current best farming practices. In the common fields, the field intended for winter-sown grain, normally wheat, was ploughed three times before being harrowed and sown in the autumn, the large clods of earth being painfully crushed by men and women swinging mallets, and the ditches cleared out and drains opened in the furrows between the ridges to allow surplus water to run away. For the spring-sown grain it was important on clay soils to get the seed in early because in a dry March the soil hardened into large unreceptive lumps, while stony ground was liable to cake over in similar weather. Ideally the seed should be changed every year, 'for seed grown on other lands will bring more profit than your own'. The field left fallow was ploughed after the spring corn had been sown, receiving a first stirring in April after the stock had finished feeding on the old stubble and weeds. A second ploughing late in June or July needed to be deep enough to destroy the thistles, and a third at Michaelmas made the little furrows small enough for receiving the seed. There was controversy then, as much later, over the respective merits of oxen and horses for the plough-team: oxen were stronger and better for heavy land, were also cheaper to feed, and when worn out provided meat for the larder; horses were faster and easier to handle but were expensive in fodder and of no use as meat (except perhaps in times of severe famine). It was not uncommon to have mixed teams, and oxen continued to be used throughout the centuries, being seen in parts of Sussex and Kent, for example, as late as the 1930s.[4]

Figure 4 Reaping in medieval times, using the sickle. Women were called in to help in this slow and arduous task.

At the beginning of haymaking in June each villein was given timber for the repair of his haywain, an allowance known as 'wenbote'. On some manors all members of the villein's household were expected to turn out and help, and in one instance an old woman had the duty of carrying water to the mowers, a service by which she held her cottage and croft. Some food was customarily provided, and as a perquisite the mowers had the right to a small amount of the grass, often just as much as could be lifted on a reaping hook or the haft of a scythe, known as 'averoc', or as much as could be lifted by the middle finger as high as the knee, known as 'medknicche', or 'midknee'. Sometimes the bundle of grass had to be raised on the point of the scythe, or its size might be as large as the amount the virgater could hold in his arms and lift on to his back; in addition he might also have the truss on which he sat to eat his lunch. By the beginning of the fourteenth century, however, these perquisites were being converted into money payments, an averoc being valued at perhaps a farthing.[5]

At Lammas (1 August) the fences round the hay meadows were removed and the cattle let in to feed on the aftermath and to manure the ground ready for the next crop of hay, hence the term 'lammas lands'. The whole community was again called out for the harvest. Scythes were used to mow the barley, oats, peas and beans, but wheat was cut by sickles, about halfway up the stalk, leaving plenty of good straw for thatching, the rest to be ploughed in or burned 'to help amend the land' after the cattle had fed on it. A band of reapers, made up of five men or women, was expected to reap 2 acres a day. The corn was

Figure 5 Carts drawn by horses or oxen were used to carry the produce to the barns. The horses had spiked shoes and the cart's wheels were fitted with cogs to help get a grip on soft or slippery surfaces.

bound into sheaves using two strands of corn knotted together by the heads, and women gleaners followed the reapers and helped bind the sheaves. Carts drawn by horses or oxen carried the corn to the great barn of the manor, there to be stacked, each sort by itself, to await threshing during the winter.[6] As with haymaking, the reapers were entitled to a perquisite, perhaps a sheaf for each half-acre reaped, or on some manors the tenth sheaf, or the last sheaf of the day. The size of the sheaf to be taken was regulated by the length of the binding, which might be measured by the circumference of the reeve's head, or by the distance from the sole of the foot to the knee, or by a more precise measure such as 52 inches.[7]

Distinct breeds of cattle and sheep developed from early times as the result of inbreeding and the natural process of adaptation to local conditions of herbage, terrain and climate. The older and poorer animals were selected in early summer for fattening and autumn slaughter, the extent of the annual reduction in herds and flocks depending on the nature of the recent seasons and the consequent variations in the supply of summer grass, hay, straw and winter fodder. Where hay was plentiful the animal slaughter might be very small, and larger numbers of stock could be carried over the winter than used to be thought. There was probably little differentiation between beef and dairy types of cattle, and the supply of milk in winter was poor or non-existent. The available milk was usually valued more for making cheese than for butter or for drinking. Sheep, however, were valued most for their wool and their manure, the former constituting the raw material of the largest branch of the textile industry and providing the major item of England's overseas trade, while the manure was invaluable for keeping the ploughland in good heart. The sheep's milk was made into butter and cheese, and the mutton was the last consideration, after the animal had outlived all other forms of usefulness. Both cattle and sheep suffered severely from 'plagues' and 'murrains' which periodically devastated herds and flocks: the centuries-old problem of liver rot in sheep was evident in the advice given to shepherds to examine carefully the flock at Michaelmas for signs of the sheep having eaten 'the little white snails from which they will sicken and die'.[8]

Other livestock included the ubiquitous pigs, which were kept in large numbers where there were woods and waste lands on which the animals could find pannage and roots, and were fattened up in late winter for slaughter. Pigsties were built in the woods or on the waste during hard weather, and a swineherd was appointed to take charge and see that weaklings were removed to the greater security of the farmyard. The flat-sided, coarse-boned carcasses provided but little meat and apparently only some 5 pounds of lard, and the peasant's profit was reduced by the lord's pannage dues, amounting to perhaps one pig in seven, or one in ten, or later a cash payment of 1d or 2d for each pig. Goats also were kept, if less commonly, partly for their milk (which was supposed to be good for many human complaints), and for the rough cloaks and coverings made from their hair. Dogs were used to guard homesteads and livestock, and both cats and weasels were domesticated to keep down the rats and mice. The tom-cat was as aggressive towards other cats then as now, making, it was complained, 'a ruthless noise and a ghastful'. Arsenic was resorted to for dealing with rats where a cat was lacking.

Rabbits were considered a delicacy and reared for the tables of the rich. They were valued as a form of fresh meat, together with hares and pheasants, and were fostered where tracts of suitable ground were available and a grant of 'free warren' was obtained from the Crown; but the depredations made on the crops of the neighbouring farmers were, and long remained, a serious nuisance to the farmers. Poultry, however, were kept by both high and low as an important element of diet, and also for making the customary gifts to the lord of a hen or two at Christmas and eggs at Easter. At Wye, in Kent, the lord's servant went round to collect the hens and eggs, and if they were not forthcoming the tenant had to bring them to the manor house himself on pain of a fine of 21d. Geese were sometimes so numerous as to require the attention of a gooseherd, while ducks and pigeons seem to have become popular by the thirteenth century, if not earlier. Dovehouses, some having as many as 600 holes, were established by early in the following century, while many lords kept peacocks, partly as a dish for festivals and partly for the brilliant feathers. Swans, too, were fattened in coops on oats and peas, and numerous hives of bees dotted the farmyards for the honey that was universally desired.[9] Fish also formed an important element of the medieval diet, brought fresh from the coast to places a few miles inland, while dried herrings were transported greater distances. Manorial lords established and stocked large ponds near the house for a ready supply of freshwater fish, and the rivers were exploited for further quantities.

In autumn or winter, or at any time when more urgent work was lacking, there was woodcutting to be done. Firewood and brushwood were collected and carted to the manor house and farmstead to be stacked against the winter, and rods and poles cut for making and repairing fences and hurdles. Turf or peat was dug for fuel where sufficient wood was lacking, and rushes collected, peeled and dipped in oxen or mutton fat to make rushlights. Early in the autumn grapes were harvested where there were vineyards, and apples, together some-times with pears, were made into cider. Even crab apples were gathered for making the verjuice used in cooking. Barley, of course, was needed for malt as well as bread, but oats and occasionally wheat, were also

Figure 6 The laborious and dusty work of threshing out the corn in the barn using the flail was a task reserved for winter, when bad weather made fieldwork out of the question.

malted, and sometimes all three were mixed in together. Since hops were not introduced until the end of the middle ages and were not widely grown until the later sixteenth century, the ale had to be drunk when new, so brewing was always going on in manor house as well as farm.

In winter, when rain, snow and frost made fieldwork out of the question, the heavy labour of threshing with the flail was performed in the barn. Villeins threshed for the lord for either a certain number of days or a fixed amount of corn. The winnowing was sometimes done by the villeins, but often by women, by the dairymaid for instance, or perhaps the wives of the oxherds. Finally, the corn was ground at the lord's mill (or in the peasant's home with the humble quern stone), and the lord's toll was fixed at a sixteenth part of the produce, or alternatively at a twentieth or a twenty-fourth part. The corn when threshed was measured by the reeve or hayward, who might assess every eighth sheaf, the writer of the anonymous thirteenth-century *Husbandrie* putting the expected yield of wheat at fivefold what was sown (usually $1\frac{1}{2}$–2 bushels per acre), barley eightfold, oats fourfold, rye sevenfold and peas and beans sixfold. Walter of Henley, perhaps the most respected authority, was less optimistic, however, putting the yield of corn at only three times what was sown.[10]

*   *   *

Except in some pastoral districts where meat was plentiful, the yield of grain was of vital importance to the community, the medieval diet depending very heavily on bread and ale, consumed in huge quantities. The poor peasants, however, relied less on wheat and more on rye and oats for their coarse dark bread and their dish of oatmeal pottage, leavened perhaps with vegetables and any meat that could be afforded, all washed down with draughts of weak 'third' ale. Eggs and dried fish could usually be obtained, and the better-off supplemented the regimen with a more ample variety of fresh fish, meat and cheese.

With low average yields of corn, livestock of small size and limited produce, and farming methods that were highly labour-intensive, it is not surprising that living standards were constantly under threat from bad seasons, natural disasters such as droughts, storms and floods, outbreaks of plant pests and livestock diseases, and pestilences among the labour force. It has been orthodox historical opinion that as the population increased during the twelfth and thirteenth centuries the cultivated area was expanded to the limit of current resources of land and labour, though more recent evidence of demesne production points to a different view. However, by the early fourteenth century a crisis developed, when a series of disasters occurred. There was, first, a run of calamitous harvests and outbreaks of disease among livestock in 1315–21, then outbreaks of plague in 1348–9, and subsequently pestilences in 1361, 1368–9, 1374, 1379–83, 1389–93 and later, which together brought about a decline in numbers. In the view of some historians these disasters may be seen as constituting a 'Malthusian check', a massive correction, arising from natural forces, to a population which had swollen to beyond its current resources of food.

We cannot be sure of the exact size of the population before the catastrophes which marked the period after 1315 but some authorities have suggested that it might have been as large as that of the middle eighteenth century, that is to say, some $5\frac{1}{2}$ million. As a result of the conditions of the fourteenth century numbers were cut back drastically, perhaps to only some 2 or $2\frac{1}{2}$ million. Recovery, despite fairly frequent years of poor harvests and near-famine conditions, and further outbreaks of epidemics in the later fifteenth and the sixteenth centuries, took the figure to perhaps $2\frac{1}{2}$ million in 1500, some 3 million by the 1550s and 1560s, and to 4 million by the beginning of the seventeenth century. The continued growth up to the middle of the seventeenth century brought numbers back to something like the figure for before 1315, that is, some 5 million, but the second half of the century was unfavourable to further growth, and the eighteenth century had dawned before the population rose permanently to 5 million and beyond.

The long-term course of change, therefore, was that the population grew in the early middle ages, reached a peak in the early fourteenth century, and then declined sharply and took another two hundred years to recover to the early fourteenth-century level. There is disagreement on the question of when the decline in numbers of the fourteenth century ceased. Some experts believe that the population was growing again in the fifteenth century, if not already in the later decades of the disastrous fourteenth century, and that the fifteenth century was in general an age of considerable economic progress and prosperity. Others believe that the decline in numbers continued to the middle of the fifteenth century and rose only slowly for the next half-century or so, and they see the fifteenth century as one of long-term agricultural depression, with few clear signs of prosperity. Whatever the real experience, the long dip in numbers between at least the later fourteenth century and the mid-seventeenth century had the effect of creating a situation similar to that of the early middle ages, where the population was at first small in relation to resources of land, but gradually increased and eventually began to press on those resources.

The fifteenth century, when numbers were still very low after the disasters of the previous century, may have seen a situation where there was such a surplus of land relative to labour as to have produced a 'golden age of the peasantry'. If not a golden age, then certainly, despite the attempts of lords to reimpose labour services, demesne farming was in headlong retreat, more and more demesne lands were leased out, and peasant farmers, released from servile status, were able to take on more land on easy terms and to farm on a larger scale. With the loosening of feudal ties the mobility of peasants and craftsmen increased, and there was much movement, especially of a short-distance kind, to take up a better holding or to pursue an occupation in a town. At this time the basis of the modern farming structure began to emerge: there were landlords, who had become for the most part *rentiers*, living on the money rents paid by their tenants; there was a tendency for holdings to grow in size, with the smaller ones declining, and the holdings were occupied by independent farmers, some of whom were freeholders, some tenants and not a few something of both; and there was a labour force made up of a variety of workers recruited from small husbandmen, cottagers, farm servants and landless labourers, and part-time workers from country towns and rural industries. Those farmers who did not own their land outright came to hold their farms under a variety of copyhold and leasehold arrangements; some former customary land was held by the hereditary copyhold of inheritance, giving the farmer a stake in the property almost equal to a freehold; other forms of copyhold, especially those with uncertain fines on succession, were much less secure, and demesne land was frequently leased for terms of years or for three lives, the latter creating uncertainty not only by the risk of the named persons dying early, but also by the possibility that the landlord might not be willing to accept new lives as the old ones dropped out.

Developments in the sixteenth century are uncertain and controversial. The traditional story has it that this period, or more precisely that between about 1500 and 1650, was one marked by the growth of large farms at the expense of small ones, and by expansion of the acreage under grass (especially for sheep grazing) at the expense of arable, encouraged by the enclosure of common fields, commons and wastes, and a variety of other factors. Prices rose, and rents and the value of land rose with them. Landlords, seeing that demesne farming could be profitable once again, revived (at least for a time) the direct farming of their demesnes, terminating leases and getting rid of the tenants by a variety of legal and non-legal, not to say violent, means. The land market was brisk, and was made the brisker by the throwing into the pot of the extensive lands of the monasteries, following their dissolution by Henry VIII in 1536. Those persons well placed to obtain monastic lands were able to acquire enlarged estates, on reasonable, if not always bargain, terms. It has been argued that those most successful in the burgeoning land market and pursuit of agricultural profits were the middling landowners, the gentry, who for a variety of reasons were able to prosper when the tradition-ridden aristocracy were handicapped by debts and high expenditure; the yeomanry also gained, though they often lacked the means to do more than modestly improve their situation.

The supposed 'rise of the gentry' has sparked off a prolonged controversy and launched at least a shelf-full of theses, but it is not our prime concern here. Suffice it to say that the drawing of distinctions between rising and declining groups in rural society has perhaps more to do with historians' attempts to provide an economic explanation for the overthrow of the Stuart monarchy and the Civil Wars of the middle seventeenth century, than with economic realities. Political factors were more immediate and significant, and, in general, there seems no good reason why the majority of sixteenth-century landowners should not have done well out of the rise in prices and the many opportunities of increasing estate revenues. There is no need to invoke the bourgeois capitalist spirit to explain why some landowners rose further or faster. The factors affecting a family's fortunes were many and complex, and the way in which they managed their estates was only one of these, though frequently an important one. Other things being equal, the families who failed to take advantage of the times were, we may hazard, those who lacked the necessary capital or who were too heavily burdened with family or other debts to hang on to their land long enough; or they may have been unfortunate in having small estates of severely limited possibilities, or perhaps estates leased out to copyholders of inheritance who were virtually irremovable. In any case there seems no good reason for supposing that the declining landowners were especially numerous or especially hard hit in the half-century before the Civil Wars: the trends of rents and estate revenues would suggest the opposite, and detailed local studies have shown that the causes of financial decline were extremely varied, including costly provision for families, extravagance in building, excessive household expenses, lavish hospitality and, inevitably, litigation.[11]

Let us return to the question of what was happening to farming between 1600 and 1750. First, we must remember that farming systems were numerous and varied, and that what might be true of one district was not necessarily so of another. In a country like England, with a wide range of soils, relief, transport conditions and even climate, and with differing regional structures of land-holding and rural society, generalization is extremely hazardous. The most we can do is to suggest possible trends, while always bearing in mind that exceptions abounded. Next, we must consider the question of improvements in agricultural techniques in the period. Medieval farm technology, let us repeat, was not unchanging, but generally its progress may well have been limited, slow and uncertain. It has been claimed, however, that subsequently there was much more rapid change: a number of important improvements marked the period after 1560, with most of them falling between then and 1673, which collectively amounted to an 'agricultural revolution'. These advances included developments in the floating of water-meadows (valuable for providing an early spring bite for the stock); the substitution of 'up and down', or convertible, husbandry for permanent tillage or permanent grass (making it possible to keep more stock and obtain higher yields from the ploughland); the introduction of new fodder crops and selected grasses (such as carrots and turnips, sainfoin and clover); and also improvements in marsh drainage, manuring and stockbreeding.[12]

However, as critics of Professor Kerridge's claims have pointed out, the rapidly rising prices of the sixteenth century are not consistent with a very large increase in farm output, nor indeed for most of the period were trends in the market consistently favourable to convertible husbandry, which increased the supply of stock, rather than encouraged the growing of grain. Furthermore, the changes he pinpointed were certainly of limited geographical extent, and in the case of the new fodder crops and grasses took effect mainly after 1650 or 1660; they came about only gradually, and in any event too late to have had much effect on output before the second half of the seventeenth century. It may well be true, however, that long before this average yields of arable crops had been improving, growing in the fifteenth century to levels well above those prevailing in the 1250–1350 era – not because of the developments highlighted by Kerridge, but simply because with the fall in population the cultivation of grain retreated from marginal lands and became concentrated on the better soils. Moreover, the greater profitability of livestock at that time ensured that more were kept and so increased the supplies of manure; further, the growing of peas and beans for feeding stock made progress, and these crops had the valuable quality of fixing nitrogen in the soil. Consequently, the greatly improved yields claimed by Kerridge for the period after 1560 may well have been appearing for more than a century earlier, while it seems that his vaunted system of convertible husbandry was also developing considerably earlier than he has suggested.[13]

It may not be simply that progress came earlier than 1560: indeed, there may well have been other 'developments within the period 1500–1650 . . . positively inimical to progress'. One such development was the revived attack on marginal lands made under the pressure of renewed growth of population. As Joan Thirsk has written: 'men made war upon the forests, moors and fens with a zeal they had not felt for some three hundred years'.[14] Some of the newly cultivated lands may well have been highly fertile, especially the freshly-drained fenlands, but generally the assumption must be that they were less productive than the lands already in cultivation, and so lowered average yields. Also, with more people in the countryside seeking land there was a growth of small, and probably for the most part inefficient, cultivators − not only in the highland pastoral areas of the north and west, but also in the forest areas and fens of midland England and the south. Many of these little farmers grew some grain for their own use, and survived (or in years of bad harvests failed to survive) on yields very similar to those of the thirteenth century. Numbers of them were migrants from lowland farming regions who found it easier as newcomers to obtain holdings in upland, forest, fen and heath areas, where there was often the attraction of some rural industry, the making of cloth, knitting stockings, lace-making or the making of nails or fishing nets. The old arable areas, with their limited amounts of commons and waste, offered much less scope for the migrant seeking land and employment: they were more exporters of migrants, younger sons with no hope of inheriting the father's holding and being able to marry, who left to establish themselves elsewhere.[15]

Possibly, as Dr Outhwaite has suggested, where there was a growth of smallholders in the areas of common-field arable this may have been a source of inefficiency. Poverty-stricken, cautious, and concerned primarily with mere survival, but sheltered by customary tenures and low rents, these petty husbandmen may have been tempted to concentrate their efforts on producing their little crops of grain rather than on acquiring more livestock, which would have improved the fertility of their holdings.[16] To what extent smallholders could survive depended not only on the harvests but also on the nature of the soil and the degree to which specialist crops could be grown for local

41

markets. Small cultivators were generally more viable in pastoral regions, and especially where the modest produce of the holding could be supplemented by part-time industrial work or by-employments.

The traditional view of the sixteenth century is of an age dominated by the rise of sheep. But how far, in fact, did the cultivation of sheep expand in the 150 years after 1600, leading to enclosures and depopulation, and complaints of 'sheep eating men'? The cloth industry was expanding, it is true, and cloth exports were growing, but only up to about 1550; and it may be significant that the prices of animal products, including wool, while rising sharply between the 1520s and 1540s, and then outstripping the rise in grain prices, thereafter failed to rise as rapidly as those of grain. Nevertheless, increased numbers of both sheep and cattle were being kept and the demand for pasture was increasing throughout the period. In the midlands, especially, this demand caused severe problems where grain cultivation expanded or the fodder crops were inadequate to meet the needs of larger herds and flocks. It was in the midlands that the controversy over enclosure was centred, though the agreements to enclose were often more aimed towards reducing the pressure on existing pasture lands than at extending them.

In the prevailing state of knowledge much of the above discussion must be speculative. Probably the optimistic accounts of agricultural progress in the sixteenth and seventeenth centuries are too optimistic, the pessimistic ones too pessimistic. In summary, it may well be that in general the reversion to a relatively plentiful land supply in the fifteenth and early sixteenth centuries had the effect of reducing the area of arable, or substantially increasing average yields above previous levels, and also of expanding the numbers of livestock. But then there may have ensued a check as the population grew more rapidly again and pressure on land resources returned. Resort was once more made to inferior soils, and average yields may have levelled out or even fallen, despite the development of convertible husbandry and the fertile land recovered from the fens, while a swelling army of small cultivators sought to sustain themselves and their families on former heaths, moors and forests. The great rise in grain prices in the years between 1500–9 and 1640–9, and the rise also of animal product prices, by as much as 350 per cent, certainly indicate that agricultural output, though expanding, was undoubtedly failing to keep up with the growth of demand. After the mid-seventeenth century a hundred years of more stable, or even declining, prices suggest that supply and a more constant level of demand were again in balance. There was more regional specialization, and the downward pressure on prices was reinforced by a farm output that was being increased by greater flexibility in land use as much more land was enclosed from common fields and commons, as well as by improved farming practices: these included convertible husbandry and the gradual introduction, mainly after 1660, of a variety of new fodder crops and grasses into arable rotations. What may be seen as the first stage of more rapid change in farming techniques was in progress, leading in time to the further advances of the later eighteenth and the nineteenth centuries.

*　　　*　　　*

After the dramatic price increases of the sixteenth century and first half of the seventeenth – the 'price revolution' – the subsequent hundred years saw much greater stability in prices, so much so that the period is often seen as one of prolonged agricultural depression. This perhaps is going too far: stable, or even slowly falling, prices need not mean depression, except for those farmers whose lands and methods could be made to pay only when prices were rising. Further, when the hundred years after 1650 is looked at more closely, one sees that it was mainly the arable farmers and sheep-graziers who experienced the worst conditions, though over the whole period grain prices fell by only 12 per cent. Furthermore, within this hundred years there were times when wheat prices were relatively high, as in the late 1640s, around 1660, the 1690s and around 1710, while the price of wool was up in the 1660s and around 1700. Apart from wool, however, livestock specialists enjoyed a substantial long-term improvement in prices of about 17–18 per cent, though the rise was concentrated on dairy cattle, pigs, poultry and horses; the price of sheep rose little and that of beef cattle fell. The period was one, therefore, in which farmers who were sufficiently flexible in their production could do reasonably well, though the conservative and inflexible certainly experienced difficulties, most of all perhaps the arable farmers on the unenclosed heavy claylands who could do little to diversify their production.[17]

The root of the farmers' problem was demand: the failure of the population to rise anything like as rapidly in the hundred years after 1650 as it had in the previous hundred years. Between 1550 and 1650, according to the estimates, some two million extra mouths were added to the market; in the hundred years after 1650, however, the rise was only of the order of half a million, and the decades between 1650 and the end of the seventeenth century actually saw a slight fall in the total. Meanwhile, under the stimulus of harder times, the progressive farmers were seeking means of moving away from unprofitable grain and wool and towards more profitable livestock, and towards also the growing markets for hay, hops, pigs, poultry and vegetables. The government stepped in to help corn-growers through bounties on exported grain, and subsequently by drawbacks of tax on exported malt. Nevertheless, relatively few farmers were in a position to take advantage of these measures, and the exports of grain at no time exceeded 5 per cent of total output. However, for well-placed producers, such as the large arable men of Norfolk, easy access to the Dutch brewing market was undoubtedly beneficial. Steps were also taken, in the form of the Irish Cattle Acts, to protect the cattle specialists, but nothing was done for the sheep-graziers.[18]

Although for a large part of the hundred years the population was stationary, or even falling, farmers benefited from the gradually improving living standards of consumers, and from the movement of people to areas of expanding industries, such as the textile districts of East Anglia, the West Country and the West Riding, and the coal-mining and iron-working districts of Northumberland and Durham, South Wales, and the Black Country. Farmers, especially those conveniently placed for water transport, tailored their production to meet the needs of this industrialized population, sending supplies of wool, flax and hay, bread-flour, malting barley, cheese, bacon and mutton. But the biggest centre of food consumption was London, which, with well over half a million inhabitants at the beginning of the eighteenth century, housed 11 per cent of the country's population and was the biggest city in Europe, drawing its supplies by river, coastal shipping and road from areas as remote as Leicestershire and Lincolnshire for livestock, East Anglia for grain and poultry, and Cheshire and Gloucestershire for cheese, to take but a few examples. From districts nearer at hand came market-garden produce, the fruit and hops of north Kent, butter from Epping, ducklings from Aylesbury and corn from Guildford, as well as fish from a myriad of little ports strung round the coasts of eastern and southern England.

The larger, more enterprising farmers thus learned to cater for the expanding demand from the growing ports and industrial centres as well as from market towns and industrialized villages. Beyond London food-stuffs were cheap, as that indefatigable traveller, Celia Fiennes, noted with the eye of a late seventeenth-century lady housekeeper: at Borough-bridge, for instance, where 'a very large Codfish ... above a yard long and more than halfe a yard in compass, very fresh and good', could be bought for no more than 8d, while in the market at Ripon she saw two good shoulders of veal, one at 5d, the other at 6d, and good quarters of lamb at 9d or 10d; at Chesterfield she bought two fat pullets for 6d the two, which in London would have cost '18 pence or two shillings apiece'; and at Preston she observed on market day 'all sorts of things, leather, corn coales, butter, cheese and fruite and garden things'.[19]

Daniel Defoe, writing a little later, in the early eighteenth century, noted how a variety of areas were drawn into the supply of London and the rising industrial districts. The woollen manufacturers of the West Riding, for example, obtained their corn from Lincolnshire, Nottinghamshire and the East Riding, their black cattle and horses from the North Riding, 'their sheep and mutton from the adjacent counties every way, their butter from the East and North Ridings, their cheese out of Cheshire and Warwickshire, more black cattle also from Lancashire'. The Black Country, similarly, obtained its corn from Staffordshire, Shropshire, Herefordshire, Buckinghamshire and the Vale of Evesham. And coming to the supply of London, Defoe expatiated on the Scots cattle fattened in the midlands and East Anglia and finished on the Essex marshes; the sheep driven from Leicestershire and Lincolnshire, and turkeys and geese from Norfolk and Suffolk, brought to the capital on foot in droves 500 strong; the Cheshire cheese transported to London by sea, 'a terrible long, and sometimes dangerous voyage', and the Gloucestershire cheese (much of it actually hailing from Wiltshire) carried down the Thames in barges. Not only cheese, but Wiltshire bacon was similarly despatched, 'esteemed as the best bacon in England, Hampshire only excepted', the hogs being raised on 'the vast quantity of whey and skim'd milk, which so many farmers have to spare, and which must, otherwise, be thrown away'.[20]

Farmers having good access to near or distant markets set about producing more of the things in growing demand, and, moreover, they compensated for sluggish or falling prices by introducing new crops and improving their ways of producing old ones. 'Necessity', as Joan Thirsk has remarked, 'was, indeed, the mother of invention'.[21] The lead was taken by gentry landowners who had come across new crops and practices in their travels, especially in the Low Countries, and who were no doubt the most attentive readers of the farming works produced by contemporary writers such as Sir Richard Weston, Samuel Hartlib, Walter Blith, Andrew Yarranton and John Worlidge.

The gentry encouraged the cultivation of new fodder crops and grasses, such as turnips, clover, sainfoin and ryegrass. They also engaged in the commercial production of fruit and walnuts, as did Sir Edward Filmer on his estate at East Sutton, near Maidstone in Kent, and many landowners specialized in the careful management of woodlands, for timber was in demand for house-building and shipbuilding. The timber of the Kent and Sussex Weald was painfully hauled to the banks of the Medway to be shipped down to Chatham dockyard, one large tree on a long carriage, called a 'tug', said Defoe, 'drawn by two and twenty oxen, and even then, 'tis carried so little a way, and then thrown down, and left for other tugs to take up and carry on, that sometimes 'tis two or three years before it gets to Chatham'. Other gentlemen's specialities included an interest in improving the breeds of livestock, and in establishing deer parks, rabbit warrens, fishponds, duck decoys, dovecotes and vineyards, as well as the cultivation of crops used for dyeing cloth, such as madder and woad, the latter giving rise to so strong and offensive a smell when crushed that Celia Fiennes could not force her horse near a woad mill. Not all the innovations depended on the gentry, however: vegetables, fruit, tobacco, hops, clover and coleseed were grown by yeoman farmers, humble husbandmen and even poor cottagers.[22]

By experimenting with lime, chalk and marl to ameliorate the soil, and by utilizing a wide variety of fertilizers, from oil-cake, seaweed, soot, ashes, 'town muck' and old rags to the waste products of slaughterhouses, breweries and distilleries, farmers moved slowly towards making the best of their land. And where possible, they introduced new crops into rotations in order to obtain more fodder. Thus a greater number of livestock could be carried on a given acreage, while the yields of grain crops were improved. Contemporary evidence suggests that average yields of wheat rose to between 18 and 23 bushels per acre, probably the highest in Europe excepting Holland, and approaching two-thirds of the average yield of the early years of the twentieth century. Livestock, too, may have improved substantially in average weight, though the supposed revolution in animal sizes is a myth. Certainly there were wide differences between breeds, but it may be suggested that sheep averaged something over 50 pounds, and the larger breeds of cattle some 500–900 pounds (liveweight) in the first half of the eighteenth century.[23] The pastures themselves were also improved, not least by the creation of temporary leys of improved grasses in systems of convertible husbandry, while water-meadows, where in use, helped to fill the 'hungry gap' of early spring.

Although there was interest in selective breeding, and some early specialists in stock improvement were already at work near the middle of the eighteenth century, advances in this area were not as yet very marked. On arable lands the progress of the new crops was limited, except in some areas especially favourable to their introduction, such as parts of Suffolk and Norfolk. Away from East Anglia and some few other areas, turnips were slow in appearing and spread widely only after about 1730. One reason for the limited nature of the changes was the poverty and conservatism of many farmers, another was the practical difficulty of introducing innovations. Although noblemen and gentry might experiment with enthusiasm on their home farms, their tenants were likely to look on novelties with a jaundiced eye, taking much time to be convinced of their advantages. Those advantages, too, had to be perceived in a profit-making or cost-cutting way, for farmers would not concern themselves with what would not pay. Sometimes their scepticism was justified: in the early days of the new crops seed was difficult to obtain and might be expensive; and when the first working seed drill appeared soon after 1700, following the initiative of the celebrated Jethro Tull, there was always the difficulty of getting one made, quite apart from the question of its efficiency in operation.

SOUTH DOWN RAM, *bred by M.ʳ Ellman of GLYND, SUSSEX.*

Figure 7 The great age of selective breeding of livestock began in the middle of the eighteenth century, and subsequently a series of famous breeders produced a wide variety of improved cattle, sheep, horses and pigs. Bakewell's New Leicester was the most widely known breed of improved sheep, though Ellman of Glynde, in Sussex, had a more lasting influence with his celebrated Southdowns.

In 1748 Pehr Kalm, the Swedish botanist, undertook a special visit to see William Ellis, a well-known agricultural writer of the time, at his home at Little Gaddesden in Hertfordshire. Kalm was particularly interested in Ellis's seed drill, but it evidently worked badly, and Kalm noted sourly:

> when we first came to Little Gaddesden he had his four-wheel-drill-plough which stood out on the farm; but directly afterwards it was locked up, so that I did not get to see it any more than when Ellis, with two carls, devoted a whole afternoon to sowing out with it about a pint of seed.[24]

Other problems which defied solution were the limitations of heavy soils and destructive outbreaks of animal disease. The heavy clays were not suited to the growing of turnips or the new grasses, and the cultivation of such soils was both difficult and expensive. Even when enclosed, heavy clays could seldom be adapted to convertible husbandry, although they might be laid down to permanent pasture. Where they remained in arable the old medieval one or two crops and a fallow perforce persisted. Little wonder that Arthur Young, writing soon after the middle of the eighteenth century, advised his friends to have nothing to do with such land. And on the lighter soils, where the

47

Wheel Turnrist Plough used in Sussex.

Figure 8 The advance of farming techniques was considerably slowed down by the conservatism of many farmers. In particular, farmers often preferred their own local designs of ploughs, no matter how cumbrous they were or how large a plough-team was required to draw them.

new crops came in much earlier, farmers began to find their turnips affected by disease (as well as frosts), and their clovers by poor crops as the land became 'clover-sick'. There were few effective remedies for the numerous diseases of livestock, and some epidemics were particularly widespread, such as the 'cattle plague' (rinderpest) which raged destructively in 1714–15 and again between 1745 and 1758. Liver rot among sheep was an ancient problem, long to remain so, an Oxfordshire farmer once stating: 'I have known years when not a single sheep kept in open fields escaped the rot. Some years within living memory rot has killed more sheep than the butchers have.'[25]

In common-field villages of this period the holdings were still often extremely scattered: thus the farm of Richard Derby of Hanslope in Buckinghamshire, whose $26\frac{1}{2}$ acres of common-field land was spread over the three great fields in twenty-four separate parcels, some as small as a quarter of an acre. Enclosure, and the consequent extinction of common fields and common rights, was proceeding however, although the era of the rapid sweeping away of the common fields by the new device of private Acts of Parliament came only after the middle of the eighteenth century. In the previous hundred years large-scale enclosure of the whole of a village's common fields and commons was carried out by agreement among the landowners, though there was also a gradual process of piecemeal enclosure. As a result of these and earlier enclosures, over extensive parts of the country the common fields either

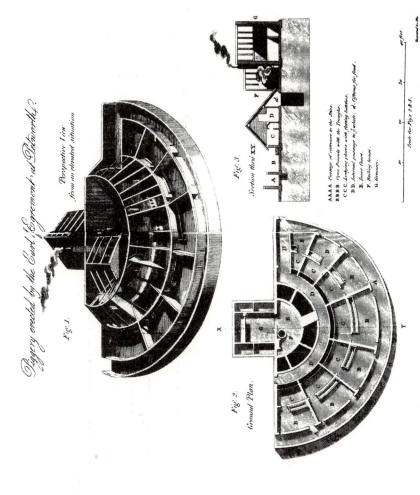

Piggery erected by the Earl of Egremont at Petworth?

Fig: 1.

Perspective View
from an elevated situation

Fig: 3.
Section thro' X Y.

Fig: 2.
Ground Plan.

AAAA *Passage of entrance to the Sties.*
BBBB *Open Pounds with the Troughs.*
CCC *Lodgings places with fitting heather.*
DD *Internal passage to feeders. d. Opening for food.*
E. *Inner Court.*
F. *Boiling house.*
G. *Granary.*

Scale for Figs 2 & 3.

Figure 9 Enthusiasts among the large landowners sometimes went in for palatial farmhouses, huge barns, decorative dairies and geometrical piggeries, as in the example shown here (1813).

A DRILL

for sowing all kinds of Grain in any Quantity and at any Distance.

Figure 10 An improved design of seed drill of about 1805. The invention of the drill had a history going back to the later seventeenth century, but weaknesses in its design and its often limited utility restricted its widespread adoption before the early nineteenth century.

disappeared completely or were much diminished. Already by 1500 most of Essex and Kent, the south-west, most of Wales, and north-west England were already enclosed, while in the districts surrounding the midland plain, in Norfolk, the Chilterns, Somerset, the Vales of Gloucester and Glamorgan, the north-west midlands and west Yorkshire, piecemeal enclosure had made great inroads into common fields and waste lands.[26]

In the common-field lands which survived, only to succumb to the parliamentary enclosures after 1760, there were many signs of change. Fields were divided so as to allow more complex rotations and to reduce fallowing, and holdings were consolidated by exchanges among the owners. New crops were brought in, and grass leys appeared within the common fields. At Wigston Magna in Leicestershire as much as a fifth of the land in the fields was in grass leys long before the middle of the eighteenth century. In this same village a new stint of the common was agreed in 1707, and was enrolled in Chancery to give it greater legal force.[27] The stinting, or rationing, of commons became a quite usual practice at this time, especially in the midlands. Here the limited area of the commons proved inadequate for the growing number of beasts which the commoners wished to put on them, and made it necessary to impose restrictions for fear of their being eaten bare. Not infrequently the farmers also found it advantageous to agree on taking land out of the common fields in order to make additional pasture closes for dairying, breeding or fattening, or perhaps for growing some special crop such as hops, liquorice or woad. As a result, the common fields sometimes shrank appreciably, and in some villages by the end of the eighteenth century there was as much or more land in what came to be called the 'old enclosures' as remained in the common fields. Indeed, this position had sometimes been reached much earlier: at Laxton, in Nottingham-shire, the famous common-field village which still survives today, half of the land was in small closes as early as 1692, and by a hundred years later the proportion had risen to nearly 70 per cent.[28]

The initiative for such changes must often have come from the principal landowners in the village, or at least have received their sanction. Where farms were let on lease (rather than by unwritten annual agreements or 'at will'), tenants might find the landlord inserting new covenants in order to enforce more up-to-date practices. Thus on the Coleshill House estate, in Oxfordshire, the leases signed from the 1730s included covenants regarding the sowing of sainfoin, clover and turnips, while the landlord interested himself directly in small-scale enclosures and exchanges of land, and reserved the right to introduce other improvements, for example schemes for better drainage. In a lease of 1736 the tenant was enjoined 'to lay 6 load of dung yearly on ye said Great Redmead and to float the same every winter with thick water, to open all ye old Trenches and to destroy the moles'.[29] The landlord–tenant system which had evolved out of the decline of demesne farming was in effect a partnership between owner and tenant farmer, where the landlord provided the land and buildings and the tenant the working capital of the farm. On progressive estates the owners encouraged the farmers by providing the conditions – ideally, enclosed and compact farm units, sound buildings and adequate access to markets – in which their enterprise could succeed. In the long run this enabled the tenant to make greater profits and the landlord to reap higher rents. One feature of the hundred years after 1750 (as until quite recent times) was that landlords in general showed little interest in reverting to demesne farming. They preferred their tenants, rather than themselves, to take on the larger risks of the farming business, and were themselves satisfied with receiving a moderate rental, which in the eighteenth century averaged only some 3–4 per cent of the capital value of the land. It became axiomatic among landlords that everything possible should be done to avoid farms falling into hand, which would mean having to find a bailiff to run them (who might be neither competent nor honest), and also the capital with which to stock the farms. Consequently, in the badly depressed arable areas during the low price years of the 1730s and 1740s landowners did all they could to help hard-pressed tenants keep going: by themselves spending more on repairs and improvements, by taking over responsibility for parochial taxes, by paying for some of the normal husbandry expenses, such as seed and fertilizers, and, not least, by allowing arrears of rent to accumulate, sometimes to the extent of double the value of the rental.[30]

*　　*　　*

Partly as a result of the need to cater for expanding urban and industrial markets, and partly because of the natural weeding-out of the inefficient in an era of difficulties for farmers, there was a renewal of the old tendency for farms to grow in size. The process was a slow one and far from revolutionary, but where it can be observed in surviving records substantial changes occurred over periods as long as half a century or so. Generally it was the small farmers, of some 20–100 acres, partially dependent on the market and inefficient in coping with its variations, who declined. Of course, where small farms were well suited to the nature of the enterprise, as in dairying, fruit, market-gardening and hops, they survived and, indeed, multiplied. And the smaller cultivators who farmed mainly for subsistence and could support their incomes by working for larger farmers or at some local craft or trade often increased in number, more especially in upland forested and pastoral regions.

The holdings of the declining 20–100-acre group went to swell the number of larger, more highly commercial farms of over 100 acres, many reaching 200 acres or more. The decline of small farmers was as marked a feature of common-field villages as of those recently enclosed or long-enclosed: the gradual engrossment of farms does not appear to have been particularly associated with enclosure, as is sometimes supposed. This slow and partial decline of small farms arose primarily from the landlord's decision, when a tenant died or failed, to transfer all or part of his lands to a larger farmer, a change which might involve only a single close or a few acres of common field at any one time. The situation of farms held by freehold or by copyhold of inheritance, where the land was passed on from generation to generation, was quite different, and here decline might be due to the old custom of partible inheritance, the division of lands among heirs, which could result in fragmented and uneconomic holdings, and might also cause the passing of land into the hands of heirs whose occupation was unconnected with farming and who might be disposed to sell the land. Partible inheritance in its various forms existed alongside descent by primogeniture, as in Swaledale in Yorkshire. In this district the holdings were mostly used for keeping cows, this being a centre of the Wensleydale cheese-making area, but the small size of the holding and the seasonal nature of dairying brought partial reliance on lead-mining or hand-knitting or other by-employment.[31]

A similar combination of a little farming with non-agricultural employment was found in wooded areas, in Sherwood Forest, for example, where little intakes from the forest for arable and the keeping of a few of the small 'forest' sheep were supplemented by framework-knitting of stockings. In the royal forests of Northamptonshire, Rockingham, Whittlewood and Salcey, many of the woodland settlements had no resident lords and were freely open to immigrants, the villages reaching an average size of some 300 inhabitants. Their economy was largely based on the grazing of sheep and cattle, and in addition to some common-field arable these villages had pasture closes taken in from the forest and common rights on the waste lands that had been cleared of wood.[32] Frequently the working of small farms depended heavily on the help of neighbours for ploughing and harvesting, and the help of the community was particularly necessary where the farmer had a variety of occupations. At Chapel-en-le-Frith in Derbyshire, for example, one of the farmers, James Clegg, was also resident minister and medical practitioner. His farm was cultivated on a communal basis, with up to eight or nine plough-teams helping during March. Although a busy man, spending time on preparing his sermons and often called away to attend on patients, he was not an unenterprising farmer, using lime, and experimenting with rotations which included clover.[33]

While the small artisan-farmer tended to grow in forest and upland regions, and the larger commercial farmers gradually expanded their operations in lowland districts, there were other places where a sudden disturbance uprooted a community and forced on it a much changed way of life. The parks created by landowners to embellish their new mansions, or for keeping deer, along with their game preserves and large plantations of commercial woodland, caused the destruction of some dispersed settlements. The squatters on former waste land were evicted, and on occasion a village was removed wholesale, sometimes to a new site nearby. The enclosure of waste, fenlands and forests, and of common-field arable for pasture might also lead to some local depopulation and shrinking of villages. But most disruptive was the large-scale drainage of the vast fenlands around the Wash and in Lincolnshire, an area of some 1,300 square miles. This began in earnest in the first half of the seventeenth century and proceeded apace in the second half, though less so thereafter, as the price of corn languished and landowners proved unwilling to spend money in scouring field drains and keeping sluices and drains in repair. One cause of the eventual decline in interest in fen drainage was the occurrence of the technical problems which arose as the dried-out peat shrank and land levels fell, leaving the land lower than the channels supposed to drain it. But although incomplete, and often defective, the attempts to drain the fens inevitably aroused the hostility of the inhabitants who formerly lived by fattening cattle and sheep, and by fishing, water-fowling and cutting osiers, and who resented the replacement of their watery wilderness by new stretches of fertile arable farms. Opposition from this 'meaner sort of people', together with legal, administrative, financial and technical difficulties, and not least the declining price of corn, all helped to discourage the progress of enterprising landowner-drainers.[34]

*   *   *

By 1750, on the eve of the first prolonged rise in prices for a century, agriculture stood poised to respond to a renewed expansion of the market. Many improvements had been introduced, especially the advances in fodder crops and convertible husbandry, the enclosure of land for more flexible use under individual occupation, the reclamation of wastes, woodlands and fenlands, and the development of the land-lord–tenant system and more efficient estate management. Agriculture had certainly increased its productivity, both that of land and capital, and, in addition, that of labour. In the hundred years before 1750 there was some expansion of the cultivated acreage and a considerable development of new techniques, while as a proportion of the working population the labour engaged in agriculture probably shrank sub-stantially, though still constituting perhaps a half of the total in 1750. (The proportion is estimated to have been about three-quarters in 1520, and only 36 per cent in 1801.) The innovations of 1650–1750, especially those in arable farming, may be seen as a response to generally unprofitable grain prices but, as Sir John Habakkuk has pointed out, they might actually have helped cause the fall in prices, by producing a surplus over previous levels of production in face of a demand that was at one time declining and later was rising only slowly. There is evidence to suggest that arable output and productivity were rising fastest in the early decades of the eighteenth century, when corn prices were particularly low. It is possible, also, that the returns to innovation were so high as to encourage landowners and farmers to go in for new developments, even though the markets were unfavourable.[35]

Whatever the causes of improvement, the agriculture of 1750 was improved and still improving. But much yet remained to be achieved – through the transformation that was to be achieved by parliamentary enclosure, through selective breeding, still more new crops, and further changes in estate management and increased size of farms. Already, however, through successive eras of expansion and stagnation the structure of farming and its methods had continually evolved, matching changing economic circumstances with appropriate changes on the land, a process that enabled the agricultural industry to fulfil its essential role in economy and society.

3

IN SICKNESS AND IN HEALTH:
DISEASE AND FAMINE

When a large proportion of the population lived at or near the level of bare subsistence hunger was never long out of the common experience. Townspeople as well as country-dwellers were heavily dependent on the size of the harvest and the well-being of the flocks and herds – a murrain among the livestock was as big a disaster as the much-feared combination of a cold backward spring and a wet August and September. Less direct, but still powerful, was the influence of fluctuations in trade: a decline in the staple export of wool, or later cloth, meant a fall in the employment of many people, in their incomes, and in their ability to feed themselves.

Hunger, a common evil among the poor, deepened in some years to the greater calamity of famine, when harvests failed over large areas. The chroniclers of medieval England left graphic eye-witness accounts of the worst years of dearth, calling up a picture of misery and desolation. One such year was 1143 when, wrote an observer, the desperate were obliged to resort to the flesh of dogs and horses, and to raw herbs and roots. Houses stood empty, their inhabitants dead or fled away, while the ripening crops of the next harvest stood untended in the fields for lack of hands to gather them in. Many such years of want were recorded, with certain ones standing out in contemporary observation: thus, especially, 1315, when starved corpses could be seen by the roadside, and again horse-flesh was eaten and fat dogs stolen for food, while it was even rumoured that parents ate the flesh of their children and that prisoners in the gaols devoured the bodies of the fresh inmates newly incarcerated.[1]

The terrible shortage of 1315 followed on a bad harvest in the preceding year, the dearth being compounded by a second disastrous harvest resulting from torrential rain. Wheat rose from 8s a quarter in 1315 – already a tremendous price – to reach the fantastic level of 26s 8d in the summer of 1316, and other victuals were also frighteningly dear since the bad seasons were accompanied by outbreaks of disease among the cattle and sheep. The harvest of 1316 was also a bad one –

the third disaster in a row – so that it provided little relief, and conditions improved only with the better crops of 1317 and 1318. There followed further harvest failures, and indeed most of the period between 1315 and 1321 was marked by severe shortages of grain and devastation among livestock. The high mortality rate – possibly accounting for a tenth of the population – resulted not only from hunger but also from famine-related diseases, including dysentery arising from the eating of rotten food, a putrid sore throat and an epidemic of fever which may have been typhoid.[2]

Famines continued in subsequent periods – there were severe ones, for example, in 1555–7 and in 1594–8 – while Professor Hoskins tells us that as many as thirty-seven of the harvests between 1620 and 1759 were deficient and that twenty-two of these could be classed as bad. The famine-stricken spring of 1623, which followed on the disastrous harvest of the previous year, saw, according to a Lincolnshire squire, thousands of the poor reduced to eating dogs' flesh and old horse meat. Food prices again reached great heights in 1631, in 1647–50, 1661–2 and all the years from 1692 to the end of the century, while subsequently 1708–9, 1729 and 1739–40 were landmarks of distress in the next half-century.[3] From the records it is not easy to ascertain causes of death, nor yet how many people died of starvation rather than from famine-related diseases, but investigation suggests that the high mortality rate of 1596–7 in Cumberland and Westmorland may well have been caused by a series of four successive bad harvests which began in 1594. In these years not only grain but peas and beans were also very dear, a matter which greatly affected the poor who were used to ekeing out their flour by mixing in 'podware' in times of shortage. For a subsequent period of high grain prices, in 1622–3, there is explicit evidence of starvation in this region, with the parish register of Greystoke, Cumberland, recording the burial of such unfortunates as 'a poore hungersterven beger child' and another 'poor hungerstarved begger boye'.[4]

In the experience of contemporaries, famine and disease were closely related. Thus, writing of the conditions preceding 1597, the Dean of Durham recorded that in the north want was then so prevalent that people came as far as 60 miles from Carlisle to Durham in order to buy bread, and corn had to be fetched from Newcastle, 'whereby the plague is spread in the northern counties: tenants cannot pay their rents, then whole families are turned out, and poor boroughs are pestered with four or five families under one roof'.[5] Later years of great dearth, the result of abnormal weather conditions, were noted as leading to a number of epidemics. The winter of 1683–4 was so cold that during the whole of January an ice carnival could be held on the Thames. This severe winter was succeeded by an excessively hot and dry summer, such as 'no man in England had known'. The drought was then followed by another bad winter, while the spring of 1685 was again dry, the second successive drought not being broken until the end of May. From the February of 1685 a heavy mortality from fevers was recorded, especially from typhus and smallpox. Then in the next decade came the infamous run of 'seven ill years', with 1698 as their climax. That year saw a late spring succeeded by a wet summer and much of the harvest lost: in the north of England some of the corn was not got in until Christmas. Again, a high mortality was experienced in some places, and subsequently, in 1727–8, another period of corn shortage was accompanied by outbreaks of a variety of fevers. Once more, in the dry spring and very hot summer of 1741 fever was very general over England, following on the acute grain shortage of 1740. This dearth was the result of what was probably the hardest winter of the whole eighteenth century: the Thames again froze over, permitting a 'frost-fair', but also preventing the Newcastle colliers from reaching the city with their coal; and on the cornfields the frost was so severe and prolonged that the autumn-sown wheat was destroyed in the ground.[6]

Poverty was a major cause of the heavy outbreaks of disease which marked other years. With many people living always on the edge of subsistence, on a meagre diet and with minimal clothing, warmth and shelter, it is not surprising that when the winter was especially severe the poor were, as a contemporary noted in 1727, 'much exposed to the injuries and changes of the weather' and 'probably wanted the necessary assistance of diet and medicines'.[7] Bodies weakened by an unusual degree of hunger and privation were the more susceptible to the common epidemics which stalked the villages and towns of England. In the later seventeenth century and first half of the eighteenth century there was a high incidence of rickets, and the poor seem to have succumbed especially to the ravages of typhus. This complaint, with its deliriums, its great prostration and its eruptions of purple spots – and so commonly called 'the spotted fever' – was a disease of dirt and overcrowding as well as poverty, though the three frequently went together. Probably, many of the fever epidemics which periodically flared up in densely packed and insanitary institutions, in gaols, barracks, ships, work-houses and factories, were outbreaks of typhus spread by the lice that infested unwashed bodies and filthy clothing. On occasion, as at the 'Black Assizes' at Taunton in 1730, the 'gaol fever' spread from the prisoners at the bar to infect judge, lawyers and court officials, striking down the high sheriff, the noted lawyer Sir James Sheppard, the crier of the court, two of the judge's servants and the judge himself, Chief Baron Pengelly.

Historians have argued that the great famine of 1315–16 was the more severe in its mortality because of the much increased population that was seeking to obtain a subsistence from the land at the beginning of the fourteenth century. The population had grown by then to probably some 5 million, a modest figure by modern standards, but the largest to be supported in England until the eighteenth century. Given the state of medieval technology and the low yields of the soil, the pressure of numbers obliged people to resort to increasingly poor land, with cultivation extended to former woodlands, fens and wastes, driving the plough into areas which were rarely, if ever, to see it again. The population, it is argued, had outstripped the available resources, and the famine when it came acted as a Malthusian check, reducing the population to what could be adequately fed in years of normal harvests. Numbers fell back drastically from their early fourteenth-century peak, and did not recover to even as many as 3 million for some two hundred years, probably not rising substantially over this number before about 1570, and not reaching 4 million until about 1600. A temporary rise above the 5 million mark may have occurred in the middle decades of the seventeenth century, but a permanent level in excess of 5 million was achieved only in the first half of the eighteenth century.

*   *   *

The fall in population in the later middle ages was accelerated by disease as well as famine. Famines, through the weakening of the body's resistance and the consumption of inferior and harmful food, brought on numerous complaints, though it is interesting that Charles Creighton, in his massive study of the subject, could find little or no evidence prior to the eighteenth century of one result of famine, ergotism. The terrible sufferings of this disease – including chronic gangrene and the loss of fingers and toes – were brought on by eating bread made from spoiled grains, especially rye.[8] The common complaints of the middle ages were, in general, much the same as those of later periods: cancers and tuberculosis (notably scrofula or the 'king's evil'), typhus and typhoid, the stone, the 'falling sickness' and St Vitus' dance, apoplexies and palsies, dropsies and fluxes, quinsies, anginas, sore eyes, putrid mouth, carbuncles, boils and 'wildfire' (erysipelas), agues, influenza, rheums and coughs. The identification of disease in modern terms is made difficult by incomplete or confusing descriptions, and by a tendency for symptoms to be noted as causes of death, such as 'lethargy', which may have been coma in a fever or a paralytic stroke, and 'phrensy' which may have been mania or a delirium of plague or typhus. Leprosy was not as widespread as the early provision of leper hospitals might lead one to suppose, and indeed it may have been confused with the similar symptoms of syphilis, or possibly with pellagra, the latter brought on by the inadequacies of the medieval diet, especially the heavy reliance on salt meat and salt fish, and the lack of fresh fruit and vegetables. The same dietary deficiencies were also responsible for 'land scurvy', the effects being similar to those suffered by sailors on long voyages.[9]

Plague, after its first appearance in England in 1348–9, was certainly one of the greatest and most feared killers, though its heaviest toll was taken in the original great outbreak of the 'Black Death'. Plague first entered the country in the summer of 1348, brought, according to contemporary account, from the Continent in a vessel which came to the port of Weymouth, and spread rapidly from there through Dorset and neighbouring Devon and Somerset, reaching Bristol by 15 August. From Bristol it spread to Gloucester, thence to Oxford, and so to London, arriving in the capital by Michaelmas, 29 September, according to one account, or at All Saints, 1 November, according to another. After causing fairly general and often very severe destruction, it declined and disappeared, to erupt again in 1361–2 and 1368–9, and at intervals until its eventual final disappearance from the country about the beginning of the eighteenth century.

As is well known, the plague bacillus could be conveyed to humans by the bite of an infected flea which had deserted its usual host, a rat. It used to be thought that the flea was carried only by the black rat, the common house and ship rat of the time, and not by the brown 'sewer' rat of a much later period; however, more recent evidence suggests that both types of rat can carry the offending flea, and that a human flea of a different variety might also act as an agent of the infection. In the mysterious outbreak in Suffolk between 1906 and 1918, it appears that pneumonic plague was transmitted by direct human-to-human contact, or by the human–flea–human route, the rat playing no further part after the initial infection – a possible explanation of the explosive nature of the pandemic of 1348–9.[10] In the bubonic form of plague, some two to six days after infection the characteristic sign of the disease appeared in a 'bubo', the swelling of a lymphatic gland, most frequently in the groin, but sometimes in the neck or armpit. It has been held that in the European plagues of the fourteenth to sixteenth centuries death resulted in about three-fifths of the cases. A second form of plague, pneumonic, was extremely infectious, being conveyed through the inhalation of droplets coughed or sneezed by an affected person, and was almost always fatal. A rare third variety of the disease, septicaemic plague, was unusually virulent, invariably causing death in a matter of hours rather than days.[11]

Since ship and house rats were the main hosts of the infected flea, plague tended to be concentrated in ports and urban centres, but could be spread to sparsely settled rural areas in the pneumonic form by travellers, or when rats or fleas were accidentally conveyed in bulky merchandise, such as sacks of grain or bundles of wood or cloth. The black rat, the one implicated in medieval and early modern times, was apparently a timid creature of sedentary habits and with a very limited natural range of migration, so that even the width of a street might serve as a barrier to its spread, and the alacrity with which people fled plague-stricken towns for the countryside shows a contemporary recognition of the plague's limited powers of movement, at least in its bubonic form. As the infected flea was weakened by cold weather, and its eggs destroyed by cold, plague assumed a marked seasonal pattern, the mortality occurring mainly in the late summer or early autumn, and ceasing when cold weather set in about December. However, it has been pointed out that the plague bacillus itself could survive in a house kept warm during the winter, and also in the nests of the rodents. Sometimes the plague would disappear completely and not reappear when the winter was over, unless reintroduced; at other times it reasserted its frightening presence in the spring.[12]

The plague was extremely erratic in its toll, leaving some places untouched, others completely or largely stripped of inhabitants, if only temporarily. An interesting aspect of the effects of the Black Death is that despite its toll – possibly on average a quarter or third of the population was destroyed – the immediate consequences of the reduced population for wages and prices were small, and most holdings left vacant by plague-stricken families were rapidly filled up by new tenants. People moved quickly to occupy vacant land, despite the 1351 Statute of Labourers, which aimed at preventing all kinds of workers from transferring from one master to another. It has been argued that such circumstances suggest the existence of a very large surplus of labour in the early fourteenth century, so that, before the late 1370s, even the recurrence of famine and a succession of plague outbreaks could not so reduce the labour supply as to force up wages very suddenly or very violently; nor did any lack of demand act to bring prices down sharply, while even in some poorer and less densely populated areas landlords found little difficulty in re-letting their lands without making rent reductions. Only in the closing years of the fourteenth century did landlords complain of fallen rents, of abandoned holdings and of demesne farms surrendered to tenants on almost any terms they cared to offer. The economic decline of the later fourteenth century, indeed, may have been due not so much to the Black Death, which after mid-century seems to have been increasingly confined to the dense populations of the towns, but to irruptions of other epidemic diseases.[13] What the Black Death did was substantially to reduce an early four-teenth-century surplus of numbers; subsequently, other epidemics may have cut back further into the population to an extent that delayed recovery until about the later fifteenth century.

Although it may be possible that plague was sometimes confused with typhus, the pestilence undoubtedly recurred in England many times between 1348 and the time of its mysterious final disappearance after the last great outbreak of 1665–6. In the seventeenth century alone plague appeared in the provinces on several occasions and, in particular, movements of troops and refugees encouraged its spread during the Civil War. The outbreak of 1665–6 was not confined to London; in the Derbyshire township of Eyam a sudden irruption swept away perhaps as many as half the population.

It was no doubt the most dreaded of all the great pestilences, though by no means the only cause of high mortality. Other scourges, frequent, painful and often fatal, haunted the land. In 1488, and at various times in the sixteenth century, there appeared the sweating sickness, or 'English sweat' as it was called since it seemed peculiar to this country. It was possibly a millary fever, allied to rheumatic fever, caused by a virus which at present is unknown. Probably it had existed on the Continent for a long time and, being introduced into England, found a highly susceptible community in which to spread. According to a contemporary description of 1552 the disease began without warning, usually at night or towards morning, with a chill and tremors. Fever and profound weakness followed, accompanied by cardiac pain and palpitation, and sometimes severe headaches and stupor. The profuse sweating set in soon after the fever. Death came with astonishing speed, sometimes within the day or even in a few hours.

There were also outbreaks of what was termed 'influenza', and apparently a considerable incidence of syphilis, commonly known as the 'French pox' or 'great pox', the latter to distinguish it from smallpox, which was rife from at least the early part of the sixteenth century. Periodically, epidemics of 'influenza' caused heavy mortality, as in 1557–8, 1580–2, 1623–4, 1628, 1638–9, 1643–4 and 1651, to mention some of the early outbreaks.[14] There were also 'agues', some of which at least were malarial fevers. They were a constant curse of country people living in low-lying, ill-drained and marshy areas, the heavy outbreak of the early 1780s, for example, being particularly felt, apparently, in the lower parts of Leicestershire, Northamptonshire, Bedfordshire and the fen country. Contemporaries sometimes connected ague with stagnant air and water, as did a correspondent of *The Gentleman's Magazine*, who in 1785 contended that its prevalence was due to 'putrescent air caused by the number of enclosures, and the many inland cuts made for navigation'. In this outbreak, it was reported, sufferers 'went abroad more like walking corpses than living subjects'. The treatment of the malady with Peruvian bark (the basis of quinine) had been practised from at least the 1660s, but as this seemed to be ineffective, physicians resorted to doses of arsenic as a remedy.[15]

Malarial ague was particularly common in the Thames-side marshes of Essex and north Kent. A seventeenth-century apothecary, who professed to be able to cure the Kentish ague, resided at Rochester, where he was well situated for a steady flow of patients coming from the marshy districts of the Thames and lower Medway.[16] Some fifty years after this time, Daniel Defoe remarked on the fatal character of the Essex marshes for those not used to living among them. Visiting 'this damp part of the world' he 'took notice of a strange decay' there of the fair sex, finding that 'it was very frequent to meet with men that had from five or six to fourteen or fifteen wives; nay and some more' – indeed, there was reputed to be one farmer presently living with his twenty-fifth wife. The explanation given to Defoe was that the men, being bred in the marshes, were seasoned to them, but they always went out of the district for a wife. The young lasses from the uplands, reported Defoe, originally 'healthy, fresh and clear', once taken out of their native air into the 'fogs and damps' of the marshes soon 'got an ague or two', and seldom lasted above half a year, or a year at most, when the bereaved spouses again resorted to the upland country for new partners.[17]

We must allow for Defoe's hyperbole and his delight in a tall story, but nevertheless there can be little doubt but that the basis of his account was accurate. Those people who did not have to live in the marshes moved some distance away to higher ground, where the malarial mosquito was not so troublesome. Parsons of marsh parishes, for instance, commonly resided a few miles off in a healthier situation – when, that is, they were not complete absentees. But mosquitoes could travel, and even Parson Woodforde's parish of Weston Longville, though a few miles west of Norwich, was apparently still too near the Broads for complete safety. In 1783, during the severe ague outbreaks of the early 1780s, almost all of Woodforde's household were affected by 'the present disorder and which is called the whirligigousticon by the faculty', he noted in his diary.[18] Outbreaks of malaria were still rife in subject areas late in the nineteenth century, and in the fenlands around the Wash the prevalence of agues was a main factor in the high consumption there of opium pills.

Agues, however, were sometimes confused with other fevers, and those with one another. Eighteenth-century terminology included 'continual fever', 'spotted fever', 'putrid fever', 'intermittent fever' and 'relapsing fever'. Epidemics of enteric fever were not distinguished from typhus, nor was typhoid, sometimes called 'brain fever' or 'low fever', always distinguished from typhus, relapsing fever and febricula. Scarlet fever was recognized in the later seventeenth century but was still often confused with measles and diphtheria.

There seems little evidence that that great nineteenth-century scourge, tuberculosis, was a major killer prior to the later eighteenth century. There certainly was, however, some incidence of scrofula, glandular tuberculosis; and the belief that the 'king's evil', as it was commonly called, could be cured by the touch of the monarch or his queen was held from as early as the time of Edward the Confessor. So strong was the faith in the efficacy of the royal hand that until the time of George I sufferers journeyed to the king's palace and thronged the courtyards to await his coming, and cities such as York laid out not inconsiderable sums of money in conveying afflicted citizens to the capital.[19] For those who could not obtain the funds to enable them to reach the king, there was resort to other, equally strange, remedies: weasels' blood or doves' dung, or in the early eighteenth century, as advocated by a farming writer, William Ellis, quicksilver or mercury. This he held to be a general cure-all, valuable also for treating 'pox, leprosy, itch, gout, rheumatism, scurvy, mange, scald-head and worms', not to mention its success in dealing with bugs in beds and furniture.

*   *   *

Professional medical care before the nineteenth century lay in the hands of physicians, apothecaries and surgeons, although there were also many unqualified practitioners. Some of these had expert practical experience, while others were rank amateurs, including village black-smiths and farriers, the latter being called in even as late as the close of the eighteenth century and after to set bones and draw teeth. Attempts to restrict medical practice to the qualified had little effect, despite such measures as the Act of 1512, which required practitioners who had no Oxford or Cambridge degree to obtain a licence from the Bishop of the diocese, and a subsequent Act of 1523 which authorized the College of Physicians to license all physicians. Unqualified practitioners abounded, and even among the qualified there was outside London little specialization of function.

The city barber-surgeons were organized in craft guilds, such as that which trained and regulated its members in medieval York. The York guild appointed officials to lecture on anatomy and to demonstrate on the corpses of condemned criminals, the only legal source of cadavers. Masters of the guild took apprentices, who were not allowed to practise surgery or draw teeth unless supervised by a master, and the academic training included study of a variety of books, diagrams and charts. At this early period medicine was associated with astrology, and the charts in use indicated the relationship between blood-letting, the moon and signs of the zodiac which were ascribed to various parts of the body. A chart of bleeding points indicated that bleeding from veins under the tongue would relieve quinsy, from veins in the 'neckhole' relieve wind, and on the outer side of the ankle cure sciatica. The limitations of the York barber-surgeons' remedies are shown by the willingness of the city's corporation to pay for patients to be sent to London for consultation or to be touched for the king's evil, or merely to take the hot baths at Buxton.[20]

By the eighteenth century a clear division of function between the three classes of medical practitioner was evident, at least in London. The physicians, who in London acted only as consultants, and did not operate, had a strictly academic training but gained general clinical experience by taking unpaid hospital appointments, thus discharging the obligation imposed by the Royal College of Physicians of providing free attendance on the poor. The surgeons, on the other hand, had a severely practical training and specialized in operations, fractures, wounds and ulcers, removal of teeth, opening of abcesses, eye and skin complaints, and venereal diseases. The coming of age of surgery was marked in 1745 by the dissolution of the old Company of Barber Surgeons and the formation of the Surgeons' Company, followed by the success of the Hunterian school of teaching. In London there were other famous surgeons besides the Hunters, such as William Cheselden and John Abernetty. Cheselden was especially noted for the speed at which he could operate for the stone, performing the work in less than a minute – a prime consideration when the patient was rarely drugged but given only a glass of brandy. Last came the apothecary, who originally sold fine groceries as well as drugs, and, like the surgeon, had a practical training by means of apprenticeship; he was not allowed to advise patients, but frequently did so and escaped penalty by charging only for the drugs he dispensed.

In the countryside these functions merged in the figure of the surgeon-apothecary, who practised all or most branches of medicine according to what competition existed from other practitioners in the neighbourhood. Country doctors' lists of patients ranged from members of the gentry and middle classes down to craftsmen, clerks and artisans. Labourers did not appear in their lists, the fees being too high for them, hence the labourers' resort to 'wise men' or 'wise women' and to folk remedies; and at a later date to friendly societies for insurance against sickness and to medical clubs run by doctors. Records of country practices indicate that the most numerous complaints treated included the effects of accidents, such as falls from horses or from ladders, sore throats, ulcers of the legs, boils and abcesses, ulcers of the mouth, sore eyes, and pains in the limbs. Major operations, such as amputations, were rare. Country practitioners made a large part of their income from the dispensing of great quantities of medicine, and also from the standard treatments of bleeding, provision of blisters and the keeping open of issues.[21] Some more well-to-do persons had themselves bled regularly as a means of maintaining good health, though for convenience and economy they might employ a servant to perform the task rather than a doctor; and many people kept wounds and abcesses open as long as possible since there was a school of thought which held that this allowed evil properties in the body to escape.

Modern opinion holds that by the eighteenth century medical practitioners had at their command a considerable range of effective medicines and procedures (as well as many irrational and bizarre treatments). Nevertheless, owing to unwillingness or inability to pay their fees, or perhaps a fear of getting into incompetent hands, many people, even among the well-educated and wealthy, preferred to resort to quacks, to homely treatments passed on in families or by friends, or to a growing variety of publicly advertised patent medicines. In the countryside such resort was sometimes enforced by distance from a qualified practitioner or by difficulties of travel — and qualified practitioners might be thin on the ground. As late as 1804 the medical resources of a substantial part of the large county of Lincolnshire consisted of five Edinburgh-trained physicians (the Scottish universities had a good reputation for their medical training), eleven surgeon-apothecaries, twenty-five druggists (only one of whom had served an apprenticeship), sixty-three untrained midwives and as many as forty quacks. Even in 1858, when the Medical Register was formed, only one in three of practitioners across the country was found to be qualified. Perhaps not untypical of the village doctor of a hundred years earlier was James Clegg, a farmer and Nonconformist minister, who practised in the countryside round the Derbyshire village of Chapel-en-le-Frith. Clegg possessed no medical degree but managed to conform with the Act of 1511 by obtaining a degree *in absentia* from the University of Aberdeen, which institution considered him qualified by experience and reputation. From his diary it is clear that he followed the standard medical practice of the first half of the eighteenth century in administering treatments of bleeding, purging and vomiting, as well as blisters, plasters and poultices, cordials and juleps; and occasionally he used a clyster, or enema, injected into the rectum to cleanse the bowels. Smallpox he treated with opiates, 'dexipharmics' and blistering poultices.[22]

Some of the treatments recommended by doctors were so grotesque and unsavoury that they must have appeared to differ little from those of quacks or folk medicine. Thus a Lancashire squire, Nicholas Blundell, who suffered from sore eyes, found that his oculist's treatment consisted of making an issue in each of his ears. Another doctor called in to examine the eyes of one of Blundell's daughters advised pulling the hair out by the roots, and as this appeared beneficial, Blundell himself carried out the same treatment on his younger daughter. Another victim of poor eyes was the great Duke of Chandos, a man of large wealth, who warily essayed the effect of such specifics as Portuguese snuff, urine and viper's fat. Sometimes a wealthy sufferer would try out a new treatment on a servant before submitting to it himself. The willingness to experiment, to try almost anything, arose from the scarcity of reliable remedies and the limited means of killing pain. Laudanum was in fact widely used for relieving pain, and continued to be used through much of the next century, in the form of various patent mixtures or as pills bought cheaply for a penny or two. Working people took it to relieve rheumatic and muscular complaints, dropping a pill in their beer, and farm animals also were treated with it. Well-to-do sufferers rubbed it on the gums for toothache, as appears in the inquest on Charles Bravo, whose mysterious death in 1876 was the subject of a great scandal.[23]

Since doctors' remedies might be unattractive, or simply unavailable, large numbers of people, even among the wealthier classes, doctored themselves. Old prescriptions were passed down in families and collected from friends and recorded in notebooks. John Fuller, a leading Sussex landowner and ironmaster, noted in his letter book the diet to be followed 'preparatory to Dr Sutton's inoculation against smallpox'. The Blois family, gentry landowners in Suffolk, had an old prescription from the seventeenth century: 'Lady Brookes purging beer that she used to give her servants in the spring'; its ingredients included scurvy grass (mustard and cress), watercress, liverwort, rhubarb, red dock roots, raisins and oranges, and so it was probably effective. The notebook kept by a professional gardener in the 1750s had its memoranda concerning plants and shrubs interspersed with prescriptions for a variety of complaints. These included one for the flux, a recipe using boiled flour in a rice gruel – 'this cured one who had been afflicted one year and been under the care of most eminent Fisicians' – and 'Mr Manley's receipt for ye Rheumatism (had of Mr Dannels)':

> Take ground pine and red sage, of each one a handfull, boil them in 5 half pints of spring water for 5 minutes, strain it off clear and when cold bottle it. Drink a quarter of a pint warm in a morning fasting and also betwixt dinner and supper, putting into each dose 30 drops of Sal Volatile. Continue to drink it for a month. Abstain from malt liquor and drink small rum punch.

Down in Norfolk the gourmandizing parson Woodforde had a pet remedy – one that must have been in constant use – for overeating and wind: 'a good half pint glass of warm rum and water', followed by a regimen of water gruel with two small tablespoonfuls of rum in it and 'a good dose of rhubarb and ginger'. In Woodforde's parish old John Reeves, the farrier, practised 'something in the doctoring way', and despite his poor eyesight also went in for pulling teeth: he once made a bad job of pulling a tooth from the parson's mouth – 'broke one of the fangs ... exquisite pain all the day after, and my Face swelled prodigiously ... too old I think to draw teeth, can't see very well'. When the parson was troubled by a painful ankle he sent to Reeves for some 'yellow Basilicum ointment ... which Dr Buchan recommends.' (Dr Buchan was the author of *Domestic Medicine: or the Family Physician*, a work which went into nineteen editions during his lifetime.) Occasionally Woodforde dispensed with even Dr Buchan's advice, as when in the March of 1791 he suffered from a 'stiony' on his right eyelid, which was painfully swollen and inflamed:

> As it is commonly said that the Eye-lid being rubbed by the tail of a black cat would do it much good if not entirely cure it, and having a black cat, a little before dinner I made a trial of it, and very soon after dinner I found my Eye-lid much abated of the swelling and almost free from pain. I cannot therefore but conclude it to be of the greatest service to a Stiony on the Eye-lid. And other Cats Tail may have the above effect in all probability – but I did my Eye-lid with my own black Tom Cat's Tail.[24]

Although medical books such as that by Dr Buchan could easily be obtained, some credence was also given to published accounts of remarkable cures and treatments, such as those that appeared in *The Gentleman's Magazine* and other widely read works. William Ellis's farming books, for instance, published some such accounts, reporting how cows' milk had cured a long-standing inflammation of the face suffered by the wife of an eminent grazier near Aylesbury, even after she had spent a year and the large sum of £30 on the advice of a noted surgeon without effect. Ellis's more extraordinary stories included one detailing how a famous London surgeon had recommended thrusting a blacklead pipe into the 'violent scorbutical Humour' which festered on the thigh of a Little Gaddesden butcher: the pipe 'there to remain for the pus to evacuate through it, and as the wound heals, it will push the pipe out by degrees, which must from time to time have its end clipped off with a pair of scissors, lest the shirt catch it and tear it out, for no salve will affect this sort of wound'. There was also the Gaddesden girl who had 'the Evil' in her feet from infancy and was cured by the advice of a beggar-woman. The beggar-woman's treatment was a grisly one, involving the mutilation of a live toad which was to be left to waste away, and as it did so 'the Distemper would likewise waste and die'. For good measure there were tales of asthma cured by swallowing young frogs, and jaundice put right by a potion of lice – nine live lice every morning in a little ale.[25]

Patent medicines were advertised in London and provincial newspapers from quite early in the eighteenth century, and were sold through apothecaries and grocers, as well as by booksellers, printers, newspaper proprietors and circulating libraries. A typical advertisement concerned 'Montpelier Pectoral Lozenges', 'the most pleasant and certain remedy in sore throats, coughs, hoarseness and shortness of breath'. There were 'Dr Lowther's powders for fits and nervous disorders'; 'a certain cure for the Itch prepared by a gentleman from Oxford'; and 'George West's pectoral elixir', 'Dr Daffey's Elixir' and 'Hooper's Female Pills'. 'Dr Bateman's Pectoral Drops', for example, were advertised in the *Kentish Post* in 1726 at 1s a bottle as 'a never failing remedy against fluxes, spitting of blood, consumptions, smallpox, measles, colds, coughs and pains in the limbs and joints'; they were stated to be effective also for the treatment of fevers, gout, colic, rheumatism and the stone, and for the prevention of miscarriages. 'Dr Daffey's Elixir', advertised in the same newspaper, was already an old remedy, first patented in the middle seventeenth century, and indeed was still being sold in 1910. It consisted mainly of tincture of gentian, but was proclaimed as 'a certain Cure (under God) in most Distempers' – particularly gout, rheumatism, scurvy, colic, consumption, agues, smallpox, the stone and gravel, worms, yellow jaundice and the king's evil – and in addition was 'a Noble Cordial after Hard-drinking'. 'Hooper's Female Pills', patented in 1743 by John Hooper, man-midwife and apothecary of Reading, contained aloes cum myrrha with sulphate of iron, and so may have been beneficial in treating chlorosis and anaemia. The various purgatives on offer were probably also effective and catered for the contemporary faith in purging as an aid to health. Most patent medicines were reasonably cheap, costing less than 2s; and some less than 1s, though the latter amount would represent a day's wage for a farm labourer at the end of the eighteenth century.[26]

Old-established patent medicines, and newer ones, continued to be popular in the next century, being widely advertised in country-town newspapers and journals such as the *Farmer's Almanac*. An issue of the *Almanac* of 1853, for example, included advertisements for 'Dr Baillie's Aperient Pills for both sexes', said to deprive intemperance of 'its pernicious effects', as well as possessing the power of destroying worms and beautifying the skin. There were also 'Abernethy's Pile Ointment' and 'Paul's Every Man's Friend' for treating corns, together with 'Dr Locock's Pulmonic Wafers', 'Antibilious Wafers' and 'Female Wafers', not overlooking various beauty preparations, such as 'Rowlands' Macassar Oil' for the hair, 'Rowlands' Odonto or Pearl Dentifrice', and 'King's Curious Essence', the 'Ladies' Favourite' perfume. From early in the eighteenth century, if not before, dentures, spectacles and steel trusses for ruptures could be readily obtained in London, the first held in place by wires and springs. The wealthy sometimes preferred to have their black and rotten stumps removed and replaced in their gums by the newly extracted teeth of a young person, though this practice was abandoned after about 1790 when it was found to cause the ulceration of the gums and other severe adverse effects.[27]

Patent medicines were heavily relied upon even when their contents were worthless or dangerous. 'Dr James's Fever Powder', produced by a Robert James, consisted of antimony and phosphate of lime, and may have hastened the end of the poet, Oliver Goldsmith. A fortune was made out of an antimonial pill (together with a headache essence) in the 1730s and 1740s by the ingenious Joshua Ward, whose 'marvellous and sudden cures' were established by the certain, if fraudulent, procedure of hiring patients at 2s 6d a week to pretend the symptoms he professed to cure. Another successful swindler, Joanna Stevens, was paid £5,000 by Parliament to reveal the secret of her remedy for the stone: it included a powder of calcined eggshells and snails, a decoction of soap and swines' cresses, and pills of snails, alicant soap and honey. Sir Robert Walpole's course of this treatment involved a consumption of some 180 pounds of soap.[28]

Quacks abounded at all levels of society. Most successful, perhaps, was the 'Chevalier' John Taylor, who described himself as 'Opthalmiator Pontifical, Imperial and Royal', and who indeed did possess some genuine skill and was in demand at the courts of Europe, though once described by Dr Johnson as 'an instance of how far impudence will carry ignorance'. The great majority were of a humbler stamp, itinerants who travelled from town to town and village to village, peddling their elixirs and attracting in the customers with clowns, tumblers and musicians. There was the 'water-doctor', known also as the 'urinarian' or 'piss-prophet'. He would establish himself at an inn and invite all sufferers to bring a sample of water for his inspection and advice. Sometimes he first took care secretly to obtain details of his clients so that he could astonish them with his powers of diagnosis. A Dr Myersbach, who came to England from Germany, acquired in the 1770s considerable wealth in this way. However, the good doctor was at last exposed when presented with a phial of urine from a gelding, from which he diagnosed a lady's disorder of the womb.[29]

Among the poor who could not afford doctor, quack or patent medicine, there was considerable dependence on charitable care. Some squires paid for a doctor or apothecary to look after the sick of the village by contract, as for example did John Emerton, the owner of the village of Thrumpton, a few miles from Nottingham in the Trent valley. The apothecary at Thrumpton was paid £16 a year in the early eighteenth century together with a little extra now and again for bonesetting.[30] The visiting doctor might be supplemented by an expert bonesetter, where the doctor was unwilling to include this branch of work. There were, indeed, a great many accidents — from clothes catching fire to falls out of windows and spills from carriages, from taking poison by mistake to being bitten by a mad dog. Some kinds of accidents in the countryside were very numerous, arising in part from the employment of untrained young boys and feeble elderly men, and from working in unlit barns and yards in the winter half-light of early morning and evening. Squires, farmers and their workers fell from ladders, haystacks and wagons, and were kicked by horses or fell under carriage wheels. They were thrown from their mounts, shot themselves accidentally while out shooting, cut themselves on sharp implements, or trapped limbs and fingers in turnip-slicers, chaff-cutters and threshing machines. They were crushed by overturned carts, or by falling trees or collapsing buildings in storms; and not infrequently they fell into rivers and ponds, or down wells and disused mine shafts, this misfortune often arising after a hard night's carousing.

Quite often the squire's wife would help sick villagers and travellers, keeping a stock of homely remedies and dispensing them at the kitchen door. Some parsons, too, like Sidney Smith, the humorous incumbent of Foston-le-Clay, near Leeds, supplied the place of doctor, at least for what he considered simple complaints. Smith performed 'miracles' in his parish with 'a pennyworth of salt of tartar', and brought his own children 'through a good stout fever of the typhus kind without ever calling in an apothecary, but for one day. I depended upon blessed antimony, and watched anxiously for the time of giving bark.' Smith had his own dispensary, and when one night his eldest son alarmed him with an attack of croup he 'darted into him all the mineral and vegetable resources of my shop, cravatted his throat with blisters and fringed it with leeches, and set him in five or six hours to playing marbles, breathing gently and inaudibly'.[31] In the cholera epidemic of 1832 the Revd John Skinner, rector of Camerton in Somerset, went round his parish to warn the inhabitants of necessary precautions, including the refusal of shelter to beggars who might be carrying the infection. Preventive measures included the whitewashing of houses and their fumigation by burning camphor and juniper, tobacco, or tarry rope (the burning of juniper had been used as far back as the Black Death). The parson complained of dungheaps neighbouring the houses, and the 'filthiness of the children before the doors', while the burning of the bedclothes of infected persons was recommended. The disease was frightening, not least for the suddenness with which it might strike down its victims: one boy in the village was at evening school and seemed quite well only the day prior to his death. So fearful were the villagers of infection that burials were carried out hurriedly and without services.[32]

Where no benevolent squire, squire's lady or conscientious parson was present, village people resorted to folk remedies, sometimes consulting a local 'wise man' or 'wise woman' who was reputed to possess secret knowledge of many mysteries. Although some folk remedies were very old – for example, the use of garlic mixed with butter and a clove as a treatment for the plague – many were still in use well into the twentieth century. Strange as they might be, the prescriptions often followed a certain logic, such as the belief in the benefit of high ground and a change of air for sufferers from consumption and whooping cough. Thus the patient was to be taken to the top of a hill, or in the North Riding to a place 'where three roads meet'. In Essex it was recommended for the sufferer to follow a plough and inhale the smell of newly turned soil. The smell of sheep in a sheepfold was also held to be beneficial, especially early in the morning, as was the odour of a pigsty or fox's lair, and 'taking the horse's breath' too – that of a stallion in Suffolk, or of a piebald horse in Herefordshire. Another basic idea was the transference of the complaint from the sufferer to an animal or inanimate object. In East Anglia the remedy for whooping cough was to dig a hole in a meadow and get the child to place his or her head in it until a cough came. In Essex the hole was then to be filled in to keep the cough there. From Shropshire came the remedy of holding a frog or toad in or near the mouth so that the whooping cough was transferred to the animal, while another suggestion was to drink the cat's milk after it had lapped it, or the water in a horse trough after a horse had drunk from it.[33] Even as late as the First World War, soldiers were eating or smelling live snails and maggots as a remedy for sore throats and coughs.

More scientific was the inoculation – often given by an unqualified person, however – which was developed in the eighteenth century for the prevention of smallpox deaths. Smallpox had long been recognized as a distinct disease, and was much feared, especially for its toll of children, though it seems to have varied in virulence: it may have been past outbreaks of low mortality which encouraged some parents to allow their uninfected children to play with a young sufferer, hoping that a mild illness would follow and confer subsequent immunity. One person who certainly understood the willingness of parents to take the risk was John Evelyn, the diarist, who himself lost two daughters to the disease within the space of six months. In 1685 Evelyn, in the company of another celebrated diarist, Samuel Pepys, made a visit to the home of Mrs Graham, wife of a member of the royal household. There they found her eldest son lying sick of smallpox,

But in a likely way to recovery, and other of her children ran about and among the infected, which she said she let them do on purpose that they might whilst young pass that fatal disease she fancied they were to undergo one time or other, and that this would be for the best: the severity of this cruel disease so lately in my poor family confirming much of what she affirmed.[34]

Inoculation as a preventative of fatal smallpox, that is, inserting a small amount of infected matter from a sufferer into an issue on the body of an uninfected person to induce a mild attack, had been practised in the Far East since early times, and was used in the Near East since at least the later seventeenth century; it was known of in medical circles in London from early in the following century. John Woodward, a London doctor, described the method at a meeting of the Royal Society, and a report of his statement was published in 1714; this was influential, and its acceptance in England was encouraged by the support given by Lady Mary Wortley Montagu a few years later. Lady Mary had already had her infant son inoculated when she was resident in Constantinople, and in 1721, when a serious smallpox epidemic broke out in London, she had her 5-year-old daughter inoculated in the presence of several physicians. These gentlemen were so favourably impressed that royal permission was obtained to make the experiment on three male and three female volunteers found from among criminals under sentence of hanging at Newgate, and subsequently on eleven charity-school children. The resulting attacks were so mild that the king ordered inoculation for two of his grandchildren.

However, at first inoculation was not always successful. It is estimated that some two or three of every hundred inoculated experienced a severe attack and died; and it is also argued that inoculation tended to spread the disease more widely than would have happened in the natural course of events. By the 1750s or 1760s, at all events, the practice had become quite commonplace; indeed, at this time some overseers of the poor were prepared to meet the cost of inoculation – a matter of pence per head – of all the poor of the parish. A major reason for increased acceptance of inoculation was the improvement effected by the Sutton family, specialist inoculators of Framlington Earl, Norfolk. They perfected a technique of inserting the smallest possible quantity of infectious matter into the lightest of scratches, although the idea of attenuating the virus had been originated in England and elsewhere some years earlier. The safer 'Suttonian method', as it was dubbed, led to an extensive practice, and after about 1768 the method was widely adopted in England and in other countries. The brothers Robert and Daniel Sutton, though unqualified, became highly successful in the business, Robert establishing himself at Bury St Edmunds and Daniel at Ingatestone in Essex, where patients from all parts were boarded and subjected to his regimen. In the three years 1764–6 Daniel himself inoculated 13,792 persons, and his assistants some 6,000 more – all without a single death. Within two years his income exceeded £6,000 a year.[35]

Very quickly other practitioners learned of his success, adopted his methods and developed high-class establishments of their own. Thus a Sussex newspaper advertisement of 1770 reads:

Gentlemen, Ladies, and Others, desirous of having *the Small Pox*, may be exceedingly well-accommodated at a very good large, and airy house on Heathfield Down, by Mr and Mrs Burfield. Eighteen days for one guinea (*Tea, Sugar, and Wine Excepted*), and longer, if necessary, paying *One Shilling* a Day; and prepared, inoculated, and diligently attended during the *Distemper*, by THOMAS BALDOCK, *Surgeon*, at Burwash, for *One Guinea*, common price.

Among the poor inoculation was carried out not by medical men but by anyone who cared to set up in practice, including, so it was said, farmers, farriers, customs officers and liveried servants. When Parson Woodforde's village was struck by the disease in 1791 steps were quickly taken for the farrier to inoculate all the children. 'It is a pity that all the poor in the parish were not inoculated also', wrote Woodforde, 'I am entirely for it.'[36]

According to the historian of inoculation, P. E. Razzell, the effect of the popularizing of the safer Suttonian method was so great as to provide a likely explanation for the remarkable growth of population which occurred in England after about 1750. In Maidstone in Kent, for instance, smallpox burials fell from 252 in the period 1752–63 (when they were nearly 15 per cent of the total) to only two in 1792–1801.[37] The country's population appears to have increased only slowly in the first half of the eighteenth century, but then rose by over 60 per cent in the next fifty years. At the first census of 1801 the population of England and Wales was assessed at 9.3 million, and in the following half-century it almost doubled, to reach 17.7 million. The latest research on this subject concludes that the main cause of the upsurge was a fall in the age of marriage, resulting in higher fertility; though in the past some historians have argued that the more likely cause was a fall in the death-rate, especially in that of young children. Here the significance of inoculation enters into the picture. Razzell's main point is that the beginnings of rapid population increase coincided with the growth of inoculation, and well before the discovery and application of vaccination as a superior method of reducing mortality from smallpox. Of course, the validity of his argument turns not only on the argued effectiveness of inoculation but also on the incidence of deaths from smallpox as compared with other causes of mortality, and whether even a greatly reduced smallpox mortality prior to the introduction of vaccination would be sufficient to account for the massive rise in population.

The story of vaccination has very much a West Country background.

In that part of the country there had long been a belief that people who handled cattle were never known to catch smallpox, though not all doctors accepted this. In fact, a person milking a cow suffering from cowpox was very liable to contract the same disease, the lesions of the ulcerated teats of the cow infecting the human through chapped hands or a scratch on the hands or wrists. Cowpox in the human was a mild affair, but did provide protection against smallpox. The first person believed to have experimented with cowpox was Benjamin Jesty, a farmer of Yetminster, near Yeovil. In 1774 he allowed two farmhands who were known to have had cowpox to nurse smallpox sufferers. Neither came to any harm. Then Jesty took matter from an infected cow and rubbed it into scratches made with a darning needle on the arms of his wife and two sons. None of them acquired smallpox, but the wife's arm became so inflamed that it had to be treated by a surgeon. Fifteen years later a doctor named Trowbridge, practising in nearby Cerne Abbas, persuaded Jesty's sons to let him inoculate them with smallpox: they experienced no reaction of any kind.

Neither Jesty nor Trowbridge followed up their experiments. The major step forward was taken by Edward Jenner, a medical practitioner of Berkeley, in Gloucestershire, who was once a house pupil of the great surgeon, John Hunter, at St George's Hospital, London. Jenner was familiar with the cowpox story, and indeed experimented with swinepox in the human. In 1778 he was consulted by a Berkeley lady who, having had cowpox herself, wished to know whether she should be inoculated against smallpox. Jenner seized the opportunity of making a trial, and found that his smallpox inoculation produced only a slight local reaction. Subsequent experiments confirmed this result, and in 1796 he inoculated a boy of 8 with cowpox matter taken from a sore on the hand of a dairymaid. The boy suffered only a mild illness, and when inoculated with smallpox showed only slight reaction. After further experiments Jenner published his findings in a famous pamphlet of 1798.[38]

'Vaccination' soon replaced inoculation since it had the important advantages that cowpox could not be spread by direct contact, and that any reaction was mild: there had always been a few deaths arising from even the Suttonian method of inoculation with smallpox. In 1808 a National Vaccine Establishment was created, and after the severe smallpox epidemic of 1838–40, which gave rise to especially heavy mortality among children, inoculation was prohibited and the voluntary vaccination of children provided at public expense. Later, an Act of 1853 made vaccination of infants compulsory, but was ineffective for lack of enforcement. A further great epidemic in 1870–1, part of a European pandemic, led to new measures, including the appointment of doctors as free public vaccinators, but a substantial proportion of children were still not treated. The disease, however, was now in full retreat. The last major epidemic here of this once feared scourge occurred in 1902–3.

As vaccination began the final conquest of smallpox a new and more fearsome horror appeared. Asiatic cholera augmented the old killers of typhoid, typhus and tuberculosis. The lack of adequate hygiene of the person and of cleanliness in home and workplace, the impurity of much of the water supply, and the foul crudeness of sanitary arrangements fostered these diseases. This was especially so in the overcrowded working-class districts of the towns, it is true, but the rich were by no means entirely immune. Typhoid was responsible for the death of Prince Albert, and nearly brought to a premature close the life of the future Edward VII; a report on the defective sanitation of Buckingham Palace had to be suppressed. But although the towns were the major seats of epidemic disease, the countryside did not escape. Many rural homes were old and defectively built, damp, cold and draughty, the cottages huddled together to share one well and quite often a single closet. Piles of refuse were heaped against porous walls, and ill-fitting and broken windows failed to keep out the stench of neighbouring ditches and pigsties. Floors were sometimes laid directly on to the damp earth, and in low-lying situations were flooded in rainy periods. The old fevers and the new as readily found victims in romantic thatch-roofed and rose-hung country dwellings as in the bleak jerry-built slums of Milltown.

In the 1820s a cholera pandemic covered great areas of the Far East, and by 1829 had extended to central Europe and to Sweden. The cholera reached England in October 1831, when the first cases were reported from the port of Sunderland: before November five deaths had occurred. The government, observing the westward march of the disease across Europe, had time to prepare plans to meet the emergency. Local boards of health were formed with authority to remove the infected persons to lazarettos, or isolation homes, and to clean the houses and destroy the clothing left by the sufferers. The epidemic died away in December of the following year, having caused some 22,000 deaths in its first months. A Cholera Prevention Act that followed was aimed at local provision of nurses and medicines, the covering of drains and cesspools, destruction of infected bedding and clothing, and general removal of nuisances, but it failed for lack of effective means of enforcement. In 1849 a new cholera epidemic dramatically reinforced the very limited authority given to a new General Board of Health appointed under the first Public Health Act of 1848. But when the cholera abated, the General Board, dictatorial and unpopular, was allowed to lapse. Its main achievements had been its experimentation with new systems of sewage removal and the awakening of some town authorities to the need for public health measures. However, it was not until 1872 that a new Public Health Act divided the whole country, except London, into sanitary districts, each with its own Medical Officer of Health and a Sanitary Inspector.

The true factors in the spread of cholera had been suspected by some English observers since the first outbreak of 1831–2, and in 1849 Dr John Snow published his findings indicating the key role played by the contamination of water supplies by sewage, and the contamination of food prepared by unwashed hands. The incident of the Broad Street pump, when cholera devastated the district round Golden Square in London, confirmed Snow's theory. A very high proportion of the people infected had drawn their water from the contaminated source of the pump. Snow found also that houses served by certain water companies were much more liable to cholera than those supplied by other companies, who drew their water from a different and purer source. In Devon a Dr William Budd noted that cottages in North Tawton drawing their water from one particular well were the ones struck down by typhoid. The later work in England of Sir John Simon, Medical Officer to the Privy Council, and that in France of Louis Pasteur, professor of chemistry at the University of Lille, paved the way to a much fuller understanding of the origins of disease and the importance of pure water and proper sanitation in creating healthy living conditions.

Epidemic diseases, nevertheless, continued to rage in the towns and countryside of late Victorian England, though typhoid and cholera became less common as water supplies and sanitation were gradually improved. The great and persistent killer was tuberculosis, which in 1838–43 was responsible for 60,000 deaths a year. With advances in housing, diet and general living standards even this scourge was in retreat, and at 1.9 deaths per thousand of population in 1900 was responsible for only half the mortality that it had caused fifty years before. In the closing decades of the century sanatoria and dispensaries were opened to provide treatment, but the bovine type of tuberculosis, spread by consuming milk from infected cows, though discovered early in the 1870s, was not effectively checked until considerably after 1922, when it was reported that as many as two out of every five dairy cows had the disease.

*   *   *

The public health problems, and their eventual solution, are generally thought of as peculiar to urban Britain; indeed most of the experimentation with new kinds of treatment and new precautions occurred in the towns. But a row of country cottages, though housing only a tiny fraction of the slum-dwellers of London or Liverpool, could be just as insanitary and just as dangerous to health. In 1850, it should be remembered, the rural population was still nearly as large as that of the towns. The main advantage of the country-dweller lay in the smaller numbers in any one place, the relative isolation and the large proportion of workers whose days were spent in the open breathing clear country air. But the towns, on the other hand, had their improvement commissioners who, whatever their failings, gave some attention to the cleaning of streets and the removal of nuisances. The towns, too, had their 'night-soil contractors' or 'nightmen' who for a fee emptied cesspools, cleared out privies and unblocked drains. The villages rarely had such professional cleansers, and in them the manure from the byre, the sty and the chicken-house was mixed with the emptyings from the privy and heaped in the midden or spread on the garden, a fertile source of plagues of flies in summer. Infection from the manure heaps was washed into neighbouring streams and percolated down to corrupt the drinking water in shallow wells and ponds.

It is interesting that in 1838, the first year in which registration of births and deaths became compulsory, a rural county like Devon had as many as 615 deaths from typhus and scarlatina, 460 from smallpox – despite Jenner and his vaccine – and 1,649 from consumption. Not that Devon was particularly unhealthy, far from it: its mortality from all causes, at 18 per thousand, was bettered only by Lincolnshire, Rutland and the North Riding. When Edwin Chadwick, the public health reformer, collected the evidence for his *Sanitary Condition of the Labouring Population*, published in 1842, he received many alarming reports from the medical officers of rural Poor Law unions. These doctors gave a great deal of emphasis to the nature of the location and the freshness of the air, showing particular concern about low and damp situations, the proximity of undrained marshes, which were productive of fevers and the ague, and to neglected ditches, which were often filled up with all kinds of refuse. Among the other conditions which they believed dangerous to health were dung heaps intended for manure, 'cesspools or accumulations of filth' close to cottage doors, the keeping of a pig hard by the dwelling, which 'in the heat of summer produces a stench quite intolerable', and a 'stagnant pond in the immediate vicinity'. In numbers of villages and country towns few of the homes had drains, and some not even privies, so that 'rubbish is thrown within a few yards of the dwellings, and there is no doubt but in damp, foggy weather, and also during the heat of summer, an exhalation arising from these heaps of filth must generate disease, and the obnoxious effluvia tends to spread contagion where it already exists'. Some houses had mud floors 'much below the level of the road, and in wet seasons they are little better than so much clay'; 'brick or boarded floors are seldom or never scrubbed ... and the walls never get lime-washed from one end of the year to the other'. Overcrowding 'is fearful. I have seen six or eight sleeping in one apartment, with every crevice stopped, and have more than once been nearly suffocated by entering the apartment even after several of them were up and out.' And in another instance of eight sleeping 'in one small ill-ventilated apartment',

> the smell arising from want to cleanliness, and the dirty clothes of the children being allowed to accumulate, was most intolerable. Considering the situation of the house, its filthy state, and the vitiated air which must have been respired over and over again, by eight individuals sleeping in one confined apartment, it is not surprising that this family should have been afflicted with fever, and that of a very malignant type; the mother and one child fell victims to it in a very short time.[39]

Nevertheless, it is necessary to remember that not all country housing was bad, and that the medical officers were drawing on their experience of visiting the homes of sick paupers, homes likely to be the worst in the district. In fact, whatever the shortcomings of the housing, the mortality rates of farm labourers improved steadily in the second half of the nineteenth century. About 1880, according to figures collected by Professor W. A. Armstrong, the farm labourer was among the most long-lived of all workers. At the age of 20 he could expect a further 45.3 years of life, and at 30, 30.7 years; even at 60 he could expect to reach the good old age of almost 76. Charles Booth, the investigator of London poverty, remarked that countrymen could work effectively for ten years longer than townsmen, 'as seventy to sixty'; and this is borne out by the much higher proportion of elderly workers found on farms than in other occupations. But though long-lived and commonly at work in his sixties, the farm labourer had a good deal of sickness and fairly high average losses of working time from this cause.[40]

In 1911 infant mortality in farmworkers' families, though more than twice as high as that for the families of solicitors and clergymen, was still relatively low for the poorly paid: it was much better, for example, than the rates for dock labourers' families, carters and carriers, bargees and bricklayers' labourers. Relatively low infant mortality, and a tendency to high fertility, made for large families and a heavy burden on small incomes for food, clothing, boots and school fees. If the families had been smaller the infant mortality rate itself would no doubt have been lower; and also perhaps there would have been less child employment in the countryside and better attendance at school. At this time, 1911, the farm labourers' working conditions and living standards were subjects of much controversy, arising in large part from public concern over the state of the nation's health, and how this was being affected by the decline in numbers of the healthier section of the community, that living in the country. The Registrar-General's returns for 1911 showed that infant mortality under one year in rural districts was only three-quarters as great as in urban areas, and that at all ages the health of country-dwellers was superior when examined over a considerable range of disease. The two exceptions were that deaths from influenza were more numerous in rural areas, as was also tuberculosis at the age of 25. (At other ages country districts had lower rates of death from tuberculosis.)

This is not to say, of course, that there was not a great deal of room for improvement in country districts or that country people suffered little from poor health. Country children when examined by medical officers were often found to be badly undernourished, and were much in need of the cheap school meals which were first introduced in the mid-1870s in Devon and in Forfar, but became widely adopted only in large towns. Country children were still undernourished in the 1930s, when adults were found to suffer considerably from such complaints as rheumatism and pleurisy, influenced no doubt by having to work in the wet and cold, and by living in damp and draughty cottages. There was also in the countryside, as in the towns, the well-known differential between the infant mortality of the middle classes and that of the working people. Indeed, it might be said in conclusion that the brightness of the rural health picture gained a great deal by the comparison with the blackness of the towns. The era in which the typical English inhabitant was transformed into a town-dweller was one in which the urban drift meant a move to a probably more prosperous but almost certainly less healthful environment.

Part of the background to the country-dweller's state of health was the gradual improvement in the provision of medical care over the course of the later eighteenth and the nineteenth centuries. Curiously, the 'paupers', the recipients of public poor relief, were among those members of the labouring class who had access to qualified medical practitioners. Moreover, from the later eighteenth century the authorities began, during epidemics, to establish 'pest houses' or houses of refuge where the infected could be isolated, while the newer workhouses, at least, were kept regularly whitewashed and adequately ventilated. Current views on the causes of infection also encouraged official efforts towards greater cleanliness. It was generally supposed among the medical fraternity that infection was spread by an invisible vapour, or 'miasma', emanating from the bodies, clothes and beds of the sick, and that unpleasant smells indicated the presence of such miasma. After the Poor Law was reformed in 1834 part-time medical officers were appointed to look after the paupers in the unions of parishes. This meant travelling the length and breadth of several parishes and attending to some hundreds of patients in their homes and in the workhouse. The salary offered for this work was generally of the order of £150 or £200 a year, but could be as low as £50: a Dr John Fox of Cerne in Dorset was paid £70 for looking after the pauper sick in twelve parishes. Soon after 1834 the typical Norfolk medical officer shouldered a case-load of 275 a year for a salary of £65, though by the middle of the nineteenth century both areas and case-loads had been reduced.

The medical officer was often required to provide the standard drugs himself, including quinine and cod-liver oil, and some tight-fisted Boards of Guardians looked askance at expensive extras, and even disliked paying an additional fee for the setting of fractures and attendance at deliveries. Doctors often found their patients to be seriously undernourished, and their prescription of 'luxury' items such as beef and mutton, port wine and porter frequently dismayed the Guardians.

After 1858 the medical officer was obliged to be qualified in both medicine and surgery, while many country doctors remained without any formal qualifications. The Poor Law requirement thus had the strange result that paupers were treated by better-qualified practitioners than the generality of the population, and often in their own homes when the independent poor had to attend at the doctor's home or surgery. However, the cumbrous nature of the Poor Law administration, requiring the production of a relieving officer's note to the doctor before he could act, was responsible for irksome delays, sometimes with fatal consequences. And not all Poor Law doctors were very prompt or conscientious; on occasion there was a failure to appoint a substitute when the doctor was away from the district.

Inside the workhouse conditions of medical care varied greatly. In 1834 there were some 10,000 workhouse inmates needing medical care, and in 1861 as many as 50,000. Improvements were very slow in coming. Some old-established, pre-1834, 'Houses of Industry' in East Anglia had long possessed hospital wards, a dispensary and a pest house for infectious cases located some hundreds of yards from the main buildings; and a surgeon and midwife were appointed to look after the sick. The new, post-1834, workhouses lacked such comprehensive facilities. It was not until the 1860s, Anne Digby tells us, that rural workhouses in Norfolk provided this accommodation. As the numbers of inmates fell away in the late nineteenth century more rooms became available for conversion into sick wards, though the Guardians were not disposed to spend much money on medical appliances or furniture. Trained nurses were in short supply, mainly because of the low pay, low status and unattractive nature of the work, and the nursing was often done by pauper inmates. In 1844–5 the Norfolk unions could boast only four nurses between them. The use of inmates as nurses continued even after 1897, when officially prohibited. As late as 1909 there were still many rural workhouses without even one trained nurse, and scores with no nurse, trained or untrained, for night duty; there were even some with no kind of salaried nurse at all. Medical officers' requests for adequate dietaries, more attention to hygiene and ventilation, and reduction of overcrowding were frequently ignored by unsympathetic Boards of Guardians. Lunatics and the weakminded posed a special problem. Guardians were reluctant to remove lunatics to an asylum because of the higher cost of maintenance there, and it was long before separate wards were provided within the workhouse. Once admitted, the mentally ill tended to remain inside indefinitely.

The Guardians' sense of responsibility for the general health of the area was awakened by their awareness of the recurrent connection between bad water supplies, insanitary housing, disease and pauperism, and was forced upon their attention by the severe outbreaks of cholera which occurred in 1848–9, 1853–4 and 1866. Even then the Guardians reserved their medical facilities for treating paupers, and, ever conscious of their responsibility to the ratepayers and the need to prevent the expansion of free services, refused help to the independent poor.[41]

For country residents at large there came gradually some increased availability of medical care, though many practitioners remained unqualified. Among those with qualifications country practices seem to have appealed to retired or half-pay army and navy surgeons who were used to less than ideal conditions. By the time that country practices came to be advertised in *The Lancet* (founded in 1823), it seems that the country doctor's income was only of the order of £200, £300 or £400 a year, and a practice, together with the surgery, drugs and equipment, could be purchased for something between 500 and 1,000 guineas. Country doctors had to be physically tough and inured to travelling through muddy lanes and over windswept moors in all weathers. Only the country towns and larger villages had a resident doctor, and so much journeying on horseback or in a gig was necessary to treat distant patients. Some doctors charged a higher fee if called out beyond a circuit of 7 miles from their home. They often dispensed their own drugs and had to be prepared for all emergencies. Amputations were carried out on barn floors and kitchen tables, teeth were pulled by the side of the road and babies delivered in a cramped corner of a cottage. Edward Jenner once turned out in cold so severe that he arrived at his destination almost frozen and senseless, unable to dismount. But he warned the servants against taking him to a fire, and thawed out gradually in the stables.

The income of the country doctor depended very much on the wealth of the district. G. M. Porter, who practised at Caistor, in Lincolnshire, around the middle of the nineteenth century, had among his patients the Earl of Yarborough (who paid him a retainer of £100 a year), the well-to-do farmers of the Yarboroughs' Brocklesby estate and the paupers of the Caistor union. But if he had no wealthy patron and few well-heeled farmers and professional people in his practice then the doctor's outlook was less promising. Bad debts were an annoying aspect of the doctor's lot, as were the many patients who preferred to pay their bills in kind, while many of the independent poor were too afraid of the doctor's fee to call him in at all.

It was to bring in this last class of patient that country practitioners formed medical clubs, whose members paid a small subscription in return for free treatment and medicine. Clubs of this kind had been tried by some Poor Law unions in the 1830s: one in Norfolk provided free treatment, free vaccination and cut-price confinements in return for subscriptions ranging from 1d a week for an adult to $2\frac{1}{2}$d for a large family. Only families with a weekly income of less than 18s were eligible, and drunkards, profligates and those already sick were excluded. Private clubs were set up by doctors who devised their own rules and means tests, and employed canvassers to rope in new members. At Batheaston, near Bath, a medical club charged from 4s 6d to 11s 6d a year according to size of family, with members providing their own bottles, leeches and bandages. Membership was restricted to those earning less than a guinea a week, and in addition to the exclusion of drunkards and those known to be idle and disorderly, sick persons could join only if they procured two healthy members at the same time. A society for the relief of lying-in women was also established in this village, and in return for a 5s subscription provided bags containing linen, bedgowns, towels, soap, rushlights, sugar, a paper of grits and a small bottle of castor oil, as well as other necessaries.[42] In industrial districts some doctors were appointed on contract to treat all the workers in collieries, quarries, factories and railway shunting yards, as well as by friendly societies and benefit clubs. Even at the end of the century the rates paid by individual members of sick clubs were still as low as 4s or 4s 6d a year – in 1911 the average was estimated at this figure – and could even be as little as 2s 6d, while country doctors continued to augment their incomes by extracting teeth and supplying dentures.

Meanwhile the medical provision in the countryside had been supplemented by two innovations, the district nurse and the cottage hospital. The district nurse, riding through the lanes on her bicycle and calling at farms and cottages over a wide area to visit patients, dress wounds and give advice, became eventually a familiar figure. The first was trained in London and served in the large village of Cawston, near Rugby, in 1857. The early country nurses were generally skilled ladies with a social conscience and sufficient leisure to undertake unpaid care of the poor in their own homes. They were originally employed by charitable bodies who also used many other, untrained, women. By the end of the century untrained country nurses were paid about 15s or £1 a week to provide a homely service, not pretending to command the skills of a qualified nurse. The villages raised public subscriptions to help pay the nurse, and small charges were made for her services, such as 2s 6d at a confinement. In addition, at an even lower level, simple village women, including many married women and widows, turned to nursing as they might do charring, and earned about the same money, 4s or 5s a week. They met the demand for 'the sort of woman who would go to a village and help clean up the cottage, put things generally straight, and see the children go to school all right, and so on'. Many of their patients were senile or chronic cases who but for this help would have received no nursing at all.

Early in the twentieth century the training of a district nurse was usually six months in midwifery 'and another six months in district work among the poor'. Many of them would not have been able to take a standard nursing examination, though gradually the less-well-trained village nurses and midwives came under the supervision of a qualified Queen's nurse, a nurse supported by funds from the money subscribed to Queen Victoria's jubilee. In Rider Haggard's village of Ditchingham a meeting was held in his house to find means of paying for a Queen's nurse; there had been several cases, said Haggard, of persons dying for lack of timely nursing care. In 1898 the village of Batheaston obtained the services of a trained nurse at £30 a year. In 1911, according to the records, her salary was £46 16s, and during the year she made a total of 1,747 visits, an average of about six a day. Later in the twentieth century, after the introduction of the nurses' register in 1921–3, the larger hospitals and district work became the two fields most attractive to trained nurses.

In the middle of the nineteenth century hospitals were confined to the larger towns, and in a sense it was the workhouses, in country and smaller towns, which came to provide a basic hospital service. The voluntary hospitals, apart from being few and far between, limited their admission to subscribers and those whom the subscribers were prepared to sponsor. In 1861 there were only about 11,000 beds in the whole of England and Wales, a proportion of one to every 1,800 members of the population. Subsequently, in 1868, a new Poor Law Act authorized Guardians to provide separate infirmaries, but progress in doing this was very slow. Nearly thirty years later well over half of the sick poor were still being cared for inside general workhouses. A new development was the cottage hospital, founded through the enterprise of a local doctor or the beneficence of a wealthy philanthropist, or perhaps by one of the big national friendly societies such as the Oddfellows, Foresters, Druids or Buffaloes. In most cases the capital cost and part of the maintenance came from donations or from the pockets of employers. An example quoted by Pamela Horn is the

Basingstoke Village Hospital which cost about £600 in the mid-1870s and had beds for eight patients.[43]

The first cottage hospital was opened at Cranleigh, in Surrey, in 1859. Six years later there were eighteen of them, and by 1880 as many as 180. Their numbers continued to grow, though each hospital, as the name implies, tended to be small: in 1935 there were 600 cottage hospitals with about 10,000 beds, an average of under seventeen beds per hospital. An important feature was that, unlike the old voluntary hospitals in the towns, maintenance and treatment were not free. The fees charged were moderate, however, between about 2s and 8s a week, and as they did not cover all the costs donations and subscribers were sought. A small committee managed the hospital, often with the parson playing a prominent role. Every doctor in the neighbourhood was entitled to send suitable patients, and was entitled, too, to perform operations and be paid any fee that was forthcoming, as in cases sent by the Board of Guardians. Thus the country-town and village practitioners now had hospitals to work in, simple and underequipped as they were, and could treat their own patients instead of transferring them to a larger hospital and a specialist at a distance.

Control by general practitioners and the charging of fees enabled the cottage hospitals to escape much of the controversy which arose over the methods of the larger voluntary hospitals. There, the general practitioner complained, a patient could get a specialist's opinion for only 1s or 2s 6d, a fee which undercut his own, while many patients – 'gentlemen's servants, clerks and well-to-do tradespeople' as well as 'yeomen' – who could well afford to pay a general practitioner's fee, obtained free attention in the out-patients' clinic. The eventual arrival in 1911 of national sickness insurance, which applied to about 15 million wage-earners receiving less than £160 a year, did not affect the hospitals or the controversy over charitable hospital care: the 'panel' doctor could deal only with minor complaints and some chronic diseases; the more seriously ill still had to go to the voluntary hospital, Poor Law infirmary or cottage hospital.

A persistent historical tradition tells of the healthy country-dweller. In past centuries it was taken for granted that country occupations, especially those on farms, produced strong, healthy bodies, and town occupations the reverse. In Tudor times one of the objections ranged against the extension of sheep-farming was the adverse effect it had on the reserve of able-bodied men required in time of war; especially serious was the decline of ploughing for, it was said, 'shepherds be but ill archers'. Remarks of this kind continued to be made over the years, and once again at the end of Victoria's reign concern was expressed about the labourers' flight from the land since, it was asked, who would provide the supply of police officers and fill the ranks of the army in years to come? Moreover, country-dwellers possessed not only better physique but were more restrained in their habits: 'the husbandman works regularly, is sober and industrious, and poorly paid', expostulated John Byng in 1791, 'but the artisan will work (from high wages) but four days in a week and wallow in drink the other three, and if unemployed, will be ripe for, and active in any mischief'.[44]

We have seen that country people, for long the great majority, were in fact exposed to recurrent famines and epidemics, and suffered largely from other disabling complaints. Although nineteenth-century evidence goes some way to bear out the tradition of the healthy country-dweller, we should not forget that the work of producing the country's food and many of its important raw materials was performed by a labour force that was at various times weakened by famine and decimated by disease, and that the yield of the land was always liable to be affected by some considerable incidence of illness and physical weakness. Rural England was not lacking in vigour and, at times, in good living; but there were many other times when farm and cottage were struck by sickness and pain, when work was badly done for lack of physical strength, or not done at all. The effects of hunger, illness and early death on the rural economy can only be guessed at, but they cannot be left out of a balanced picture of the past.

4

PLENTY AND WANT

The fundamental factors in the living standards of the past were broadly the same as those of today. That is to say, standards depended on the amount of the family income and the size and age of the family, together with the effects of movements in real wages, that is, the relationship between money income and the prices of consumer goods. Generally, small families were better off than large ones, and living standards rose when prices fell relative to money incomes, and *vice versa*. Of course, the price of some goods was of much more importance to people than that of others: for the poor the price of bread or of bread-flour was always of critical importance since it played so large a part in total spending. Unfortunately, it is far easier to state the nature of these factors than to discover what their dimensions were in the past, and this is true of even the relatively recent past, such as the first half of the nineteenth century.

Over a period population trends, and wage and price movements, could exert considerable influence on living standards. When the population was growing fairly rapidly, as in the early middle ages, again in the sixteenth century and first half of the seventeenth century, and in the 170 years after 1750, the average size of family rose and living standards came under pressure. This pressure, however, was partly offset by expanding opportunities for employment and the additional income which a larger number of children in the family might produce. Very possibly, the bulk of labouring families were better off when different conditions prevailed, the population was more stable and there were fewer mouths to feed. Also, such families might be better off when prices were low or falling, and especially when favourable prices were combined with a stable or falling population, as was the situation in the later middle ages and in the hundred years between 1650 and 1750. In these conditions land was more readily available and wages improved.

Evidence suggests that the average size of family changed considerably over time. Some studies of medieval population have assumed that the average then was 3.5 persons, though this may be too low, and investigations of records for later periods have found that it might fall between 3 and 5 persons; the average for Canterbury in 1563 was 3.4, and in mainly rural communities between 1650 and 1749 as high as 4.75 persons.[1] The village of Shepshed, in Leicestershire, which was undergoing gradual industrialization as the stocking-knitting frame became established there, had an average family size which rose from 3.62 persons in the sixteenth century to 3.88 persons in the first half of the eighteenth century, and then jumped to over 5 persons thereafter.[2] In this village industrialization was accompanied by a fall in the mean age at marriage, a change particularly evident after 1750, and indeed this was the general experience, as shown by broader evidence that the age at first marriage of women fell from 26.5 years in 1740 to 23.5 years in 1800. This change was accompanied, too, by a dramatic fall in the proportion of spinsters, that is, women who never married, and by an increase in the proportion of births that were illegitimate.

There were then, as later, substantial differences between the various social classes. Among the wealthy, where large inheritances, dowries, and political and dynastic objectives were at stake, marriage was a matter of great consideration and prolonged negotiation, and was usually early. Heiresses were widely sought after, and a girl might be promised to a suitable husband at a very early age, even if the marriage itself was postponed. Lower down the social scale, farmers and crafts-men who had the expectation of inheriting a farm or a workshop showed greater prudence than poorer people who were without such prospects. They married later, often waiting for the father's death so as to have an income adequate for supporting a family. As George Ewart Evans has pointed out, among the farmers marriage was designed to conserve family property and to maintain a traditional way of life, some families often being associated with a particular occupation. He instances, as example, the Groom family of the Claydon district of Suffolk who, most appropriately, had always been connected with horses.[3] Thus a period of exceptionally heavy mortality, as occurred in the first half of the eighteenth century, might well produce a lower age of marriage among farmers and craftsmen since expectations were achieved earlier than before, and younger sons might find themselves unexpectedly in pos-session of property as death claimed the father and first-born at an early age. In a later period, after 1750, the expansion of industry, trade and agriculture created many new openings for employment and helps to explain the marked fall in age of marriage (and consequently the increase in family size) which is associated with the era of industrial revolution.

Historians have been able to gain some detailed knowledge of living standards (as well also of occupations, farm stocks and farming methods) from records known as probate inventories, the valuation of people's possessions at the time of death. From these documents it is possible to see that certain areas were substantially wealthier than others. For example, in the later sixteenth century Hertfordshire labourers enjoyed a much higher level of personal wealth than those in the midlands, while the midland labourers in turn were much superior to the northern ones. A similar picture emerges for the three decades between 1610 and 1640, except that it is then possible to place Somerset second to Hertfordshire, with the eastern counties falling between the wealthier midland woodland areas and the less wealthy midland fielden districts.[4] An analysis of the distribution of wealth in the Vale of Berkeley in the closing decades of the seventeenth century also shows the marked differences which existed between occupations. Some 60–9 per cent of the personal wealth was held by people leaving less than £50, while 7.5–10 per cent was made up by possessions of mercers, clothiers, gentry and clergy who individually left property worth over £250. In between these extremes, 11–15 per cent of the wealth was that of artisans, husbandmen and suppliers of food and drink, people leaving between £50 and £99; and 12–16 per cent was that of comfortably-off yeomen farmers, butchers and bakers, leaving between £100 and £249.[5]

To take a more specific example, we have a prosperous Kentish yeoman, Nicholas Wigmore of Goodnestone Court, near Faversham, whose will and inventory have been studied by Dr Dennis Baker. When Wigmore died in the spring of 1560 he left domestic goods and farming assets together worth over £240 – and this at a time when the average country-dweller of east Kent had property worth less than £30. The inventory reveals that in a wool loft Wigmore had stored for future use or sale a hundredweight of raw wool and over a hundredweight of woollen yarn, together with spinning wheels and the carding implements needed for preparing the raw wool for spinning. In his poultry yard ran eighteen chickens, six geese and some ducks, as well as two turkey hens and a cock, the last a quite recent addition to the range of English poultry. His house possessed at least twelve rooms, and the existence of silver plate, joinery-made furniture, bedcoverings, wall hangings and an ample supply of linen indicates a very superior standard of living. The kitchen boasted its kettles, stewpots, chafing dishes, spits and dripping pans, and the meals were served on pewter, though possibly only for the family, since there were also a dozen wooden trenchers, relics of a more primitive past, which perhaps were still used by the servants. Also indicative of the insecurity of the time was the armoury, which included a sword, a hand gun, daggers, bows and sheaves of arrows.[6]

Inventory material reveals that often there was no clear division of occupations. Even Nicholas Wigmore, a substantial and well-off farmer, evidently dealt in the yarn spun at home from his own wool. The combination of a craft or trade with the working of some land was very common. At Otford, in west Kent, Samuel Walker, a blacksmith, who died in 1667 leaving personal property worth £39 5s 10d, had wheat, oats and hay in store, as well as a sow and four pigs, the corn and pigs being worth together considerably more than his blacksmith's tools. Daniel Marlin, a weaver, who died in 1676 leaving goods worth over £95, had nearly half of this sum in farming assets, when his loom and other cloth-making equipment came to only £6. John Stileman, a brickmaker, had corn, other crops and farming gear worth £72, when his stock of bricks amounted to less than £19.[7] There were, of course, a great many people with sufficient land to be full-time farmers, or nearly full-time ones, but even some of these might run a secondary business connected with the farm, such as selling wood or delivering coal from a nearby port or river, or they might hire out their carts and wagons for more general use when not needed on the farm.

Access to land, whether owned or rented, made a great difference to the well-being not only of such people as craftsmen, dealers and innkeepers, but also of many humble labourers. From evidence collected by Professor Alan Everitt, it seems that although very few labourers of the sixteenth and early seventeenth centuries had as much as 4 or 5 acres of land, there were a large number who had some smaller quantity. And of course, the labourer who was almost or entirely landless had appeared on the scene in the early middle ages. By the sixteenth century two out of three labourers probably had little more than a garden, with perhaps a small close or two attached, though the situation varied widely from one part of the country to another.

In the course of the later eighteenth and the nineteenth centuries the growth of the rural population resulted in an increase in the numbers of labourers who had little or no access to land. Further, since in the same period the average size of farms was tending to get larger, there was also an increase in the ratio of labourers to farmers. Many small farms continued, however, farms where hired labour was not commonly found, and where, indeed, much of the fieldwork, even heavy tasks like ploughing, were performed by the farmer's wife and daughters. But on the larger farms, the hard work was undertaken solely by the workfolk, male and female, and on really large farms a sizeable labour force was deployed under the orders of the farmer or his bailiff. Many of the farmworkers came to be day labourers, a wage proletariat living in the farmer's cottage and having no land beyond a garden, if as much. By the nineteenth century this situation came to be commonplace in the southern counties of England, where farm servants living in with the farmer had become much reduced in numbers, and it was especially marked in those districts given over to large-scale grain production.

Figure 11 Farm labourers of the late eighteenth century, as pictured by Stubbs. By this time many farmworkers were without land of their own and were entirely dependent on their wages, being frequently hired and paid by the day.

In the absence of a little holding of his own the key factor in a labourer's fortunes was access to a common. Rights of common varied greatly, but in the best circumstances they might include the right to depasture any number and any kind of beasts, to lop trees for timber and gather fallen wood or cut turf for fuel, and to quarry stone and gravel for building and repairing the cottage, as well as rights of fowling and fishing. Frequently, too, poor people could snare rabbits and take hares, wood-pigeons and birds' eggs, as well as gather beechmast for the pigs, collect crab apples and cobnuts, pick berries from the hedgerows to enliven the diet, and search for herbs on waste ground for culinary and medicinal purposes.

However, the extent of these rights and perquisites varied greatly, and they were often closely regulated by the community in order to protect the woods and commons from excessive depredations and over-grazing.[8] Over time the commons and waste lands were nibbled away by farmers seeking additional land, by landlords making parks and game preserves or seeking minerals to exploit, and by squatters who settled and took in a piece of waste land for a cottage and some pasture. Commons diminished, and they often became closely stinted in common-field areas, or they disappeared altogether as villages became enclosed. By the early decades of the nineteenth century, as William Cobbett noted, the labourers were best off in heavily wooded districts – Cobbett remarking here on a circumstance which perhaps had long been significant. Traversing the Isle of Thanet in September 1823, he was struck by the beggarly appearance of the cottages and the dirty, ragged character of their inhabitants: 'Invariably have I observed that the richer the soil, and the more destitute of woods; that is to say, the more purely a corn country, the more miserable the labourers.' In the wealds and forests of the southern counties which he knew well, labourers had fuel for their ovens and winter fires, and the woods themselves provided work in the planting, thinning, cutting and carting of the trees, and in making such things as poles, hurdles, fencing, posts and charcoal from the wood.[9]

Piecemeal encroachment on the commons gave way to wholesale enclosure where the land was good enough to warrant the expense. The incorporation of commons and waste lands into the farms had been going on for centuries, but proceeded most quickly during the period of parliamentary enclosure which began about the middle of the eighteenth century, and was especially rapid during the wars of 1793–1815, when corn prices reached famine height and almost any piece of uncultivated land was worth the cost of enclosing it. The effects on the labourers of the loss of commons in this period have long been debated by historians. How serious for them was the loss of the right to pasture a cow in the summer, to gather winter fuel, snare rabbits, and all the other little perquisites that the commons and wastes had previously afforded? On this there is no agreement, and a major difficulty in the way of reaching a positive conclusion is that we do not know what proportion of cottagers actually enjoyed common rights; nor for those who did, how valuable they were to them. We have seen that the extent of the rights varied widely, and this may well explain why contemporaries differed in their opinion of that value. It was argued then, and since, that enclosure, by extending the area under cultivation, increased the availability of employment, so providing the labourers with a more secure living than before. However, although employment increased where the area of arable was extended or some form of convertible husbandry was adopted, it would certainly decline where the former common fields were put down to permanent pasture. It has also been pointed out that the compensation for loss of common rights awarded by the enclosure commissioners was often an allotment of the order of only an acre or two, or even less, suggesting that the common right was valued at only £10–40, or often less. Further, it is argued that an acre or two of land was not a fair compensation for access, even if it was restricted access, to a wide expanse of common and waste.

The problem is highly complicated, and indeed is one which very much interested contemporaries as well as modern historians. Arthur Young, for instance, made notes on a number of instances of varying effects which he found in enclosed villages in Norfolk. He noted that at Carleton, for example, 40 acres had been allotted to provide fuel for the cottages, and that where a cottager held a common right by virtue of owning a small tenement, the commissioners had allotted in compensation land worth £10. At Cranworth, however, the poor were now deprived of the geese they formerly kept on the common, and the allotment for fuel that had been given was inadequate because of their number. At Ellingham there were formerly 'scarcely any cows kept by the poor, as they would have been starved by the sheep', while at Felthorpe, on the other hand, the commons had previously been so valuable that the farmers could not get labourers to work for them; here a common of 50 acres, allotted after enclosure for providing fuel, was grazed by the small occupiers and the poor continued to keep cows. Cottage cow-keeping had come to an end at Fincham, however, though many persons had formerly grazed the common without possessing the right, paying fines for their trespass. At Heacham 'the really poor had no stock on the fields or common, further than geese, and could suffer by the enclosure to no other amount; abundantly made up to them by an ampler and better paid employment'; while for the common-right owners of Heacham the stinted common remained in being and 2 acres of middling land had been allotted as compensation for the loss of grazing in the former common fields: 'there are from twelve to fifteen little and very comfortable proprietors and renters of small plots from two to ten acres, who have cows and some corn'.

At Langley, again, the commoners formerly derived little benefit from their rights: 'they used to beg for straw, etc., and often lost their cows; and went begging to get others'; after the enclosure the landlord had provided small grass closes to all who were able to get a cow, and so many had become better off. But at Marham, on the other hand, the cottages did not belong to the poor, and neither did the common rights, though they had exercised them; thus the allotments went to the larger proprietors who owned the cottages; 'many cows were kept before, few now'. At Northwold enclosure had tripled the market value of a house and allotment, and after the enclosure the cottagers of twenty years' standing who had no common rights were allowed to cut 800 turves a year from the fen for fuel. Some twenty cottagers who had kept cattle and geese without a right now had no possibility of continuing to graze their former half-starved beasts. And at Shropham the poor 'used to have cows, mares, geese, ducks, etc.; but now nothing, and their language is (I talked with several) that they are ruined ... The account a farmer gave me was, that many poor kept cows before; now not more than one or two.'[10]

Clearly, the great variety of circumstances that existed prior to enclosure, the differing practices in detail of enclosure commissioners in the matter of compensating both legal and customary rights, and the initiatives sometimes taken by landlords to provide cow pastures and vegetable plots for rent after enclosure, make it impossible to come to a general conclusion. In some places, where the common had formerly been of value to the poor and the compensation awarded by the commissioners was niggardly, the poor were undoubtedly worse off; in other places, especially where the common was small and had been strictly stinted before enclosure, and was of little value to the majority of labourers, they might be no worse off than before; and in others still, where compensation was more generous or landlords provided land for the labourers to rent, or where employment was greatly increased by the expansion of arable farming, the poor might well have been made considerably better off by the enclosure. Whatever the consequences might have been in particular circumstances, it has to be borne in mind that even had there been no parliamentary enclosure, the growth of numbers in the countryside would have put increasing pressure on the commons, and must have resulted in tighter restrictions on their use, and, eventually, the exclusion of all those who could not prove a legal right of access.

Moreover, it is also important not to exaggerate the extent of any changes which occurred. Where parliamentary enclosure was most heavily concentrated, in the midlands, it affected over a period of some eighty or ninety years about half or slightly more of the total acreage. But very large areas of the country, in the eastern counties, the south-east, south and south-west, saw little parliamentary enclosure because most of the land had already been enclosed in some earlier, perhaps much earlier, period. And in Wales and the north of England most of the parliamentary enclosures were concerned very largely or exclusively with waste lands in areas of sparse population. Overall, across the whole country, some 24 per cent of the total land area was affected by parliamentary enclosure, and of this figure a large proportion, about three-fifths, represented enclosure of pasture and waste, which must have tended to extend cultivation, to increase livestock numbers and generally to raise the local demand for labour. Only a third of the newly enclosed land was previously in common fields. In some areas, like the North York moors, where land was of marginal value for cultivation, the enclosures were permissive rather than mandatory, and might not in fact be implemented for periods of years, perhaps not at all: and even in areas of widespread specialized arable farming, in Norfolk for example, some common land was not worth the enclosing and so remained in being.

On balance it is probable that parliamentary enclosure did constitute in some degree a landmark in the gradual growth of a rural proletariat, of a rural labour force which had little or no access to land beyond a cottage garden and perhaps a rented vegetable patch. But the change was not sudden or sweeping, and we must recall Professor Everitt's conclusion that perhaps as many as two-thirds of labourers had little more than this, if any more, in a period stretching back over 200 years before the onset of parliamentary enclosure; and, indeed, the existence of landless villagers was already evident far back in the middle ages. Nor did the era of parliamentary enclosure see any revolution in farm sizes, although it appears that there was a general slow increase in the average size of farm units, a development that was not, in fact, very closely associated with enclosure.

*   *   *

Despite enclosure, relations between farmer and his workers remained for the most part what they had always been, close and personal, if not always amiable. There were, of course, some areas of large farms, those of 500 acres and over, which if largely in arable employed upwards of fifteen or twenty men and boys regularly, as well as women and children, and great numbers of seasonal workers at busy times. But taking the country as a whole, large farms like these were exceptional. Even in the middle nineteenth century the 'average' farm (a statistical rather than realistic concept) was only a little over 100 acres, and a large proportion of all farms, as much as 30 per cent, covering nearly a

95

half of the total acreage, fell into the 100–300-acre range; such farms employed from two or three to between five and a dozen regular hands, depending on the extent of the acreage that was in pasture as against the much greater labour demands of the area of arable.

Most labourers, therefore, worked on small or medium-sized farms, and had a close personal relationship with the employer, who as a working farmer laboured alongside them. A substantial number of the labourers, especially among the younger ones, had a very close relationship, since they lived with the farmer, sleeping in a loft or outhouse, and eating at the farmer's kitchen table. These farmworkers, mostly aged between 11 and the early twenties, were known as farm servants. They were usually hired and paid by the year, and they very frequently changed employer, moving from farm to farm within a distance of a few miles, generally less than 12 or 13 miles. Farm service ended when they married and set up home in a cottage, often one provided by the farmer; they then became day labourers, paid by the day, though quite frequently they would work for one farmer on a regular basis. Even having a family and a cottage did not always serve to tie a man to a particular farm. In Dorset in Thomas Hardy's time, and doubtless elsewhere, it was common for labourers to change employers, and consequently cottages, quite frequently. Those seeking new masters stood, like the farm servants, in the marketplace when the local 'statute' or 'statty' was held, bearing some mark of their calling to indicate the nature of the employment required – a shepherd held his crook, a carter had a piece of whipcord twisted round his hat, a thatcher carried a bundle of woven straw.

Of course, not all labourers were so footloose. Some stayed on the same farm for decades and never travelled more than a mile or two. Celia Fiennes, traversing the Peak District of Derbyshire in the course of her travels in the late seventeenth century, noted that strangers were obliged to hire guides, 'the common people know not above 2 or 3 mile from their home'. And over a century later, Cobbett found the same difficulty when riding near Ludgarshall, west of Andover. He asked a cottager, a smart young woman of about 30 years of age, the way to the village, which he knew could not be more than about 4 miles away.

> She did *not know*! ... 'Well, my dear good woman,' said I, 'but you *have been* at Ludgarshall?' – 'No.' – 'Nor at Andover?' (six miles another way) – 'No.' – 'Pray, were you born in this house?' – 'Yes.' – 'And how far have you ever been from this house?' 'Oh! I have been *up in the parish* and over *to Chute*.' That is to say, the utmost extent of her voyages had been about two and a half miles![11]

Just what made some labourers move is difficult to determine:

perhaps a farm changed hands, perhaps a labourer decided to seek better accommodation or a more affable master, perhaps there was a dispute between employer and employee over the management of the flock, the making of the hayricks or some other detail of running the farm – matters of slight import to an observer, perhaps, but highly important to skilled farmworkers who took a pride in their work and liked things done in a certain way. At all events, despite the fixity of a minority, the mobility of rural people, though usually confined within a limited district, was generally much greater than is often supposed. At Otford, in Kent, in 1851 only a half of the householders had been born within the parish, while seventeen out of the eighty-four were born in neighbouring parishes, twelve in other places in Kent, and thirteen outside the county altogether. Thus 30 per cent of the householders had come to live at some considerable distance from their place of birth. The same sort of movement may be seen in other parts of the country.[12] At Batheaston in Somerset the 1851 census shows that well over half the population had been born elsewhere, and the figure for agricultural labourers alone was 40 per cent. Twenty-eight per cent of agricultural labourers had been born within 10 miles of Batheaston, and 12 per cent came from further afield.[13] Evidence from other places at an earlier period shows a similar position, with a high proportion of both men and women coming from outside the parish, many of them from places more than 10 miles away. There is no doubt that, within broad districts, the movement of people was considerable, and those who spent the whole of their lives in their native parish were in a minority, if a substantial one.

The division of the regular farm labour force into farm servants living in, and day labourers living out, was one which changed over time. Ann Kussmaul's study suggests that the rise and fall in numbers of farm servants was connected with movements in population and changing labour demands on farms. Farm servants, constituting between a third and a half of all hired labour, were less readily hired by farmers when the population was growing and the supply of alternative labour was rising; conversely, servants were more eagerly sought after when population ceased to grow rapidly and labour surpluses disappeared, as in the later seventeenth and early eighteenth centuries. From the later eighteenth century the effect of the renewed growth of population on farmers' attitudes to the hiring of servants was reinforced, among other factors, by the consolidation of farms, the expansion of grain production and the decline of commons – changes which influenced both the nature of the farmers' labour demands and the availability of day labourers. After the French wars the fall in prices and glut of labour combined to give a fatal blow to living in, especially in the south of England, though not to annual hirings. In the north and in Wales farm servants continued to be employed, and especially so where livestock, requiring constant care throughout the year, loomed large in the farm enterprise.[14] The contemporary observer William Cobbett remarked on the change and put his finger on two other factors. In a famous passage he pointed to the higher social pretensions of well-to-do farmers, who banished the rustics from their homes and tables, and also to the low level of day-labourers' wages which made it uneconomic to provide board and lodging. The farmers, Cobbett expostulated, could not now 'keep them *upon so little* as they give them in wages. This is the real cause of the change.'[15]

Day-labourers, farm servants and some craftsmen also depended in large degree on their wages, though there were other sources of income. Day labourers were usually provided with a cottage, perhaps free of charge but more commonly in return for rent, and they might have their dinner at the farmhouse. At haymaking and harvest the farmer provided food and drink, and throughout the year there was usually a daily allowance of beer (or cider in cider-producing districts). There was commonly a free allowance of fuel, though this might only be turf, furze or 'culm', made from coal dust mixed with clay, and the fuel was hauled by the farmer to the labourer's cottage. On some farms labourers were allowed some produce, such as milk, bacon or potatoes, though they might have to pay for it, and it was often of inferior quality. Further, they might be allowed a corner of a field for growing vegetables, in addition to a garden attached to the cottage. The value of these perquisites is difficult to gauge because they varied so widely, but generally they formed a useful supplement to meagre cash wages, and the daily allowance of drink, in particular, was highly prized.

Farm servants living in with the farmer got their board and lodging as part of their remuneration, and so were able to save a part of their annual wages – if the attractions of the alehouse and fair could be resisted. Sometimes servants were allowed to keep their own sheep along with their master's flock, a deduction for the grazing being made from their wages. Apart from bringing in additional income, the servant's sheep represented an accumulation of capital, a step in the direction of becoming an independent farmer, which was the goal of many a servant. Over a few years of service the combined savings of a male servant and his bride (often a servant too) might amount in the later eighteenth century to some £20–30, and considerably more over a period of service as long as eight or ten years.[16] With, say, a sum of £30, a farm servant might be able to stock a holding of between 15 and 20 acres, according to contemporary estimates of the minimum farm capital that was generally employed.

Craftsmen worked for wages when employed as journeymen by a master, but the majority were small independent jobbing entrepreneurs who undertook work on commission and supplemented the income from their craft by keeping livestock and perhaps a few acres of arable. In Lincolnshire, for example, agricultural assets, especially livestock, accounted for over half of the personal estate of a sample of mainly rural carpenters, masons and thatchers. One, James Eagle of Navenby, who died in 1598, left three horses, twenty-one cattle, 140 sheep and lambs, a few pigs, poultry and husbandry equipment, as well as crops in the ground valued at £20.[17] Many other craftsmen and some country professional people supplemented their commissions and fees with the income from various kinds of by-employment. This was so even with such notables as village clergy, notaries, scriveners and barber-surgeons, as well as the more commonplace shoemakers, tailors, blacksmiths, brickmakers, brewers, butchers and bakers. By-employments which were seasonal or part-time fitted in well with a profession or craft that might have a too small or erratic demand to provide round-the-year work. Apart from farming, there were in woodland areas the felling and carting of timber and the making of such wares as gates, posts, handles, brooms, besoms or even wooden spoons; in addition there were potting, tiling, mining, carting, thatching, ditching and a host of odd labouring jobs. More regular employment was afforded by spinning, weaving, fulling and dyeing, but the burning of charcoal and making of iron were generally confined to the winter months; the summer, when the roads became drier and more easily passable, was reserved for the transport of the iron to foundries, slitting mills and other points of consumption.

Wages, therefore, were of minor importance, or even of no importance at all, to many people in the rural past. Those most dependent on them (though only to a degree) were the day labourers and farm servants. The amount of wages paid varied regionally, and also of course over time. In money terms farm wages rose and fell with the movement of prices, though not necessarily to the same extent. On a group of estates in the south and east midlands the rise between 1500 and 1640 was threefold, from an average 4d a day to 1s a day, without allowance for meat and drink. In the same period, however, the cost of living rose sixfold, so that by 1640 the purchasing power of a day's wage was only half of what it had been formerly. Wage rates were rather lower in the north of England, and somewhat higher in the west and south, but in all areas the general trend was much the same.[18] Labourers could earn more on piece-rates and for performing special tasks, and there was often a marked seasonal variation between the higher summer rates and the lower winter ones. Again, higher rates were paid in the busy seasons of haymaking and harvest, when, however, the hours worked were also longer. In the middle seventeenth century rates considerably above 1s per day were paid for such work as haymaking, ploughing and lading water; as much as 1s 6d for felling timber and reaping, 1s 9d for hedge-mending and 2s to 2s 6d for thatching, though such work might involve labourers in putting in longer hours, and perhaps they would be expected to supply their own carts or horses.[19]

But, as we have noted, money wages tell only part of the story, and of course the value of perquisites was increased when prices were rising. Allowances of a free cottage and fuel, of beer, clothing and shoes, of milk and of corn and malt, and of the keep of a few sheep or a pig, were all the more considerable when their value rose sharply in the course of the sixteenth century.[20] Subsequently, when prices fell in the late seventeenth century and the first half of the eighteenth century, labourers' wages ceased to rise and may even have declined a little, while the value of perquisites certainly fell. In the later eighteenth century seasonal differences were still marked. In his northern tour of 1770 Arthur Young found that the average of eighty-two places from which he collected figures was 7s 1d per week, a figure made up from an average 6s 5d a week for the forty-one weeks of 'winter', 9s 5d for the normal six weeks of haytime, and 10s 8d for the five weeks of harvest. His methods of collecting and analysing his data, however, were unscientific and suspect, but the results are not without interest. Women labourers averaged about half the men's rates, at 3s, 4s 4d and 6s 3d respectively. The wages of farm servants, living in and paid by the year, Young found to average £10 8s 6d a year for 'first men', £6 11s for 'second men', £3 2s for 'lads', £3 19s for a dairymaid and £3 5s for other female farm servants.[21]

It has to be remembered that Young's figures were taken from widely scattered places, from as near to London as Kensington, and as far away as Alnwick in Northumberland, and there were wide differences in the wages paid in neighbouring districts, even on neighbouring farms. He speculated on the influence of proximity to the capital, and was surprised to find that in places between 100 and 300 miles from London the rates were similar to those near London, while in other nearer and more distant areas they were lower. It was also remarkable that he found the presence of manufacturing made no difference, a very different conclusion from that of Sir James Caird eighty years later. The man's average rate for the great bulk of the year, 6s 5d per week, does not appear to be very different from the 1s a day mentioned by Professor Everitt for the middle seventeenth century, suggesting that money wages had not changed very greatly in the interim, although real wages had risen substantially since food, the major item in the labourer's budget, had fallen in price. Young, incidentally, found that the cost of board in the north of the country averaged 8d per day, and in the south 10d (with a dinner valued at $4\frac{1}{2}$d in the north and 6d in the south).[22] This suggests that in the north the cost of keeping an experienced male farm servant, a 'first man', was about £12 on top of his £8–13 in annual wages, a total of £20–25, and in the south about £22–26 (since the generally lower wages in the south partially offset the increased cost of board). These figures may be compared with the earnings of a day labourer which, assuming full employment throughout the year, varied between some £38 and £66 a year, according to Young's figures. Clearly, if Young's evidence is to be relied on – and this is subject to question – the keeping of a farm servant at this time was cheaper for the farmer, though on the other hand, day labourers, being older on average, were probably more useful and more highly skilled, and also offered the advantage of greater flexibility, since they could be laid off in bad weather or other slack periods.

Sir James Caird's figures for 1850–1 were more precisely divided between north and south, since he found wages in the north to be much superior on average owing to the labour demands of industry, which served to put a floor under farm wages. The growth of industrial occupations in the north of England had evidently brought about a major change in the pattern of farm wages since Young's time, eighty years before. Now the north showed higher than average wages, the south lower than average. Caird's figure for northern counties' weekly wages was 11s 6d, and for southern counties 8s 5d, producing a national average of 9s 6d.[23] If this last figure is compared with Young's 7s 1d we can see that by 1850, after falling somewhat after the end of the war in 1815, farm wages had settled down at a rate about 35 per cent higher than in 1770. By 1850, too, the prices of food, clothing and housing had fallen from wartime heights to levels which were probably not very different from those of 1770 (though the nature of diets, cottages and clothing had changed considerably in the meantime, making comparisons very difficult). However, over the space of eighty years the labourer's purchasing power had suffered not only from the wartime high prices but also from the growth of winter underemployment, which became especially marked in some southern districts after 1815 as rural population increased, while farmers were hit by lower prices and accordingly cut back on their labour demands.

To take the story on, between 1850 and the First World War money wages slowly improved, particularly as more men and women left farming for other kinds of employment, or emigrated, and the farm labour force gradually shrank. After about 1870 real wages rose more quickly as the prices of common foodstuffs and cheap clothing fell. The beneficial rise in real wages came to a halt about the beginning of the new century, however, as prices began to rise again as fast as, or faster than, wages, but over the period 1870–1914 real wages may have improved by as much as 25 or 30 per cent.

* * *

In the past, as now, the earnings of the husband may give only a partial picture of the family's financial situation. Wives commonly worked on the farms, full-time or part-time, tending the dairy and the poultry, hoeing and singling, helping with the haymaking and harvest, and cutting roots for the stock in the winter. In some counties, such as Dorset, many farmers would not hire a man unless he had a wife able and willing to work, and preferably one with children old enough to help, while in the north the old tradition of the man providing a wife, daughter, sister or other young woman, a 'bondager', died out only gradually in the course of the nineteenth century. In districts where large acreages had recently been enclosed from the waste, as in parts of Lincolnshire and East Anglia, male labour was scarce and the farmers resorted to gangmasters who recruited bands of women and children to work by contract on such tedious and backbreaking tasks as clearing the ground of stones and weeds, spreading manure, hoeing roots and lifting potatoes. The work was often excessively arduous, and women and children laboured in bitter winds, snow showers and rainstorms, often spending most of a long day in the open, half-frozen in wet clothes. But it was not so much the physical strains imposed by gang labour that troubled observers, rather the moral dangers to which young people were exposed when constantly in the company of adults of intemperant habits, doubtful morals and foul speech. Eventually the Gangs Act of 1867 established a licensing system for gangmasters, forbade the employment of women and girls on a gang in which men worked, and prohibited the employment of children under the age of 8. To evade the limitations imposed by this Act many public gangs transformed themselves into private ones. But what really crippled the gangs was the arrival of compulsory education, the raising of the minimum age for agricultural employment to 10 in 1876, and the progressive raising of the school-leaving age in the legislation which followed the Education Act of 1870.

Outside the areas where gangs were widely used wives and children worked on the farms in twos and threes, except at haymaking and harvest when troops of women and children followed the men, raking up the hay and stooking and binding the cut corn. At other times of the year young boys were employed to help the carter or ploughman, or to serve as mobile scarecrows in newly sown fields. The wages paid to a woman ran at about half the amount paid to a man, and varied considerably with the nature of the work, more being paid for harvesting, less for taking up potatoes, and less still for such jobs as weeding and planting, or sorting potatoes. A similar variation often appeared in the even lower sums paid to children. But though the rates changed with the seasons and with the tasks performed, the earnings of women and children made a substantial difference to the family income.

Regional and local variations make it impossible to quote typical figures, but as an example from a county of middling wages (the figures kept up by the presence of alternative occupations such as coal-mining and framework-knitting) we may quote the earnings of Nottingham-shire farmworkers: in 1833 the average weekly wage was about 12s 6d, but in favourable circumstances the earnings of the wife and children could bring the family income up to as much as 20s. In 1838 the Assistant Poor Law Commissioner for Norfolk and Suffolk, one of the less well-paid areas, found that the earnings of each child over the age of 10 added about £5 a year to the family income, suggesting an average wage of about 4d a day. In Dorset, another low-paid county, as late as the 1890s ordinary labourers could earn only about 10s a week, with carters, shepherds and cowmen receiving an extra 1s to 3s (though for longer hours). Women were paid 9–10d a day, and boys from 4s a week upwards. An extra 1s 6d or 2s a week was paid if no cottage was available. With a wife and two boys earning, therefore, the total family income of an ordinary labourer might come to about 23s a week if the farmer provided a cottage – a sum well over double the man's earnings.

Labouring families spent a life that took them through a cycle of changing fortunes. In early married life, when the children were small and the wife could earn little, times could be very hard. Then, as the children became old enough to earn and the wife was free to work, the situation improved, and might become better still when the daughters were old enough, at 12 upwards, to leave home for domestic service. Later, as the children all left home and the parents became elderly their position would deteriorate again, perhaps to the point where eventually the workhouse loomed as the last bleak resort at the end of their days. All this assumes full-time employment. In practice earnings were reduced by seasonal unemployment, which was more marked in arable districts than in pastoral ones, and especially by spells of severe winter weather when farmers laid their hands off. Many farmers, it was reported, did not hire their hands 'for wet or dry', and perhaps about one-half of men were laid off in bad weather, while a large proportion of even the labourers hired by the year received no pay in sickness. In some years, too, low prices caused farmers to economize in labour, employing only the best of their workers for the essential tasks. Sickness and accidents were grave misfortunes for labouring families, most particularly when it was the husband who was laid up, perhaps for months on end. The early death or permanent incapacity of the husband reduced the family to a life of unending poverty, only somewhat relieved perhaps by the occasional charity of the farmer or parson and the help of kind neighbours. And compulsory education, universally enforced from the later 1870s (though often evaded), meant that for much of the year the children's earnings were reduced, while school fees (not completely abolished until 1918) were a heavy drain on the labourer's income.

As the nineteenth century advanced women became less frequently employed on the farm, especially out of doors, so that by the end of the century a woman working in the fields had become an uncommon sight. The number of female farmworkers recorded in the census fell quite sharply in every decade between 1851 and 1891, falling by 65 per cent over the forty years, a considerably more rapid fall than that of the men on farms. After 1891 the numbers of women employed rose somewhat and stabilized, reflecting perhaps the growing scarcity of men and boys, and the expansion of those branches of farming in which women could readily be employed: dairying, fruit, poultry, potatoes and market-gardening.

The decline in female employment before 1891 owed something to the partial mechanization of some field operations, such as haymaking and the harvesting of corn crops; more perhaps to the slow improvement in men's wages which made families less reliant on the wife's earnings; and in some districts more still to the growth of cottage industries. Straw-plaiting and pillow-lace-making spread through the villages of Bedfordshire, Buckinghamshire and parts of neighbouring counties, while further west in Oxfordshire and elsewhere glove-making occupied many of the cottage women. These women's trades flourished for a few decades, being especially active between the 1850s and the 1870s, but by the end of the century they were far gone in decline. In Bedfordshire, for example, there were over 20,000 female straw-plaiters at the census of 1871, but only 485 in 1901; and in Buckinghamshire the 1851 census recorded over 10,000 female pillow-lacemakers, still over 8,000 in 1871, but only 789 in 1901.[24] A combination of changes in fashion, the introduction of cheap imports from abroad, and in some cases the competition of factory production, were the main factors in the collapse of these and other cottage employments. Occasionally, if distance was not a problem, women and girls could move from cottage work to employment in a factory making the same goods, as in gloves. There were also many other kinds of small country-town factories, for making butter and cheese, jam and pickles, cloth, hosiery and collars, steam laundries, bakeries and the like. The menfolk, too, could now find some local alternatives to the attractions of the large cities and emigration. While some rural industries, such as iron-making and cloth-making, had disappeared in areas such as the Kent and Sussex Weald, the Forest of Dean and the old cloth-making towns of East Anglia, new types of work began to appear. In Norwich, for example, the making of wire for fencing replaced the old cloth trade, and ornamental iron-working for gates and railings developed in the Sussex Weald. Everywhere small ironworks produced the improved ploughs, harrows and other

Figure 12 Charcoal-burners in the New Forest. Families engaged in woodland occupations took caravans or built crude huts to set up home in the woods. Until fairly recent times charcoal-burning and a variety of woodland crafts provided some country-dwellers with a livelihood.

implements now used in farming, corn and cattle cake mills flourished, and both the blacksmith's and the wheelwright's trades grew with the expansion in the number of horses used in country and towns. Brickworks expanded in areas like north Kent, Sussex and the district around Bedford, agricultural machinery at Lincoln and Ipswich, furniture-making at High Wycombe, and every country town of any size had its waterworks, gasworks, breweries and warehouses, and numbers had nearby paper mills, quarries, sandpits, cement works or railway workshops.

Some of these occupations declined, as did the women's trades, with changes in demand and in production, as, for example, with the increasing concentration in a few centres of flour-milling and brewing.

Country people had to change with the times, some moving into nearby towns for alternative employment, some emigrating, some remaining in the village but turning to other occupations such as dealing in wood and coal, shopkeeping or the carrying trade. Before the country motor-bus began to appear at the very end of the nineteenth century the village carriers provided the essential link between villages and nearby towns and railheads. Serving regular routes on fixed days of the week, usually coinciding with the market days of the towns, the carriers' carts and vans collected parcels and passengers and carried out commissions for customers, buying the ordered articles in the town and bringing them back the same day. Carriers offered a convenient door-to-door local transport service which the railways, not even touching the great majority of villages, could not begin to provide. In the nineteenth century the carriers multiplied, operating many thousands of routes, and offering an occupation which, if not full-time, could be combined with general cartage, higgling and shop-keeping.[25]

Where cottage industries failed, or had never appeared, the women-folk might still turn a penny in a variety of small but profitable ways. Early in the nineteenth century William Cobbett had written his *Cottage Economy* to instruct labouring folk in the mysteries of keeping cows and goats, and the making at home of bread, candles and rushlights. Pigs, especially, Cobbett enthused over, claiming that a couple of flitches of bacon were 'worth fifty thousand Methodist sermons and religious tracts. The sight of them upon the rack tends more to keep a man from poaching and stealing than whole volumes of penal statutes.'[26] Cottagers kept chickens and sold the eggs, made jams and pies, collected cockles and mussels from a nearby stretch of shore, went out as charwomen and took in washing, just as their young sons went before and after school to run errands, clean boots and cutlery or sweep the yards at the home of the squire, parson or doctor. Home-made produce was exchanged with that of neighbours, acorns were harvested in the woods for the pig, and fruit for the pies and jams gathered from the garden and hedgerows. The ancient custom of gleaning, the collecting of the fallen heads of corn from the fields after harvesting, was still widely practised, though many farmers had long frowned upon it. A family might glean enough corn to keep them in bread for the winter, or to pay the cottage rent. When the church bell rang out the hour for gleaning to commence all the women trooped into the cornfield, wearing huge bonnets to keep off wind and sun and carrying their babies on their backs, giving the mites 'a little bit of laudanum on sugar to keep them asleep'.[27] And although cottages were often small and unhealthily overcrowded, a spare bed might yet be found for a lodger, not infrequently an Irishman, especially in places where some

Figure 13 Dorset village women returning home with their loads after gleaning in the fields. Although increasingly frowned on by farmers, gleaning was an important supplement to the cottage economy, and a family might gather enough corn to keep them in bread over the winter.

casual employment was available, in quarries, brickworks, the railway, road-making and the like.

Nevertheless, seasonal unemployment, illness and accidents, the burden of a large family, and perhaps fecklessness and drink, kept many families near or below the edge of extreme poverty. Destitution could sometimes be staved off with the aid of a local charity or the occasional gift of coal and blankets provided by the squire's lady or the parson. Most families ran up debts with the village shopkeepers and relied on extra harvest earnings or the sale of a pig to square the account. But there were many who could not live on what they were able to earn or

107

what they were given or could borrow – families with many young children, families who had lost the earnings of the husband through death or disablement, deserted wives, elderly widows, the handicapped, including the severely crippled and the mentally defective. For all these the Poor Law stood as the last refuge, the safety net drawn between hunger and starvation.

This is not the place to explore the complexities of the Poor Law. At any one time it consisted of a confusing variety of measures which differed greatly from place to place. From its early beginnings in the sixteenth century down to the major reform of 1834, relief was on a parish basis, each parish adopting whatever forms of relief seemed best suited to its needs at the time. After 1834 relief was still geared to local conditions though responsibility was shifted to an elected Board of Guardians, which administered a union of some ten or fifteen parishes. Prior to 1834 relief was predominantly of the 'outdoor' kind, that is, given to the pauper in his own home, while a parish poor house or workhouse was available for the homeless and those who needed institutional care. After 1834 the workhouse regime was made much harsher, with the object of discouraging able-bodied paupers from seeking relief there and so forcing them, through the denial of outdoor relief, to fend for themselves. However, for other large sections of the poor, the widows, the able-bodied sick and others who could carry on in their own homes if given a little help, outdoor relief was continued much as before. Outdoor relief was cheaper and much more flexible than workhouse provision, so that despite the bleak image which the post-1834 Poor Law has acquired, the great majority of paupers continued in fact to be supported in the traditional manner, with only a small minority enduring the rigours of the dreaded workhouse.

Outdoor relief included doles of cash, food, fuel, clothing and household necessities, together with free medical attention. It was certainly less degrading and more humane than the reformed workhouse. None the less, any form of public relief carried with it a stigma, and assistance was often grudgingly given, which helps to explain why the numbers receiving relief were much smaller than the total of very poor people living below the poverty line. Late nineteenth-century investigations put the latter at some 10 per cent of the population, while those in receipt of public relief represented in 1851 only a half of this figure, and by 1901 only a quarter. The Poor Law was thus the resort of a declining element of the poor, the larger part managing to survive through unimaginable frugality or by begging, borrowing and stealing.

Rural crime was not of course confined to the very poor, though the trivial nature of much of the stealing – bits of wood for the fire, a few carrots or turnips taken from the field for the pot – imply poverty as the cause. At all events much of the stealing, as well as poaching, was put down to the presence in the neighbourhood of vagrants or gypsies. There were organized poaching gangs who operated on a commercial scale, often made up of groups of industrial workers, railway navvies or harvesting gangs, and there was also the persistent individual, often a well-known character who acquired a local reputation for his skill. However, judging from the appearances in the magistrates' courts, the typical poacher was a young man in his twenties, often a village craftsman or labourer. It is subject to question how far the poaching of such young men was habitual and induced by necessity, and how far it simply represented the urge for a little sport and excitement in an otherwise unexciting existence. Certainly poaching was not without its dangers. Spring-guns and mantraps were outlawed before Victoria came to the throne, but the old hatred between keepers and poachers persisted to the end of the century and beyond, producing its annual toll of violence. In some counties the keepers considerably outnumbered the police, though the latter were drawn more closely into the matter by the unpopular Poaching Prevention Act of 1862, which authorized officers to hold and search persons merely on suspicion.

*   *   *

The labourer's home was not often such as to offer an inducement to keep away from the alehouse or the game preserves. Over the centuries, it is true, it had improved in its ability to keep out the elements, and in comfort. The medieval framed construction in timber, once widely found, had all but disappeared by 1750, while stone continued to be used where it was readily available, brick became more widely employed, and unfired earth, the cheapest material, became more common. Tiles, and later slates, replaced stone and thatch for roofing, tile-hanging as a waterproof finish for framed houses began near the end of the seventeenth century and bricks began to be used for flooring. The changes were neither uniform nor complete: stone and thatch continued to be used for roofs, and even in the nineteenth century some cottages continued to be built with mud walls as a cheap and durable form of construction. It is no longer accepted that a 'Great Rebuilding' took place in the later sixteenth century and early decades of the seventeenth century: new building was in fact more common after 1640 than before, with a peak about the end of the seventeenth century followed by a trough in activity in the middle years of the eighteenth century.[28]

The size of the house and the number of rooms it contained varied with wealth and status. Better-off peasant farmers in the 1660s had between two and eight rooms, the average varying somewhat from one region to another. Husbandmen had fewer rooms in their houses, labourers fewer still, generally not more than three. Rural craftworkers had about the same number as labourers, but in addition they had their shops and other workrooms. New houses came to have two full storeys, instead of merely lofts or chambers in the roof space which were lit by dormers or windows in gable ends. As new and superior farmhouses were built so the old ones, if still serviceable, were used for housing labourers, being subdivided into smaller dwellings as necessary. This process continued in the eighteenth and nineteenth centuries as farms increased in size and successful farmers took over neighbouring lands, installing bailiffs in the former farmhouses.

The typical labourer's cottage of the later seventeenth century contained a living-room and a ground-floor sleeping-room, with perhaps a milkhouse or dairy as well, and there was often room at the back for keeping livestock and stocks of fodder. Of course, wide regional variations existed, and generally the improvements in construction and in numbers of rooms came later in the north than in the south: many northern labourers lived in a single-storey house with only one all-purpose room.[29] It was in a somewhat larger cottage that Celia Fiennes, travelling in Northumberland around the end of the seventeenth century, was obliged to put up one night despite the affront to her gentlewoman's sensibilities:

> I was forced to take up in a poor cottage which was open to the thatch and no partitions but hurdles plaister'd; indeed the loft as they called it which was over the other roome was shelter'd but with a hurdle; here I was forced to take up my abode and the landlady brought me out her best sheetes which serv'd to secure my own sheetes from her dirty blanckets ... but noe sleepe could I get, they burning turff and their chimneys are sort of flews or open tunnills that the smoake does annoy the roomes.[30]

The newer farmhouses of the seventeenth century were not only larger but also better equipped and furnished, with fireplaces and chimneys, more chairs and cushions, curtains to the windows, and, possibly, plastered ceilings. As time went by chairs replaced stools and forms, and four-legged tables were substituted for the planks laid across the stools. Dressers, chests of drawers and clothes-presses came in, more ground-floor rooms boasted fireplaces, and clocks, looking-glasses and close-stools began to appear. Nevertheless, there remained great variation in house design, as in structure, with many northern and Welsh farmers of the later eighteenth and early nineteenth centuries still living in houses having only three or four rooms with a minimum of furniture, and sometimes having homes of the 'long house' style, with one end of the house given over to the livestock.

Housing in the south was generally superior, and was indeed better in some respects than that to be found on the Continent, as foreign observers noted. Travelling from Dover on a visit to London in 1765 a

French gentleman, M. Grosley, remarked on the well-built farmhouses which he saw along the roadside, built substantially in brick and tile, with glass in the windows, and 'kept in the most exact order ... The appearance is as comfortable within as without.'[31] On a visit to Hertfordshire some years earlier, Pehr Kalm, the Swedish naturalist, commented on the pride taken by the housewives in their clean floors, observing too the presence of mats and iron scrapers for cleaning the mud off the boots before entering: the ladies being 'not particularly pleased if anyone comes in with dirty shoes'. Somewhat contradictorily, he complained of the laziness of the women, who, though they did the cooking, 'never [took] the trouble to bake because there [was] a baker in every parish'; and, furthermore, they left the care of the livestock to the men, spending their time sitting by the fire and 'prating'.

> In short, when one enters a house and has seen the women cooking, washing floors, plates and dishes, darning a stocking or sewing a chemise, washing and starching linen clothes, he has, in fact, seen all their household economy and all they do the whole of God's long day, year out and in ... They are lucky in having turned the greater part of the burden of responsible management on to the men, so that it is very true that England is a paradise for ladies and women.

Kalm was critical, too, of the draughtiness of English houses, with the wind free to whistle in round ill-fitting doors and windows and through unlined roofs and floors, and with all the warmth going up the chimney.

> Therefore, when it is cold, one can often warm oneself on one side and freeze on the other. To prevent this, there was used here in many houses a kind of settle or bench made of boards, with a very high back, so that when one was sitting therein, the head could not be seen from behind.[32]

As a more rapid rate of growth affected the size of the population from about the middle of the eighteenth century, pressure on housing became severe. It is true that ports and industrial towns grew more rapidly than country towns and villages, but the increase in numbers in the countryside was also very considerable, rising more than threefold between 1750 and 1901. A lower age of marriage among farm labourers, together with a falling death-rate, contributed to the increase in rural numbers, and when, nationally, the age of marriage rose and the number of births per marriage began to fall in the course of the nineteenth century, farm labourers followed the general trend only sluggishly. Rural workers thus tended to have larger families than did town-dwellers, and the resulting effects on rural housing were relieved only partially by the movement of country people into towns or abroad.

111

This external migration had the effect of removing the bulk of the rising rural numbers (about four-fifths of them) from the countryside, but was insufficient to prevent the total of rural families from rising.[33] Moreover, increasing numbers of homes in the countryside were being occupied by people not working on the land, by miners, quarrymen, railway-workers, road-workers, employees of brick and cement works, and the people employed in a wide variety of small country factories.

As a result, the demand for homes continued to increase. That being so, how did the supply of houses respond to this situation? The problem here is that while many thousands of new cottages were built, large numbers of old ones were pulled down or abandoned as ruinous and unsafe. The housing situation varied greatly from village to village, according to such factors as the inflow of newcomers, the extent of local out-migration, the availability of land for building, the cost of building in relation to the rents that country people could pay and the extent of cultivation in nearby areas of former waste land where existing dwellings were very few. In villages where the land was held by a few landowners, or perhaps by only one, the proprietors might follow a policy of strict control over new building and over the letting of existing cottages. Partly this was to reduce the possibility of the inhabitants becoming claimants for poor relief and thus placing additional burdens on the parish rates; more probably it was to keep undesirable characters – reputed thieves and poachers, drunkards and the irreligious – from gaining a foothold in the village. These 'close' parishes had their counterparts in the 'open' parishes which often flourished nearby, from which the farmers of the close parishes drew additional labour when required. The open parish had its property more widely distributed, with farmers, publicans, shopkeepers, petty builders and craftspeople able to buy plots of land and run up cheap cottages as a speculation. In such villages newcomers were welcome as adding to the demand for local services as well as offering a market for the new cottages.

Cottages in the open parishes were often cheaply built of poor materials and with the bare minimum of foundations, defective drainage and inadequate water supply; and since their owners often lacked the means of maintaining them they rapidly declined into insanitary slums. In landlords' villages, on the other hand, the cottages were likely to be better maintained and often better built in the first place. Indeed a number of landowners, such as the tenth Duke of Bedford, took a pride in building good cottages (which they saw as having a moral influence on the inhabitants as well as securing a better class of labourer for working the farms), and some owners went in for building on a large scale. The best of these estate cottages were quite roomy and well appointed, and, being subsidized by the owner, low in rent. The Duke of Manchester's cottages on his estate at Grafham, Huntingdonshire, had three good bedrooms and a living-room 14 feet by 12 feet; while Lord Leconfield's cottages built at North Stoke, in Sussex, in 1893 boasted four bedrooms, a living-room 12 feet by 12 feet, a kitchen and a large garden, for 1s 6d a week. But not all estate housing was so ample and up-to-date. Sometimes it was old and neglected, owned by a landlord who lacked the motivation or the funds with which to repair or rebuild. There were instances of landowners' cottages with floors below ground level, that had to be bailed out in wet weather; instances too, of desperate overcrowding, with five children sleeping in a room 9 feet by 8 feet, and the water supply drawn from a well situated close to an ancient cesspool, from whose cracked or porous walls the sewage seeped into the neighbouring soil.[34] Sometimes, also, the cottages, although new and well-built, suffered from the owner's taste for the gothic and picturesque, so that the interiors were cramped and dark, with much space lost for the sake of architectural effect.

Unfortunately, too, many owners allowed their cottages to be let with the farm, making it possible for the farmers to charge an enhanced rent. Tied cottages, which went with the job, were not, of course, confined to farming, but everywhere they had the effect of putting the occupants in the position where they might fear to lose their jobs and be afraid to ask for better wages, let alone for repairs to be made to their cottages. And where landowners kept the letting of the cottages in their own hands they often exerted an undue control over the morals, habits and leisure pursuits of the occupants, even over their religious and political views, a control which was tyrannous and confining. The economics of cottage-building made it difficult, if not impossible, to build cottages which could be let for an unsubsidized rent to the poorest of country people. A return of only 5 per cent on a good cottage costing in 1875 about £150 to build meant a rent of 3s a week, a sum which many thousands of labourers, paid only 11–13s in the later nineteenth century, could barely afford. Thus it was that many of the better houses available were occupied by those more highly paid than the agricultural labourers, by craftspeople, small tradespeople, and the employees of iron foundries, implement works, breweries and country factories. The farmworker was often left with the oldest, and the most dilapidated and insanitary – a cottage which the sanitary inspector should have condemned but was constrained from doing so because his order would have meant turning a family out into the street. And some of these old, cramped and unhealthy homes became the more overcrowded when aged and infirm parents were taken in, and when lodgers occupied one of the bedrooms to help pay the rent.

Sanitation and water supply were always problems when a row of cottages shared one or two privies and a single well or standpipe. Cottagers were notorious for keeping pigs and chickens by their back door, and for heaping piles of refuse under the windows. However, improvements in water supply began to appear around the middle of the nineteenth century. Brigg, a small Lincolnshire market town of some 3,000 inhabitants, with the densest area of the town housing 600 people in a space of 400 yards square, first obtained a water supply in 1852. By 1900 most cottages there had the convenience of a tap placed just inside the door – though without a drain and soakaway, so that a bucket stood below each tap. Lacking drains, the cottagers collected the rainwater in barrels, though sometimes the water dripping from the roof made the yards and nearby earth permanently damp. Privies were emptied at night by farmers' carts, which were supposed to have quitted the town before morning, though they often left behind a trail of spilled sewage. By 1900 a certain night, Friday night, was appointed for night-soil collection, 'Long Evening' as it was termed in the town, and in some instances the buckets had to be carried through the living-rooms for the 'dilly men' to empty into their carts.[35] Elsewhere, as at Batheaston, in Somerset, and in countless other places, sewage was discharged through pipes or open ditches into a nearby brook or river. An adequate main drainage system was not provided at Batheaston until 1908; and the collection of house refuse was begun in 1884 with a modest scheme which allowed for only three collections a year. Street lighting was also late in appearing: at Batheaston in 1881, at Dunton Green, in Kent, from 1901 and later still in nearby Otford.[36]

*   *   *

The great variations over time in the demand for and supply of housing, and in standards of construction, size and appointments make it difficult to trace the general course of housing conditions. Looking back over the centuries there were undoubtedly major advances, as when, for example, the one- or two-roomed cottage was gradually replaced by one with three, four or more rooms, and when glass became used for cottage windows, more durable materials were adopted for construction, and ultimately piped water, improved sanitation and damp-courses became mandatory. The addition to cottages of gardens, returning in a small way to the cow-pastures of an earlier age, made together with allotments a substantial difference to cottagers' resources, and notably to their diet.

Diet, indeed, was affected so much over the years by major innovations like the potato, white bread and tea, and by long-term changes in eating habits, as to make it difficult here again to assess the balance of advantage. The potato gave variety to the diet but was regarded by some contemporaries as less nutritious than bread; and, similarly, tea was regarded as an inferior substitute for beer. And when bread-flour was produced by the new roller-milling process in the later nineteenth

century, the bread certainly deteriorated in nutritional value. In medieval times and for long after, the bread of working families was made
from rye, barley or wheat, or very commonly from mixtures of grains,
sometimes with the addition of pea and bean meal when flour was dear.
In addition to any beef, mutton, pork or poultry that could be afforded,
rabbits and hares, and a variety of wild birds, blackbirds, rooks, even
larks, were made into pies. Fresh fish was eaten from rivers and from
the sea near the coast, though inland people perforce made do with the
red herring and other dried and smoked fish. Wild berries were collected
from the woods and hedgerows, as supplements to garden or orchard
fruits, which then included medlars, quinces, dewberries and bilberries.
As well as cabbages, peas and broad beans, English garden vegetables
included such now uncommon items as skirrets (a form of parsnip),
garlic, endive, fennel and common sorrel. Dishes were enlivened by
numerous herbs, parsley, sage, tarragon, thyme and mint, while saffron
was used along with many other flowers and herbs for medicinal
purposes, but also for making saffron cakes. Salads were likely to
include cowslips, violets, primroses, longwort, liverwort and purslane,
the last a specific against land scurvy.

Regional variations in common dishes differed perhaps more in the
name than in the making: oatmeal porridge was known as 'wash-brew'
in the West Country, as 'flamery' or 'flummery' in Lancashire and
Cheshire, and was still called 'frumenty' in Dorset at the beginning of
this century. Then, as now, housewives passed on favoured recipes and
noted them down, often in the back of a household account book. An
aristocratic housekeeper such as Lady Dorset was not too proud to
enter among her recipes some ones of lowly origin, such as 'Goodwife
Wells, her runnet', 'Goodwife Rivers, her liver cakes' and 'Goody
Cleaves recipe for Hogs Cheeke'.[37] Indeed, the origin of Stilton cheese
in the later seventeenth century is supposed to derive from such a
transfer of recipes.

In the eighteenth century tea, at first an exotic and expensive
beverage, came to be drunk by all classes of society. Jaundiced observers
(of whom John Wesley was one) railed against it as enfeebling and
dangerous to health; the philanthropist Jonas Hanway believed it had
caused a deterioration in the looks of young women, whom he found
to be less pretty than when he was young; and yet another critic thought
it responsible for the agricultural depression of the 1730s and 1740s,
with so many farmers' wives now consuming the upstart beverage. At
the time of Kalm's visit to England in 1748 tea and toast was the usual
breakfast of the better-off, though in the countryside, as he noted,
people had to 'content themselves with whatever they [could] get'.
Kalm observed too the absence from the country dinner table of soups,
and of the fashionable *ragoûts* and *fricassées*, though the roasted meat,

delicious in its fatness, was amply supplemented by turnips, carrots and potatoes. 'Potatoes', he remarked, 'are now very much used with the roast. A cup of melted butter stands beside to pour on them. When they have boiled meat, whole carrots are laid round the sides of the dish.' Sprouts, cabbage and fresh peas were also served with roast meat, and, more surprisingly perhaps, cucumbers and lettuce. A whole cheese, set on the table for everyone to cut as much from as was desired, nearly always concluded the meal.[38]

Here Kalm was describing the diet of the more well-to-do. For the farm labourers bread, bacon and cheese were the great standbys, and any salad they had was likely to consist of lettuce, early nettles and turnip tops. The harvest fare taken out to the men in the fields, as described by Kalm's contemporary, William Ellis, consisted basically of bread and cheese (Cheshire, Gloucester, Warwick or Somerset Cheddar) and apple pie, together with a quart of small beer. The harvesters, he thought, should have five meals in the course of their long day, the additional dishes including porridge, hashed or minced meat (with any taint taken off by a dressing of shredded onions and parsley), broad beans and pork, or beef and vegetables with plum pudding.[39] The cottagers' daily fare at other times was undoubtedly much more spartan, and a great deal depended on the supply of fuel, which regulated the frequency with which hot food was prepared. In the north, where fuel was both plentiful and cheap, hot dishes were made every day; in the south, however, perhaps only once a week, and even then the housewives took it in turn to light their ovens, the neighbours bringing round their bread, pies and tarts to be baked.

By the early nineteenth century it seems likely that the diet of the cottagers had deteriorated somewhat, especially as the price of bread-flour had risen greatly over mid-eighteenth century levels. By this time white bread, considered socially superior, had widely supplanted the former rye or mixed-grain bread, though oatmeal cakes continued to be eaten in the north. The potato had become a major item of diet, much to the alarm of those who, like William Cobbett, thought it smacked of Irish poverty. The supply of fuel was still critical in southern counties, though perhaps as much for winter warmth as for hot food, and bread, bacon and cheese, along with potatoes, were still basic to the diet. Travelling through the Sussex countryside near Eastbourne Cobbett saw 'with great delight, a pig at almost every labourer's house', and he encountered a turnip-hoer breakfasting on homemade bread 'and not a very small piece of bacon'. Asked Cobbett: 'You do get some *bacon* then?' 'Oh, yes! sir', the man replied, 'with an emphasis and a swag of the head which seemed to say, "we *must* and *will* have that"'.[40]

It is to be expected, and indeed is confirmed by modern research, that dietary standards varied not only with income but also with the size of the family which that income had to support. It has also been revealed that the average calorific value of the labourers' diets was substantially below present-day standards, approximating more to those common in underdeveloped countries of today. Surveys of diets made by contemporaries, such as the Revd David Davies and Sir Frederick Eden in the later eighteenth century, and by Dr Edward Smith on behalf of the Medical Department of the Privy Council in 1863, show the existence of considerable regional differences. These make generalizations difficult, while the nineteenth-century gap between high-wage and low-wage districts, mainly a gap between north and south, probably made the regional differences in nutritional standards greater than they had been earlier. It was shown in 1863 that each adult labourer ate on average over 12 pounds of bread and 6 pounds of potatoes a week, but only 16 ounces of meat. Many poor families never had butcher's meat but made a stew from a sheep's head, pluck or half a cow's head, while very weak tea, drunk without sugar or milk, was the common beverage of the wife and children. However, averages and general pictures are not very meaningful when regional differences were so important: the Lancashire labourer regaled himself on porridge, meat and potatoes, a baked pudding, toasted cheese and bacon; the Devonshire man, however, had to make do with tea-kettle broth (concocted from bread, hot water, salt and milk), bread and treacle, a pudding made of flour, salt and water, with vegetables and perhaps a little fresh meat.

When Dr Smith's survey was made labourers' real incomes, and hence their diets, were already advancing. The improvement continued during the remainder of the century, and in 1902 a new Board of Trade report showed not only that there was much more variety in the diet but also that many farmworkers' diets were on a par with, or even above, the average consumption for the country at large. This is not to say that this diet was now adequate: medical examination of rural schoolchildren in the inter-war years revealed certain evidence of malnutrition. At the turn of the century many working families lived still on bread, cheese and potatoes, with scraps of meat sold off cheaply by the butchers late on a Saturday evening, on 'flitters' made from pork fat, chips without fish from the fish and chip shop, and condensed milk and margarine – cheaper than fresh milk and butter, though of lower nutritional value. Although diet had certainly improved greatly over conditions found in the low-wage areas of the middle nineteenth century, when ill-fed workers made painfully slow work of every task, it was still very far from always producing the healthy, vigorous and hardy country-dweller of popular myth.

5

LANDED SOCIETY AND RURAL CULTURE

The superior classes of the countryside – the owners of landed property – enjoyed incomes and lifestyles which were light-years away from those of the cottagers. A male day labourer of the eighteenth century might not receive in cash and kind more than the equivalent of some £10–20 a year; the wealthiest of the landed aristocracy had revenues totalling in some cases £30,000 or £40,000, two thousand times as much. Only a few landowners, it is true, enjoyed incomes of this size. However, the role of great landowner, which involved running a large country mansion and making a prolonged stay in London every winter, could be maintained on some £10,000 a year, and there were some hundreds of families who could claim this status. Below this level, among the poorer aristocracy and the ranks of the gentry, incomes ran down from several thousand to only a few hundred pounds a year, but even modest country gentlemen could keep comfortable homes, ride in their own carriages, and employ several servants on only £300 or £400. In west Wales and other remote parts of the country many managed on less, and certainly there were large numbers of professional men, clergy, lawyers and surgeons, as well as retired merchants, industrialists and financiers and their widows who lived in genteel fashion on incomes of well under £500.

In general social status went with income, although there were certainly some great landowners, such as the Myddeltons of Chirk Castle, whose lack of a title did not prevent them from ranking as major magnates; and there were some peers (especially those of a naval or military background) whose title hardly consorted with their modest incomes. The seal of success, for those of ancient lineage as well as for *parvenus* from trade and the law, was the great mansion. Old houses, developed from medieval or Elizabethan roots, were added to, rebuilt, or replaced by completely new structures. The great houses of the eighteenth and early nineteenth centuries cost what were then vast sums: the rebuilding of Chatsworth over £40,000; Audley End £73,000; Wentworth Woodhouse £80,000. Later such sums were dwarfed by the

118

£600,000 spent by the Duke of Westminster on the remodelling of Eaton Hall and the Duke of Northumberland's £250,000 laid out on Alnwick Castle. In the 1820s the Marquess of Ailesbury lavished some £250,000 on Tottenham Park in Wiltshire, while William Beckford committed £400,000 to his ill-starred Fonthill Abbey, only to see its tower collapse soon after completion.[1] Not a few of the new houses, both large and small, were built by newcomers, merchants, industrialists, bankers, who desired to establish their families among the landed élite. Fortunes made in government office, in coal, iron or cotton, from the American or East Indies trades, even from railways, were poured into the costly prestige of a stately pile.

Once built or acquired a house had to be maintained and be serviced by a small army of domestics and outdoor servants. When the family was in residence there was much entertaining and great consumption of food and drink. The house itself, the stables, kennels, outbuildings, gardens and park had all to be kept in good order. In the eighteenth century a large mansion cost some £5,000 a year to maintain. Park-making, beginning in the seventeenth century, rose to a fine and expensive art, projects taking many years to complete. Great sums were expended in acquiring adjacent land, in removing inconveniently sited settlements, in shifting earth, digging out lakes, damming and diverting streams, and planting on a huge scale. Statuary, summer-houses, temples, ornamental bridges, grottoes and romantic ruins – specially constructed – were required to achieve the desired effect. The full impact might take generations to be realized, and meanwhile the maintenance had to be met. In the eighteenth-century play *The Clandestine Marriage*, a penurious landowner complains of the cost of keeping up his ruins, and in real life landowners spent good money on their follies and paid for hermits to give their parks a romantic aura; Sir Joseph Banks's correspondence includes an application from a man who desired such a post.

Many country houses exhibited a wealth of tasteful design and fine detail, often the work of amateur architects and unknown local craftsmen. They were usually furnished piecemeal with a random collection of furniture and *objets d'art* gathered from the corners of the earth: carpets from Turkey, damask from Genoa, tapestry from Paris or Brussels, linen and tiles from Holland, silks from India, *chinoiserie* from the remote East. Oriental screens and tables mingled with Roman busts, Greek goddesses, Italian landscapes, and Chippendale cabinets and chairs. Books were ordered by the yard to fill the voids of newly constructed libraries, and pictures bought in job lots – as when Lord Darnley paid £20,000 for 'all the small pictures in the collection of the Duke of Orleans'. Heirs to estates brought back from their grand tours pieces garnered in a dozen continental cities, and Italian sculptors turned out statues by the dozen, suitably scarred and stained to give verisimilitude to a claim for antiquity.

Nineteenth-century changes reflected different standards and new interests, with the addition of games-rooms, billiard-rooms, conservatories, shooting-boxes, fishing-temples and, indoors, steam-closets, hydraulic lifts and gas fittings, eventually even electricity. Some of the larger of the new nineteenth-century homes were incredibly comprehensive in their design, with a gentleman's wing centred on the library and a ladies' wing centred on the drawing-room, nurseries for the children, separate staircases for family and servants, even separate stairs for gentlemen and ladies. The servants' quarters and domestic offices were tucked away out of sight at the back, often in ill-lit and damp basements, though elaborately provided with separate rooms for the brushing of clothes and shoes, for polishing the silver and ironing the newspapers. The carrying of coal to keep going some dozens of fires in winter was a major chore, lightened in up-to-date establishments by wagon railways which brought the coal from the store right into the house.[2]

Despite all the fires the old-fashioned country house was cold and draughty, the heat making habitable only one small part of a large high-ceilinged apartment. The candles of chandeliers and candelabras gave but limited illumination, and the hand-held candle might well blow out along a draughty corridor or staircase when finding the way to one's room. To be a country-house guest in winter was a trial of endurance, and expensive too, as the servants expected their 'vails', or tips, and deliberately neglected the guest who omitted them. Little-used guest-rooms were as dank as the beds were damp, and ill-fitting doors and windows let in the rain and night frost. Rarely opened bedroom closets housed mice and spiders, and a broken bell-pull kept servants out of reach. In these respects the great house was often little better than the ancient farmhouse or parsonage. Woodforde noted in the January of 1795 how the cold inside his parsonage at Weston Longeville was so intense that the temperature in his study, though warmed by a fire, stood only at forty degrees, the milk and cream froze solid in the kitchen and the chamber pots, too, froze in the bedrooms.[3] Matters were not much improved a century later when Rider Haggard, engaged on the country-wide tour which led to his *Rural England*, commented bitterly on the rigours of the ancient mansions in which he was entertained.

Slowly, however, improvements did come about. Celia Fiennes, near the close of the seventeenth century, was one of the first country travellers to find a bathroom, a great curiosity. This was at Chatsworth, the house boasting a marble bath 'big enough for two people; at the upper end are two Cocks to let in one hott the other cold water to attemper it as persons please; the windows are all private [obscure] glass'.[4] But in most houses a bathroom was, for a long time, an unusual feature. When a bath was required the maids brought in a portable hip bath, set it before the bedroom fire and filled it with jugs of hot water; and the ewer and washstand continued to serve for a quick toilet. Water closets, first patented in the 1770s (one by Bramah, the inventor of the beer pump), were also slow to appear, and when they did were often fitted in a dangerously insanitary manner, in a cupboard or under the stairs, and without a trap to prevent foul gases from the cesspool invading the room. Only gradually did the new invention replace the commode or close-stool and the external 'Jericho'. About the same time the pervading chill of great houses began to be mitigated by early essays in central heating, using hot water, steam and warm-air ducts. Knole was warmed by steam as early as 1825, parts of Tottenham Park in 1835. But partly for technical reasons central heating remained rare and was still uncommon in old houses at the end of the nineteenth century. Even in new houses it was confined at first to the hall and corridors, and only later supplemented the fires in the principal rooms. Meanwhile draught-free ventilation, for a generation learning to value the benefits of fresh air, remained difficult to achieve, and it was again late in the century before piped hot water, and with it, bathrooms, became standard in new houses. Gas lighting was equally slow in replacing candles and oil-lamps, at least in the family's quarters. This was because each house had to manufacture its own gas, and the resultant product, dirty, hot and smelly, was considered good enough only for the servants. By the 1880s, when gas was at last becoming acceptable, it was already beginning to give way to electric lighting, superior in brilliance, cleanliness and convenience.[5]

What comfort was provided in the unimproved country house depended on servants for lighting fires, carrying coal, bringing hot water, and sweeping and dusting. The numbers of servants varied, of course, with the size of the establishment and the amount of entertaining that was done. At the Duke of Chandos's eighteenth-century mansion, Cannons, the servants were numerous enough to require four separate tables in the servants' hall, the tables ranked in status from the exclusive musicians' table down to the lowly board of the kitchen hands. The Duke of Kingston's servants' wages (paid in addition to livery and board) ranged from £100 a year for the house steward, £60 for the clerk of the kitchen, £43 for the head keeper and £40 for the head cook (evidently not an expensive Frenchman), down to footmen at £8 and maids at £4. At Boxley in Kent, the Bests, gentleman brewers removed from the naval port of Chatham to a more genteel address, kept thirteen servants in 1758: a butler, groom, coachman, postilion and gardener, and a housekeeper, cook, nurse and five maids: the yearly wages of the whole amounted to £106 14s a year.[6] At Erddig, near Wrexham, some twenty-five staff were employed in the 1720s, though fewer later on, and the Yorke family were unusual in appreciating their servants, composing verses about them and hanging on their walls portraits of their carpenters, blacksmith, negro coachboy and 'spider brusher'.[7]

The country house was a social and administrative centre as well as family seat. The land steward, later 'agent', ran the farms, woodlands, quarries, mines and brickworks from an office in the house, and he roped in the tenants on important occasions, to celebrate the birth of an heir, for instance, or to welcome home the proprietor on his return from a journey abroad. Relations and friends came to stay for long periods, sometimes being asked for a financial contribution or being allocated responsibility for some minor chores to help meet their keep. Fellow-landowners, justices, political allies, sporting friends, stopped by to discuss a forthcoming election or hunt, or the need to keep a stricter eye on vagrants, or perhaps to form a society for the prosecution of poachers. An occasional gentleman tourist called to be shown round the house, perhaps to report later on its rooms and pictures in an account of his travels. There were hunt meetings and shooting parties, balls on great occasions, fêtes and dinners on birthdays. At Belvoir Castle in 1833 the Duke of Rutland brought together the greatest in the land to celebrate his birthday, including the Duke of Gloucester, the Duke of Wellington and Sir Robert Peel, to name but a few of the distinguished company. Such gatherings often had political implications, adding to the country house's sphere of influence.

In the eighteenth century, dinner, the principal meal of the day, was seldom taken before three or four o'clock in fashionable society; in the course of the nineteenth century its hour grew gradually later, as room had to be made for luncheon – at first a snack but subsequently a more substantial meal – so that it was eventually eaten at about seven or eight o'clock. The dinner itself, lasting some two hours, consisted of a wide choice of roast meats and poultry, pies, puddings and fish, followed by fruit pies, tarts and jellies, and a dessert of fruit and nuts; the diet grew in richness and variety from the later seventeenth century onwards, and especially as home-grown fruit was supplemented by such imported exotics as lemons, oranges, limes, melons, dates and figs. When the ladies left the table to take tea and coffee in the 'withdrawing-room', the gentlemen passed perhaps another two hours over their port and brandy. Thirsts were stimulated by frequent toasts, and as a French visitor remarked, 'an alarming measure' of drinking accompanied conversation, which might become 'extremely free upon highly indecent topics'. At the Duke of Grafton's Euston, to spare the gentlemen the inconvenience of having to leave the room, the sideboard was furnished with a number of chamber pots 'and it is a common practice to relieve oneself whilst the rest are drinking; one has no kind of concealment and the practice strikes me as most indecent', wrote François de la Rochefoucauld.[8] Christmas and New Year feasts were elaborate even in the more modest houses, and at Ockenden House at Cuckfield, in Sussex, thirteen guests sat down on 1 January 1707 to a repast of fifteen dishes, which included goose, roast and boiled beef, pork, veal, capons, pullets, and calf's head and bacon. Such entertainment might consist in large part of the gifts of game, poultry, sucking pigs, wine and brandy which were furnished by friends and neighbours.[9]

Medical treatment was one of the few necessities of life in which a large income was not of great advantage. True, the well-to-do could more readily consult physicians and surgeons, but the advice and treatment offered were not always sound, nor even safe. Indeed, they were not necessarily much superior to traditional herbal remedies and old wives' cures. Patent medicines, in addition to spectacles, trusses and false teeth, could be obtained from London and provincial centres, and in desperate cases resort might be made to surgery, with all its attendant pain and risks in a pre-anaesthetic and pre-antiseptic age. Some remedies, though professionally advised, were as outlandish as they were useless. In 1679, for instance, the rector of Horsted Keynes in Sussex paid his surgeon 20s 'for advising about the turning about of my neck', and a further 3s for two dozen pills. If the pills did not work he was 'to use a large blyster behind the shoulder blade; to do it again in a fortnight, and then afterwards to shave my head'.[10] It was only late in the nineteenth century that a combination of deeper medical understanding, new surgical procedures, and a better supply of qualified doctors and surgeons gave the wealthy the advantage in preserving health that they had long enjoyed in other spheres of life.

*   *   *

Land and the church were closely connected. Pious landowners contributed to the construction of churches and paid for additions and repairs; they contributed, too, to the maintenance of the clergy, to whom they were not infrequently related by family connections. The medieval church was a major landowner, often leasing out properties to laymen, and using lay gentry and farmers as stewards or managers of their estates. Numbers of abbeys, and the Cistercian monasteries founded in upland areas, were major wool producers, whose fleeces constituted a significant element of that mainstay of the medieval economy, the wool trade. In medieval times the church was not only prominent in agricultural production, it was a force also in education, in looking after the sick and relieving the poor. The Dissolution of the Monasteries in 1536–40 came therefore as a tremendous upheaval in rural life. By 1547 some two-thirds of the church lands seized by the Crown had been sold; by 1585 as much as three-quarters had gone. A great part of England had changed hands, leaving the monks to go where they may and their houses to fall into alien hands.

Some former monastic lands were presented as gifts or conveyed on very favourable terms to courtiers and statesmen, but the majority were sold at the going market rate to a wide variety of opportunistic purchasers. The old monastic buildings, former granges and bartons, offered attractive possibilities for conversion to private residences, or at least suitable sites and ready supplies of building materials. As a further consequence of the Dissolution many lay proprietors acquired the right of receiving the tithes paid by farmers for the support of the clergy (using some part of the proceeds to maintain a parish priest), while the advowson, the right of presenting a new incumbent to a living, often fell also into lay hands.

The medieval clergy contained all manner and condition of men, ranging from the poor village priest, little superior to the peasants among whom he lived, to the bishop, who might be a landed magnate of great wealth, power and influence. The parish clergy were often ignorant as well as poor: some could not even sing the Mass, and scores, it was proved, could not tell who was the author of the Lord's Prayer, or say where it was to be found. Many were unscrupulous in squeezing poor cultivators through ruthless exaction of the full burden of tithes. Because of tithes they were in constant conflict with their flock, and disputes arose too over the farming of the glebe and competition for an additional assart or favoured close. Not a few rectors were absentee pluralists, serving as clerks or agents for the king, a bishop, abbot or lay magnate, and employed a salaried curate in their stead. Thus, through a community of private interests, there early developed the close connection between the priesthood and the landowners which was to endure to modern times. Some priests did not even trouble to find a curate but allowed the Mass to go unsung and the church and rectory house to fall into disrepair. Others engaged in common trading and usury, took to poaching and smuggling and frequenting of taverns, while charges of immorality against the clergy were commonplace.[11]

Nevertheless, the church was at the centre of the village community as the structure itself dominated by its physical presence: 'the great moments of man's stay on earth – baptism, marriage, burial – centred in the sacred building'. The church's spiritual influence extended much further than the customary services, and indeed included:

exorcisms at every turn against evil spirits and sorcery. The church bells were tolled against the approaching storms, which had been conjured by some witch; and the priest would sometimes formally curse, with sprinklings of holy water, a plague of caterpillars or locusts. Villagers felt at home within the four walls of the church, and the difficulty was rather to prevent too great familiarity. Church councils had to forbid theatrical performances and dances and semi-religious beer-drinkings within the church or its precincts, and to prohibit markets in the churchyard. Here, moreover, the clergy themselves set an example of freedom, stacking corn or even brewing beer in the nave of their church.[12]

Absenteeism and pluralism persisted through the centuries. Clergymen of influence combined two or more livings to produce a good income and lived comfortably in a more or less distant village or town where there was a more healthy environment and more genteel company and entertainment. A study of the Bishop of Ely's benefices in the eighteenth century, covering an area not noted for its wealth, suggests that the livings most frequently joined in plurality produced a total income of between £150 and £500 a year, enough to yield the incumbents a pleasant if not luxurious existence.[13] Pluralism continued to result in neglected churches and tumbledown parsonages. Cobbett remarked acidly on this phenomenon when riding through southern England in the 1820s. Near Warminster, in Wiltshire, he noted that in seven of twenty-four parishes the parsonages were such miserable dwellings as to be unfit for a parson to reside in; two, indeed, had disappeared altogether, leaving only the sites. He remarked too on the absence from church of labouring people; they had 'in a great measure, ceased to go to church'. At Goudhurst, in Kent, on one fine Sunday he counted fewer than ten labourers there in the great church. And the change was fairly recent: 'I can remember when they were so numerous that the parson could not attempt to begin till the rattling of their nailed shoes ceased.'[14]

Pluralism widened the material and social gap between the clergy and the labourers: their priest no longer lived among them to dispense some part of his income in works of charity or in feasts and celebrations. He was a stranger who lived, behaved and thought more like a squire, a closeness of lifestyles which often extended to a fondness for the bottle and enthusiasm for sport. Parsons were among the most regular supporters of hunts, and indeed some even kept their own packs of hounds. There were advertisements by those who sought a living where the duties were light and the hunting good, and one parson, when asked if Lent made any difference to his sport, answered: 'Certainly. Always hunt in black.' At Wastdale Head, in Cumberland, the sexton would appear at the door of the tiny church and shout: 'No service today. Parson's gone a-fishing.' And even George Crabbe, the poet-parson of Stathern, near Melton Mowbray, the country's hunting capital, was so influenced by the sporting clerics who surrounded him that for a while he dressed in a velveteen shooting jacket, with breeches and gaiters, and although a poor shot himself, carried a gun.[15]

But not all parsons were inattentive to the problems of the contemporary countryside: Gilbert White, the celebrated curate-naturalist of Selborne, was one of those knowledgeable on cottage economy; David Davies, rector of Barkham, in Berkshire, made one of the earliest studies of rural poverty; and the eccentric Sydney Smith, rector of Foston-le-Clay, near Leeds, was not unusual in keeping a dispensary and providing medicines for his parishioners.[16] Parsons were at the head of the movement to provide allotments for labourers in the nineteenth century, they held school classes in the church or rectory, and were instrumental in getting village schools built. Numbers of them were active, too, in drawing attention to insanitary housing and in encouraging labouring families to emigrate, with an eye to their enjoying a better existence overseas as well as relieving local gluts of labour.

One development which served to place parsons more firmly in the ranks of the ruling class was their elevation to the commission of the peace. Clerical justices first began to be noticeable in the seventeenth century. Then, as the total numbers of magistrates increased rapidly so the clerical Justice became more evident. In Hertfordshire the proportion of clergy among the Justices rose from only 2 per cent in the seventeenth century to as much as a quarter between 1752 and 1799, reaching a peak between 1800 and 1833, before falling back again subsequently. In remote Pembrokeshire, similarly, the three clerical Justices of 1727 had risen to thirty-nine by 1790, when they represented about a fifth of the Bench. By 1832 clerical Justices accounted, over the whole country, for about a quarter of the total, and in several counties they were so conscientious as to outnumber their lay colleagues at Quarter Sessions. Perhaps because they were newcomers to the Bench, and frequently originated from outside the county, they were inclined to justify their presence by being particularly active and enterprising. They took a special interest in the Poor Law and the reform of prisons, and were sometimes the most enthusiastic pursuers of criminals. It was a clerical member of the Suffolk Bench who took up the improvement of a local House of Correction ten years before the opening of John Howard's reform campaign, while in Berkshire the historic Speenhamland decision of 1795, providing a scale for the relief of men in work, arose from the initiative of a prebendary of Winchester.[17]

Perhaps a not untypical figure was Benjamin Newton, rector of Wath, near Ripon in north Yorkshire. His diary for the years 1816–18 shows him actively managing his farm, acquiring a drill and buying and selling livestock, going hunting, shooting, fishing and coursing, attending race meetings and dining at an agricultural gathering 'with forty fine fellows who talked of beef and ate pudding and drank wine like trueborn Britons'. When he received his tithe (in cash, totalling £676) he rode with it to Ripon to place it safely in a bank. Also in Ripon he was to be seen at the Assembly Rooms and the balls, though he had more intellectual interests also. A regular member of the Ripon book club, his reading included works of history and biography as well as those of Ricardo, the contemporary economist. He took time to visit the sick and dying, and was also an active magistrate, once finding himself the only one at the sessions, and noting: 'the meeting is not near so respectable if only one magistrate attends, and does not carry the same weight in the eyes of the country'.[18]

When a census of church attendance was taken in March 1851 it was found that only a half, indeed slightly less than a half, of those going to church were Anglicans. Of the non-Anglican majority the Methodists made up the largest element, followed by the older branches of Dissent and a relatively small number of Roman Catholics. The established church had lost much ground in the previous hundred years when Nonconformist chapels grew rapidly, finding their adherents principally among tradespeople, artisans and labourers. In the countryside the Nonconformist strongholds were most commonly concentrated in areas dominated by small freeholders rather than in those controlled by the gentry; and the chapels were especially numerous in upland, pastoral and forested regions where farming was small-scale and industrial occupations were widespread, as in Wales, much of the West Country and the north of England. The Church of England, consequently, became more evidently associated with the wealthier classes, with squires' villages and areas of large-scale farming. Many conservative landowners took a hostile attitude to the chapels, sometimes refusing to allow one to be built in their neighbourhood, and declining to accept Dissenters as tenants. This was not always so, however, and in England and Wales some gentry embraced the new faiths, or at least showed a degree of sympathy towards them. In terms of the number of services on offer the church could not compete in areas that had numerous chapels; nor, unlike Methodism, did the church succeed in drawing into its organization many laymen, such as those who became the stewards, trustees, class leaders and local preachers of the Methodist connection. A constant flow of new preachers emerged from the Methodist class meetings, where promising members had shown talent in leading prayers and expressing themselves, often in the homely language most likely to appeal to a rustic congregation. Furthermore, the Methodists' flocks were bound more closely to their chapels by Sunday schools, open-air meetings, choir outings, Christmas Day teas, and meetings, bazaars, concerts and lectures.[19]

Thus many country parishes came to have two ministers, an Anglican and a Nonconformist, the two strongly contrasted in their origins, education and tastes. The Anglican dined with the squire, while the Dissenter took tea with the small tenants, shopkeepers or cottagers. Rivalry between rector and minister was often acute. The minister was often an aggressive radical, a supporter of reform movements and a keen advocate of the disestablishment of the church. He had no brief for Game Laws, and was inclined to argue that the land was made to carry too many burdens, not forgetting the squire's rents and the parson's tithes, so that the farmers were prevented from giving their workers a better living. The rector in reply pointed to the difficulty of making farming pay and the clear impossibility of paying higher wages. The village school, fostered and regulated by the rector, was a sore point with the minister, for he regarded it as little more than a nursery for followers of the established order, 'worth as many as ten curates' to the church. The churchman blamed the Dissenter for promoting radical views and sowing discontent among the poor, and for stirring up antagonism between the social classes. There was, indeed, a powerful alliance between radicalism and Dissent, exemplified especially by those ministers who took a prominent role in the 'revolt of the field' in the 1870s. But many of the poor stood apart from the argument. Neither religion nor politics interested them at all deeply – they were matters better left to the 'high-ups' who understood them. Rather their interests revolved round daily life in the village, round gardens and allotments, sport and tittle-tattle, and round making do on an inadequate income. On a Sunday the labourer ignored both church and chapel: he dug his potatoes, repaired his boots, walked with friends to a pub in the next village and left rector and minister to get on with their moralizing and their charges and counter-charges.

The church's tithe was a sore point among Dissenters and farmers in general. Before 1836, when it was still sometimes paid in kind, it gave rise to all kinds of difficulties, and even when commuted to a more convenient cash payment still formed an only too obvious tax on the farmer's income and a disincentive to his making improvements. From 1836 the Tithe Commission apportioned the sum to be levied among the various occupiers of each parish, and assessed the amount by means of a rent-charge, usually based on a seven-year average of grain prices. The tithe remained contentious, however, especially in strongly Dissenting areas such as Wales, where the money was seen as going to support a church which was followed by only a small minority of the population. Grievances boiled over in periods of depression when farmers were in financial difficulties, and tithe payments were a factor in the Rebecca riots of the 1840s, and again in renewed rioting in the middle 1880s. In Wales the religious factor rather than economic pressure was uppermost, with Nonconformist preachers stirring up opposition from their pulpits, though farming conditions and national sentiment were also involved. The Tithe Act of 1891, which transferred liability to pay from the occupier to the landowner, did not entirely quieten opposition, neither in Wales nor in England – in large part because the tithe was now merely added to the rent.[20]

The Victorian clergy had much to contend with in addition to the rivalry of the chapel and hostility to tithe. They faced an apathetic, even antagonistic, community, farmers who resented criticism of their labourers' pay and cottages, and who were generally unenthusiastic about schools or anything that might affect the labourer's mobility and chance of bettering himself. They faced cottagers who attended church more with an eye to possible help from the charities controlled by the parson than from any real religious conviction. The fabric of the church building itself had to be maintained, sometimes restored from a near-ruinous condition, and eventually improved by introducing an organ and installing modern forms of heating and lighting. Some parsons thought it necessary to wage war on the private pews which had proliferated to fill much of the body of the building, leaving only a few benches for the farmers and labourers. Conscientious clergy helped run schools and allotments, visited the ailing, interested themselves in the improvement of cottages and their sanitation, and held lectures and penny readings in an effort to bring enlightenment to a benighted countryside. Their wives and grown-up daughters brought comfort to the poor and the sick with medicines, blankets and gifts of coal, and they helped provide the cottagers with boot and clothing clubs.

Beyond all this, the parson and his lady had to bring up a family and maintain a rambling rectory with its extensive grounds. Stipends were only too often inadequate and had to be supplemented, where possible, from a private income. The heavy recruitment of young clergy in the 1830s and 1840s produced an oversupply of rural parsons, which was felt particularly keenly when agricultural depression made rural livings less attractive in the later decades of the century. Poverty, and decline in status, help explain the sharp fall in the numbers of clerical magistrates after the rapid growth up to the early years of the nineteenth century. By the end of the century the country clergyman was falling behind in the struggle to keep up his social position. There was of course still much diversity, still sporting parsons who gave the hunt priority over weddings and christenings, and scholar-parsons who toiled away in their studies over obscure works of learning and piety. But perhaps few country parsonages were now turning out such distinguished writers and poets as in the past: for example, Addison, Cowper, Coleridge, Tennyson and the Brontë sisters.

One reason for the large numbers of labourers who attended neither church nor chapel was the persistence of old pagan beliefs which, even in the nineteenth century, continued to play a role in the lives of simple country people.[21] The credence given to witchcraft, still very strong in the seventeenth century, had not yet completely died out even by the opening of the nineteenth century. Unusual natural happenings and inexplicable private misfortunes were easily set at the door of some malicious follower of the devil. By 1804, certainly, it was a long time since a witch had been burned at the stake, or confessions had been made of visits to covens and worship of a sinister Man in Black. But it was in that year that a Dorset clergyman gave employment in his home to a local woman, one whom he later described as 'a Hag and reputed witch'. There was a series of strange incidents with which the woman seemed to be connected – the mysterious illness of the clergyman's baby son, the unexplained deaths of a horse and a pig, and the failure of garden crops sown by the woman – all of which combined to persuade the Revd William Ettrick that he was indeed harbouring a witch in his household. The woman, Susan Woodrowe, was dismissed, whereupon the parson's misfortunes ceased, the baby recovered, and quiet returned to the parsonage of Toner's Puddle. Nothing could be legally proved against her, as the Revd Ettrick wrote in his diary, and so the enigmatic Susan Woodrowe disappears into the mists of unrecorded history.[22]

Another manifestation of popular disregard for the church's teaching and authority was the occurrence of wife sales, of which numerous examples have been collected.[23] When Thomas Hardy's *The Mayor of Casterbridge* first appeared in 1886 the author was criticized for making so unlikely an event as a wife sale the crux of his plot. Modern research, however, has justified Hardy and confirmed his deep knowledge of rural life. Wife sales, closely associated with markets, fairs and inns, and especially with London's Smithfield Cattle Market, had, it is true, become less frequent by the close of the nineteenth century. However, they were still quite common in mid-century, where Hardy pitches the beginning of his novel. Wives were sold, apparently, because of their physical defects, their heavy drinking or their being 'damned *hard mouthed* and headstrong'. Some, presumably the less desirable ones, fetched only a leg of mutton, a gallon of beer, or 1s 6d in cash; others went for as much as two guineas or even £5. While the sellers were often castigated as dissolute, low idle fellows, the purchasers seem earlier to have been mainly artisans or members of the independent middle class, so that the transfer represented an improvement in the wife's status and well-being. By the nineteenth century, however, the purchasers seem almost always to have been of the labouring classes, perhaps marking the growth of public disapproval of the transaction.

Many old myths and magical beliefs surrounded the great events of life, birth, courtship, marrriage and death. And traditional remedies for the common ailments of both humans and animals owed much to superstition, which again survived until surprisingly recent times. Edwin Grey, writing of Hertfordshire in the 1870s, refers to the cottagers inhaling the fumes of the gasworks or eating a fried mouse to cure whooping cough, and he mentions superstitions which forbade the placing of shoes on a table and the driving of a nail into wood on Good Friday. When the relation of a beekeeper died it was necessary the same night to tell the bees in their hives, otherwise they would all die too. To encounter a piebald pony or horse was unlucky, calling for an immediate crossing of one's feet; and it was considered wicked to point at the moon. It was unlucky also for a bride to step from the church porch with her left foot, old men carried a potato in the pocket to ward off rheumatism, and warts were charmed away by rubbing them with a piece of meat, the meat to be buried and the warts disappearing as the meat rotted away.[24]

*   *   *

The long survival of such beliefs might be ascribed to the slow progress of education. It is true, of course, that by the eighteenth century illiteracy was highly unusual among the gentry, and certainly among the clergy and professions, but according to the evidence of depositions made to the Consistory Court of the Diocese of Norwich before 1700 a large minority of yeomanry, tradesmen and craftsmen could not read or write, and neither could over 80 per cent of labourers and women.[25] And, of course, even many well-educated people, such as Parson Woodforde in Norfolk and the Revd Ettrick in Dorset, were by no means uninfluenced by superstition. How far the growth of literacy was a factor in creating a more rational approach to the mysteries of heaven and earth is arguable. Arguable, too, is its influence on economic progress: the 'industrial revolution' after all, came about in a country where only some 60–70 per cent of adult males (and a distinctly lower proportion of females) were literate. Investigations of literacy indicate that there were wide regional differences: on the eve of the Civil War only 15–20 per cent of adult males in the rural north and west of the country were literate, but up to 40 per cent in the countryside near London. By the nineteenth century such differences had tended to narrow, and it is thought that average male literacy across the country had increased from 30 per cent or rather more at the time of the Civil War to 56 per cent by 1750, and 69 per cent by 1850, reaching as high as 97 per cent in 1900.[26]

Locally, before 1870, much depended on whether a village possessed a resident clergyman interested in promoting or teaching a school. While the children of better-off parents might be able to attend a country-town grammar school, or even a distant public school, the children of small farmers, artisans and labourers depended on there being a charity school, or a little private institution conducted by someone who had a room to spare and felt the need to earn a very modest income by teaching. Despite the efforts of parish clergy and some landowners, despite too the work of the voluntary National and British Societies and Methodist chapels, and the growth of private or 'Dame' schools, it was still a fact that numerous villages remained without a school of any kind until after the Act of 1870. The number of country schools, it is true, had been increasing for a very long time before this, but often from a very low starting-point. In the Kent of 1660 only thirty-two of the more populous parishes are known to have had a school, although by 1807 as many as 172 parishes, nearly half the total, had one. Still, at the later date, there was a majority of rural parishes in the county, mainly ones of small population, which had no school.[27] Similarly, in Oxfordshire in 1808, forty small parishes had no school at all, while another eighty had only Dame schools. Fifty parishes in the county could boast a Sunday school, and six offered evening classes for boys to attend after work. However, it could be said that sixty of the county's parishes possessed institutions which taught the 'three Rs', thus providing, presumably, a sound basis for true literacy.[28]

In many villages across the country the existence of a school depended on the initiative of some worthy squire or the enterprise of the church or chapel. Thus in Pembrokeshire in the early part of the eighteenth century Sir John Philipps of Picton Castle founded numbers of charity schools for poor children to learn to read the scriptures in English and gain some inkling of farming, seamanship and domestic service. This gentleman, indeed, established and financed as many as twenty-two of the thirty-one schools in the county, and by his example encouraged other gentlemen to take the initiative in their neigh-bourhoods.[29] In nineteenth-century Lincolnshire the Church of England's National Society was in the forefront of educational enter-prise, and at the end of the century a majority of the county's elemen-tary schools still held the connection with the established church. The Methodists, supporters of hundreds of Sunday schools, trailed far behind with only twenty-six day-schools in 1895. The Methodists, however, gave a great stimulus to adult education through their Bible readings and class meetings. But the curriculum of most elementary schools, like that of the old grammar schools, was often very narrow and tedious, and was little related to the needs and interests of country pupils. Nevertheless, numbers of grammar schools continued to survive, and some indeed were restored to greater popularity by moving to a curriculum less severely classical in content.[30]

Village elementary schools, even in the later nineteenth century, were too often held in buildings cramped, cold and draughty. Often there was only a single classroom, with a house or rooms attached for the master. If there was a second classroom it was frequently inadequately divided off by merely a curtain or screen. The schools were 'all-age', and consequently teachers tried to deal in the one or two rooms with youngsters ranging from 5 or 6 to 12 or 13 years old. Noise was a great problem, some children reading aloud, others chanting their tables, and yet others reciting by rote the kings and queens of England or lists of capes and bays. A fire or stove at one end of the room failed to dispel the cold in bad weather and sometimes the room was so cold that the ink froze in the stands. Wind and rain penetrated through defective windows or down the stovepipe, adding to the discomfort. Artificial light was late in coming, some schools even lacked a supply of drinking water, and children were sometimes required to fill the place of caretaker, sweeping the floors and yard, and gathering kindling for the stove.

The teachers generally did their best, but many were untrained or were inexperienced young pupil-teachers, and the masters and mistresses proper were not above giving themselves unwarranted half-holidays, or using a girls' sewing class to get their own clothes repaired. The great problem, however, was attendance. Periodical epidemics decimated the rolls, and some farmers, even those who served as school managers, employed children on the land at busy times when they should have been in school. Parents kept children at home to help look after baby or clean the house, or for lack of winter boots, or because the week's 'school pence' could not be found that Monday. And the children took themselves off when there was some local excitement, a village fête, a procession or a circus in a nearby town.[31] When, under the Revised Code of 1862, the teachers' pay depended in part on the children's performance in examinations, the visit of the Inspector was a much-dreaded occasion. As in Joseph Ashby's village school, the master would hover round, calling the children up in turn, and starting with vexation as nervous pupils stumbled over words they had read dozens of times or sat motionless staring at the sum in front of them.[32]

From quite early in the nineteenth century Mechanics' Institutes were founded in some larger villages and country towns in areas where industrial employment was important, in mining, iron-working or country textile districts. These establishments, though ostensibly concerned with the spread of scientific knowledge amongst workers, found it essential to hold classes in the three Rs in order to overcome the students' deficiencies in elementary education. Amateur monthly lectures, often given by members of the committee, might show a more scientific bias, but those given at Pately Bridge in Nidderdale in 1848 were miscellaneous in the extreme, and included such subjects as 'Macbeth', 'The Shetland Islands' and 'The Life and Character of Charles

XII of Sweden', as well as 'Spontaneous Combustion' and 'Agricultural Chemistry'. Lectures fell away, however, as they failed to attract continued support, the Institute at Ripley reporting sadly that they were 'not appreciated unless they were amusing. Now we hold that it is not the province of Mechanics' Institutes to amuse, but to instruct.'[33] The familiar problems of weak basic education and lack of interest in anything other than the immediately relevant and attractive were to plague attempts to set up adult institutes and evening classes thereafter, and indeed in periods much closer to our own.

The education of the children of landowners and the superior merchants and professional people followed a different course. In the middle ages sons of the gentry intended for the church were sent to board in a monastery and were educated with the novices in the cloisters, while others went to the grammar schools attached to cathedrals and collegiate churches. The foundation in 1382 of Winchester School marked a new epoch, for it was not only the largest grammar school but also the first to be established purely as a school and not as an adjunct to an ecclesiastical institution. Eton, founded in 1440, was the first grammar school to be called a 'public school', a term which meant that its pupils were drawn from the whole country rather than merely from the school's neighbourhood. Eton was associated with Henry VI's other foundation, King's College, Cambridge, just as Winchester was established by William of Wykeham to prepare scholars for his New College, Oxford.

Gradually public schools and grammar schools broke away from the control of the church and developed independently. For long no very clear line was drawn between grammar school and university, and boys might come up to Oxford and Cambridge aged as young as 13 or 14, though a higher age was usual. For the sons of the wealthy their education was not complete without a period of residence in the household of a noble or bishop where the emphasis fell on training in courtesy and manners, subjects somewhat neglected in school and university. Among the refinements of polite society to be acquired particular emphasis was placed on carving and serving at table, but young ladies as well as young men pored over books of etiquette, the ladies having gained skill in reading and writing from a stay in a nunnery or private tuition at home. The advice given on manners seems somewhat elementary, though perhaps it might still not come amiss today in our supposedly more advanced society. The young person was not to hang his head lumpishly or scowl sullenly when addressed by a superior; nor was he to puff or snort or scratch himself. At table he should not pick his teeth with knife or fingers, or dip his meat into the salt, or yet 'sup lowde of thy pottage'; neither was he recommended to scratch his head or spit over the table board.

This is not to say that manners were always well attended to.

According to contemporary comment the minor country gentry seem to have been thought ignorant and boorish by those in elevated polite society – too over-fond of their hounds and the bottle, and too given to carousing, brawling and swearing. Perhaps, in time, the criticisms offered by playwrights and by writers such as Addison and Steele had effect, for it seems that the later eighteenth century witnessed some improvement in behaviour. No doubt those of superior culture were always inclined to look down on 'our English Bumpkin Country Gentleman', as Lord Chesterfield scornfully put it, and his renowned partiality to the 'rustick, illiberal sports of guns, dogs and horse'. The more refined country gentlefolk, in turn, would have no truck with the independent yeomanry, nor yet with the plain farmer, whom Jane Austen's snobbish Emma characterized as lacking gentility, 'so very clownish, so totally without air'.

But merely to be able to run their estates and to have some comprehension of the advice of their stewards, lawyers and bankers, the great majority of the larger landowners must of necessity have possessed some education. They generally took the beaten path of grammar or public school, followed by a period at university, perhaps without taking a degree, or a stay at the Inns of Court, where some smattering of legal knowledge was acquired. Younger sons, too, had of necessity to gain an entry to the professions, the church, government service or the establishment of a great lord in order to provide themselves with a genteel, if modest, livelihood. And though there were undoubtedly besotted and benighted squires who fully answered Lord Chesterfield's description, there were many others whose libraries and intellectual activities proved that they truly belonged to a cultured class. Large numbers of country gentlefolk, squires, parsons and professional people belonged to subscription libraries and book societies, and ordered new books for their own libraries when they heard of ones that interested them. Some were sufficiently eminent to join such august bodies as the Royal Society, or Royal Society of Arts, or, at a more modest level, local debating societies and provincial literary and scientific circles, and thus kept themselves abreast of current advances in a variety of fields of knowledge. Music, too, they purchased and performed, or had performed for them, and they gave their patronage to individual artists, authors and musicians. And not a few pursued intellectual interests to the extent of writing volumes of poetry or works of religion, geography or history, scientific treatises, political tracts, or studies of natural history, arboriculture or agriculture.

It is true that the more elevated and comprehensive education, that extending to university, Inns of Court, and a protracted grand tour on the Continent, was reserved for the sons of the wealthiest families, and among them confined perhaps to the eldest son, the heir. Younger sons often felt themselves slighted by being allotted a more modest course, one confined to grammar school, with perhaps a period at Gray's Inn, Lincoln's Inn or another such establishment. Distinctions between schools and forms of education had the effect of creating a great awareness of social distinctions, and fostered resentment among the less fortunate. But the universal grounding in the classics gave a sense of a common culture which permeated all ranks of the superior classes, and so enabled the meanest squire or curate to communicate on even terms with the powerful magnate. Education was on the whole a cohesive influence, cementing common membership of a culturally homogeneous, if hierarchical, élite.[34]

*   *   *

The idealized view of a countryside consisting of romantic rose-covered cottages and lusty, honest peasants loses a good deal on closer inspection. There was indeed a mass of criminal activity, sometimes of a completely unconcealed kind. The lawbreakers fell into three broad categories. There were, first, the crowds or mobs that gathered to vent some grievance, more commonly one concerning a shortage of supplies of grain, less frequently the barring of a road by a turnpike gate or the fences that closed in former common land. Second, there were numerous professional criminals, such as horse thieves, poachers, smugglers and wreckers, highwaymen and footpads, forgers and coiners, many of whom tended to frequent out-of-the-way areas of rocky coastline, forest fastnesses or remote moorlands where the arm of the magistrate failed to reach. And there was, third, the individual villager who occasionally indulged in the stealing of game or other petty theft, and participated not only in drunken assaults and slander of neighbours, but also – though much less frequently – murder and rape.

The rustling of livestock, often by men on horseback, was not uncommon in pastoral areas, especially in late summer when the animals were well-fed and best able to travel. In arable areas, too, any livestock left in the fields were liable to disappear, along with crops and sundry items from homes and farmyards. Although theft was a capital offence if the value of the goods taken was over 12d, this does not seem to have been much of a deterrent. Partly this was because of a very low conviction rate, arising from the presentment of insufficient evidence or the packing of juries. Local figures of influence, the chief landowner, a wealthy farmer, even a respected parson, were themselves frequently involved in offences, especially in smuggling operations, while it was not unknown for the weak and scattered forces of the law to be intimidated by the size and weaponry of large criminal gangs.[35] On the coasts nearest to France and the Low Countries squires protected the smugglers, and the squires' tenants lent them carts and horses for transport and their barns for storage. Indeed, farmers further inland were known to complain of a shortage of workpeople, of losing hands who had drifted away to join the more lucrative business of smuggling.

Even when a lawbreaker was caught red-handed there was often a sympathetic landowner or clergyman to intervene, so that frequently the wrongdoers got away with a warning, merely being bound over to keep the peace, or perhaps, from the late sixteenth century, serving a short spell in the House of Correction. Even the sentence of a public whipping in the marketplace, or along the length of a certain stretch of village street, might not be too painful where the constable could be bribed to spare the lash (sometimes artfully concealing some red ochre in his hand to make the cord look bloody). And in times of dearth when food was costly there was much sympathy with those found committing crimes against property.[36]

To check crime the law was from time to time extended or increased in severity, with new measures such as the Black Act of 1720 which made it a felony to go abroad into woods in any form of disguise or with a blacked face – a response to the activities of notorious gangs of poachers and extortionists who terrorized the forests of Waltham and Windsor. But in the eighteenth century the great majority of capital statutes were not used at all, and the value of stolen goods was often deliberately assessed below the true figure to avoid a capital charge, while judges frequently commuted death sentences to ones of transportation. Convictions and executions were most likely to result from cases of burglary, highway robbery, horse and sheep stealing and murder; they were rather less likely in arrests for theft from dwelling-houses and forgery. The crowds of labourers and artisans who in times of shortage stopped grain carts, or who forced corn dealers and millers to sell flour at a lower price, were hardly considered as criminals, even if they used an element of force to gain their ends. The community felt some sympathy with their actions, and there was a widespread belief that the public should be protected by regulation from the vagaries of market prices; strongly held was the idea of a legally set price, or a normal or 'just' price, what E. P. Thompson has termed the 'moral economy of the English crowd'.[37]

Those involved in food riots often consisted mainly of townspeople (often led by women) rather than cottagers or farm labourers, and it was townspeople, too, who made up the organized gangs of poachers who persistently raided game preserves and rabbit warrens. Organized poaching was encouraged not only by the growth in the eighteenth and nineteenth centuries of game preservation but also by the profitable markets that existed for sale of illicit game, especially in London. The pheasants and partridges found their way through the agency of accomplices among the carriers and stagecoach drivers and guards to the counters of highly respectable poulterers, those catering for equally respectable customers in the towns. Increasingly stringent game laws, and for a period the adoption by landowners of lethal spring-guns and crippling mantraps, failed to stop the gangs, while an increasing army of gamekeepers clashed with bold bands of poachers in bloody nocturnal encounters.

Although poaching has attracted the prime interest of historians, there was much other crime, and to travel about the countryside with cash on one's person was always risky. Landowners' stewards sought to evade robbers by concealing the rents inside the carcasses of poultry taken to town by a carrier, and stagecoach travellers took pains to conceal cash, rings and watches in their hats or boots. The diary kept by John Carrington of Bacons Farm, Bramfield, in Hertfordshire, during the Napoleonic War years contains several reports of the activities of gangs of robbers, a matter which concerned Carrington closely since he was often carrying considerable sums in his role as a part-time local collector of taxes, including the land tax, the assessed taxes (imposed on luxuries such as horses, carriages, servants and armorial bearings), and the newly introduced income tax. Indeed, he was himself robbed one Sunday evening in August 1806 by two Irishmen:

> they Clapt a pistel to my Head & Demanded my money & they blow my Branes out if I made a noise, I told them to take the pistel away & I give them my money, so I went to gitt of the ass but they wont Let me, So I told them my puss was in my waistcoat pocket which they took with my knife & some halfpence & Hankerchieff, they said I had more money, I told I had no more in Very loud terms ... So off they went Down the Road towards Tewin & I walked on a Little way with my ass, then got off & Runn & hollowd Down to Marden, So I escaped with my other money, Near 20£ in Notes, in a little pocket in the Lining of my waistcoat, So my loss but small, about 4sh in my puss & knife & Hankerchieff, the 2 men was Drinking at my sons while I was their.[38]

The terribly high, near-famine prices of the Napoleonic War years saw an increase in food riots, burglaries and theft; and at the end of the Wars the onset of economic depression and heavy unemployment intensified pressures on the rural poor. In East Anglia, indeed, 1816 saw large-scale riots when crowds of country people armed with rustic weapons attacked millers, forced shopkeepers and publicans to dispense food and drink and ultimately clashed with the volunteer cavalry. 'I might as well be hanged as starved', said Richard Rutter, one of the rioters at Ely – and in fact he was transported for life. Five of his fellow-rioters were not so fortunate, paying the ultimate penalty for their part in the outbursts.[39]

The war years and their aftermath saw also a deterioration in the relations between labouring folk and the superior classes of landowners, clergy and farmers. Unemployment and inadequate wages made a potent brew of resentment and distrust, which boiled over into the burning of ricks, barns and even farmhouses, the maiming of livestock and the deliberate destruction of farm implements and machines. An unpopular magistrate, a harsh Poor Law overseer or an over-strict employer were likely targets for assaults on their persons and property. How far the incidents represented the occasional vengeance of discontented individuals, men who had been sacked from their work or refused parish relief, or perhaps the amusement of drunken youths of the neighbourhood – many riots were said to originate in alehouses – or the depredations of strangers, discharged soldiers, escaped criminals, vagrants, gypsies, itinerant 'bankers' or drainage workers, and groups of Irish harvesters, or yet gangs of habitual robbers and burglars, is difficult to say. Certainly there were some villages which gained an unsavoury reputation for drunkenness, brawling and lawlessness.[40]

To counter the violence and insecurity of property landowners and farmers formed local societies for the purposes of offering rewards to informers, paying for prosecutions, and the employing of private watchmen and gamekeepers. Frequently this private police force, together with the old-established parish constables, continued to exist alongside the new official police forces when they were gradually introduced following the County Police Act of 1839. In some counties, indeed, there was much hostility to the very idea of a publicly controlled police force, but nevertheless twenty-four counties had adopted the Act within two years of its passing. Periodical waves of widespread outbursts of arson, Poor Law offences and, especially, the increase in vagrancy, were responsible for the change. Vagrants had always been feared as potential, if not actual, criminals and as spreaders of disease, and had long been liable to be taken up and incarcerated in a House of Correction. After 1815, however, vagrancy increased with the discharged soldiers and sailors from the army and navy, the unemployed from closed-down shipyards, mines and ironworks, and those young men laid off by bankrupt farmers; and subsequently there were also the able-bodied workless turned adrift by the harsher policies of the post-1834 Poor Law, and the invasion of uprooted Irish peasants fleeing from the potato blight and the 'great hunger'.

However, after the peaks of mid-century the crime-rate diminished, and continued to fall. How far the gradual emergence of a more peaceable countryside was due to the new police and their watch on the public house, brothel and fair, and the extension of their powers to deal with vagrants and suspected poachers, is not clear. It seems likely that the police, who before 1871 were still very thin on the ground (with a total of only 15,860 men outside London, and outnumbered in some counties by private gamekeepers), were only one factor in the environment of a changing society and advancing economy. The mid-Victorian boom, the long-term rise in living standards and the wider spread of education probably had the greater influence. An expert conclusion is that the strengthened forces of the law were now able to contain the criminal class, while the great body of honest poor were encouraged to show a greater patience with their lot.[41]

6

THE TWO FACES OF THE COUNTRYSIDE

The countryside of the past presents two opposed and contrasting faces. On the one, riders in scarlet gaily halloo as they leap the fences; heavily bewhiskered men in Norfolk jackets take aim at a covey of partridges; a solitary fisherman casts his line into a silvery stream; and a cheerful group of stout labourers play at skittles in the yard of a rustic inn. On the other, a procession of ragged men, pinch-cheeked, wild-eyed, armed with staves, pitchforks and reaping hooks, march to some desperate rendezvous; bands of similar scarecrows sport a loaf impaled on a long pole, the mark of their grievance; yet others grip iron bars and hammers, intent on breaking up a hated piece of machinery; and still more, in ones or twos, flee into the night, leaving behind them an ill-fated cow or sheep bellowing in pain, or the soaring flames of a haystack lighting up the near horizon.

Both faces existed, and often enough at the same time and in the same place. The one face comes down to us as evocatively traditional, vividly depicted in the pages of Surtees or the myriads of sporting prints which enliven the walls of many a modern-day hotel, clubhouse or inn. The other seems alien, strangely anomalous, an aberration; and certainly a view of rural life that has barely survived in either art or popular literature, examined in depth only with the somewhat clinical detachment of specialist historians. Specialization apart, it would be misleading to emphasize the one at the expense of the other, and an attempt at balance must try to explain the coexistence of a Merrie England of sport and good cheer alongside a Joyless England of hunger, deprivation and unrest.

*   *   *

The ample open spaces of the distant past, the unfenced solitudes of forest, waste lands, commons, moors and hills, provided an environment which from early times encouraged men and women of all ranks of society to find pleasurable pursuits in the outdoors. The royal forests of medieval times, it is true, were protected by special laws enforced

141

by forest courts and officials, and great nobles kept their private parks and chases for their own exclusive use. But such monopolies were difficult to enforce, though everywhere rights of hunting were confined by restrictive game laws. As early as 1390 a property qualification of land worth 40s a year – then a very considerable amount – was required if one wished to keep hounds, use ferrets, or employ nets or other means of taking deer, hares and rabbits. Spaniels and greyhounds were specially bred for these sports, while mastiffs were brought in for the sterner work of tackling wild boars – a sport in which, unlike some others, the ladies did not share.

Vigorous ball games such as handball, club-ball (probably a form of fives), football and tennis were the preserve of the menfolk, although football, a rough game in which fatal accidents were not unknown, seems to have declined to become mainly a plebeian diversion by the sixteenth century. By then the more gentle bowls and skittles had been introduced and enjoyed popularity among both gentlemen and their inferiors. In summer ladies spent much time in the garden with a book of romances or playing with their Maltese spaniels, their tame larks and nightingales, or their magpies, popinjays, squirrels and monkeys. On winter evenings both men and women relished the performances of itinerant bands of minstrels, musicians, jesters and actors, although the recitation of epics and legends died away as printed books became more numerous and more people were able to read. Board games, too, were popular, chess especially, but also draughts and 'tables', or backgammon, while card games were attracting a following by the later fifteenth century.[1]

Riding, hunting and racing developed with advances in the breeding of horses and hounds, and the gradual improvement of the sporting gun, especially the introduction of the flint-lock. Riding was a recreation of both sexes, a Gloucester gentleman once writing to tell a friend 'how good a horsewoman my Sister is; She rode out yesterday with her uncle and me about seven miles, a single Horse and without being led, I assure you she almost tired my uncle.'[2] The breeding of horses led to an interest in racing, which in turn further fostered the efforts of the breeders. Race meetings were held wherever a stretch of suitable ground offered itself, but Newmarket early became established as the great centre of the sport. By the later eighteenth century the races at Newmarket were run over a period of three months, and large stables were kept there by noblemen who expended thousands of pounds on buying and breeding horses and employing grooms and jockeys – as well as on betting. At a less exalted level local gentlemen and farmers took their horses to nearby meetings, and the somewhat despised sport of steeplechasing, riding across country to a distant mark such as a church steeple, was especially popular among them. Race meetings became important social events, attracting many people from surrounding towns and villages who came to watch the sport and to drink and bet, and who might stay on (as did Thomas Turner of East Hoathly at a Lewes meeting in 1756) to observe the ball, 'an extremely pretty sight'.[3]

All classes of society patronized prize-fights and cock-fights, and country-town fairs and some village inns were known for their matches of cudgels, for their bull-baiting and badger-baiting, and their goose-riding, cock-throwing and similar vulgar and brutal amusements. The Cornish sport of wrestling spread to other parts of the country, and one Nottinghamshire squire, Sir Thomas Parkyns of Bunny, was a great enthusiast, practising the art on his drawing-room hearthrug and going to the length of writing his own treatise, entitled *The Cornish Hug*. His monument in Bunny church, erected four years before his death, depicted him in a typical wrestling stance, but also, somewhat more modestly, with Time brandishing his scythe over his prostrate form.[4]

At length two developments came to have a major impact on sport and leisure activities. From 1671 a series of new and more stringent game laws was enacted to raise the property qualifications and to discourage depredations on game reserves, the measures rising to a peak of severity in the early nineteenth century. An Act of 1803 made armed resistance to arrest a capital offence, and in 1817 armed poachers caught at night were punishable by transportation for seven years. So that country-house shooting parties might boast of their huge bags (the record for a single day's shooting of 535 pheasants was achieved in 1823), poachers and gamekeepers were killed and maimed, and offenders charged under the Act of 1817 were sent to the other side of the world to 'enjoy a better climate' in Australia. A reaction followed, however. At Winchester Assizes in 1821 two poachers in their late twenties were hanged, the only ones to be executed out of sixteen prisoners condemned to death; one was condemned for assisting in killing a keeper, the other for shooting at a keeper. The judge stated that the extreme penalty was necessary to deter others 'as resistance to gamekeepers had now arrived at an alarming height, and many lives had been lost'. The use in game preserves of spring-guns and mantraps no doubt made poachers less careful of keepers' lives, but juries became unwilling to convict, and from 1828 the severity of the law was moderated. Spring-guns and mantraps had been prohibited a year earlier, and in 1831 the legalizing of the sale of game made the operations of poaching gangs less profitable. Shooting, however, went on to renewed popularity, and poaching continued with it; and it was not until 1881 that tenant farmers were given the right to kill hares and rabbits on their farms without first seeking the landlord's permission.

The farmers, indeed, had very longstanding grievances, both against the foxes which stole their chickens, and the rabbits, hares and game

Figure 14 Game Keepers, by George Stubbs. With the growing popularity of shooting in the eighteenth century landowners created game preserves and employed keepers to patrol them, while a series of new game laws imposed harsh penalties on convicted poachers. Thus developed a rural war between keepers and poachers, leading frequently to bloodshed, a struggle which persisted to recent times.

which raided their growing crops, although often enough they received implicit compensation in the unduly low rents of their farms, and more explicitly in the sums which Masters of Foxhounds paid out for broken fences and trampled crops. And, of course, some farmers were themselves keen sportsmen who readily accepted an invitation to ride with the hounds (as some landlords expected them to do) or supported the less prestigious farmers' hunts. Farmers were rarely found in the more exclusive shooting parties, however.

The fox had come to supplant the hare in hunting folk's affections in the eighteenth century, and the faster quarry and longer chase called for speedy thoroughbred horses and faster hounds. The first Master of Foxhounds to attempt to breed hounds especially for foxhunting was Hugo Meynell of Quorndon Hall, who in the second half of the century hunted what came to be called the Quorn country. Although hunting became widespread, the midland counties, especially Leicestershire, Rutland and Northamptonshire, provided the ideal conditions of expanses of rolling fields broken by woods and copses, and the Leicestershire town of Melton Mowbray became the capital of the sport. It was not a poor person's pleasure: the Quorn, when run privately by Sir Harry Goodricke, cost him £6,000 a year – more than many middling gentry families had as their whole income – and packs of hounds could change hands for as much as £2,000. The great hunting landlords had to be enthusiasts with the length of pocket and sufficient leisure for keeping and managing large stables, a pack of hounds and professional huntsmen. Frequently the role of MFH of a famous pack was virtually hereditary in a certain family, though a change would come when an heir succeeded who had no interest in the sport, or the costs could no longer be met. One solution to cost was the subscription pack, first introduced in Cheshire in 1746; later in the nineteenth century the sport's appeal was further widened by the spread of the railways, making it possible for a businessman to spend part of the day in his office and the remainder on the hunting field. In Lincolnshire the famous Brocklesby hounds went out five days a week, and the hunt was noted for the support it received from the farmers, as many as eighty strong, on good horses and immaculately turned out. Well might the fourth Earl of Yarborough pay tribute to his tenants: 'There are no better puppy-walkers, no keener fox preservers, and no finer sportsmen than the tenant farmers in North Lincolnshire.' The Duke of Rutland, too, expected those of his tenants who could afford it to join him in the field, and the others to accept with equanimity the spoliation of their farms. Some farmers occasionally declined the compensation offered for damaged fences – 'On no account, my Lord' – a refusal as polite as it was welcome to an MFH spending thousands a year to hunt his large Belvoir country.[5]

145

Some of the great sporting figures of the nineteenth century went far beyond spending a few thousand a year. Lavish gamblers as well as keen followers of hounds, they occasionally got so far into debt as to be obliged to sell up their estates and retire into oblivion, as did Sir Vincent Hynde Cotton of Madingly Hall, Cambridgeshire, and George Osbaldeston, 'Squire of all England' – the former ending his days as a coachman driving under an assumed name on the Brighton road, the latter as a gentleman of severely restricted means, living in a succession of country villas, his wagers at the Portland Club limited to a paltry guinea an evening. The 'Squire', a magnificent marksman, fine rider, brilliant oarsman, tennis player and cricketer, could never resist a bet, and in his prime was known to play whist for £100 a trick and £1,000 a rubber. He himself admitted to losing nearly £200,000 on betting and racehorses, and when he failed to discover a much hoped for and highly providential seam of coal under his land he was forced to sell up for the sum of £190,000. Sir Tatton Sykes, the eccentric owner of the Sledmere estate in Yorkshire, never got so far into debt, although he sold a priceless Elizabethan library as well as family medals, coins and pictures, in order to pay for his hounds. In a long and colourful life he saw the St Leger seventy-four times and, a true reactionary, rode everywhere on horseback, despising the comfort of coaches, and likewise the convenience of the new-fangled railways. Dressed always in the clothes which were fashionable when he was young, he once rode from Yorkshire to Aberdeen, covering 749 miles in five days in order to win a race for Lord Huntly. Yet another prominent sporting figure was Grantley Berkeley, the second legitimate son of the fifth Earl of Berkeley: he hunted buffalo on the Great Plains of North America, defended game preservation before a Parliamentary Select Committee, and wrote a three-volume historical romance which, when severely reviewed, caused him to fight a dual with one of his critics and horse-whip the offending editor of *Fraser's Magazine*.[6]

But not all leading sportsmen were gamblers or bullies. Many combined their field sports with diligent attendance in Parliament and prudent care of their estates. Tom Smith, Master of the Craven and the Pytchley, was a progressive agriculturalist and engineer; Thomas Assheton Smith, an MFH for fifty-nine years, was a master of the classics, a man of science and a Member of Parliament.[7] It was Sir Frederick Fletcher Vane of Arrowthwaite in Cumberland who employed as his huntsman the immortal John Peel. Peel went out regularly twice a week in his grey coat woven from the local wool, often covering 50 miles in an outing.

Members of the country gentry encouraged village sports, perhaps offering prizes, providing a playing-field, or captaining their own cricket eleven, a team made up of their grooms, gardeners or keepers with a leavening of farmers and village craftsmen or tradesmen. Many a young lad acquired valuable patronage and perhaps an opening to a good career through making his mark in the squire's team. There were also many village matches in which the squire played no part, scratch teams gathered together from the village, with neighbours placing bets on the result in sums ranging from a shilling or two to several guineas. John Carrington of Bramfield in Hertfordshire recorded in his diary seeing a match played on the upper green of nearby Tewin in September 1802, a match between the married and single men – 'the Married Beat [by] 14 notches'. On another September afternoon five years later he again attended a match at Tewin, 'Lord Cowpers Carpenters Joyners and others a Building the New House at Pansanger against all Tewin for a whole Sheep Dressed at Sons Rose and Crown, 2 Leggs Boyled, Saddle Rost, 2 Sholders Baked, with 2 Large pyes of the Necks and Brests Baked, the Tewiners Beat them Shamefully, 143 Notches in Both Inings, 11 of a Side.' In the May of 1809 Carrington saw a different kind of entertainment when, on his way back from drawing some money at the Hertford bank, he 'Stoppt & Saw the Mountybanks in Mr Elleses Timber yard, Horse Rideing & Rope Danceing & Tumbling'.[8]

Carrington might well have seen other itinerant entertainers on his journeys round his part of Hertfordshire. The country was quartered by bands of musicians and actors who performed in country-town assembly rooms, inn yards and village barns; while, travelling through the lanes, came too the owners of giants, midgets, dancing bears, performing dogs, learned pigs and other astonishing curiosities. By Carrington's day travelling circuses were visiting country towns, and occasions in the village such as weddings, holiday feasts and concerts were enlivened by the strains of a homely band of fiddlers. The numerous country fairs attracted people from miles around to see the cart-horse-pulling competitions, the cudgel play, boxing and wrestling matches, the stone-lifting, foot races and football. At Yattendon, near Newbury, the 'Revel' of 1785 included cudgels played for the prize of a gold-laced hat, wrestling and boxing for a similar prize, a jackass race for half-a-guinea, and tobacco 'to be grinn'd for, by old women, through a horse-collar as usual'. Even the superior farmers and professional people were sometimes carried away by the animation of the fair, and perhaps more by the drink, one young gentleman recording how he and his brother visited Matlock fair and got into an alehouse argument with an old woman: 'she flung some hale amongst us and it hite us all, and Brother Cam and flung a hole pott of hale at her head, we was prodigious merry'.[9]

Drink was the occasion of numerous riotous nights spent by Thomas Turner and his wife in their village of East Hoathly, in Sussex. On one

December evening they and some friends gathered for a game of brag, which was followed by a substantial supper (four boiled chickens, four boiled ducks, minced veal, sausages, cold roast goose, chicken pasty and ham), and then succeeded by

> dancing or jumping about, without a violin or any musick, singing of foolish healths, and drinking all the time as fast as it could be well poured down; and the parson of the parish was among the mixed multitude ... About three o'clock, finding myself to have as much liquor as would do me good, I slipt away unobserved, leaving my wife to make my excuse. Though I was very far from sober, I came home, thank GOD, very safe and well, without even tumbling; and Mr French's servant brought my wife home, at ten minutes past five.

In the following March there was another carousal when, as the con-science-stricken Turner relates

> We continued drinking like horses, as the vulgar phrase is, and singing till many of us were very drunk, and then we went to dancing and pulling wigs, caps, and hats; and thus we continued in this frantic manner, behaving more like mad people than they that profess the name of Christians.[10]

*   *   *

More elevated, and perhaps more restrained, persons preferred a formal dinner, concert or ball at a nearby town, while those who could afford to travel took themselves off to a spa, where polite entertainment, paying calls, taking tea, playing cards, attending receptions and dances, occupied the large part of the day not spent in taking the waters. There were, of course, the famous and fashionable spas, some dating back to the time of Charles II, such as Tunbridge Wells, and much patronized later ones, such as Bath, Cheltenham and Harrogate, but hundreds of lesser resorts also existed. Celia Fiennes noted a number on her travels. There was one at Alford in Somerset, its water 'a quick purger good for all sharpe Humers or Obstruction'. It was not a fashionable place, however, 'there being no good accommodation for people of fashion, the Country people being a clounish rude people', and so the water was sent for 'several miles' in order to brew beer from it, rather than being taken on the spot. Another spa, at Astrop, in Oxfordshire, was more to her liking:

> a Steele water much frequented by the Gentry, it has some mixture of Allum so is not so strong as Tunbridge; there is a fine Gravell Walke that is between 2 high cutt hedges where is a Roome for

the Musick and a Roome for the Company besides the private walkes.[11]

The better spas offered numerous attractions: Epsom had racing on Banstead Downs, and Box Hill boasted mazes, which made it 'very easy for amorous couples to lose and divert themselves unseen'. Bath offered good houses to board in, where the hostess 'keeps us like fighting Cocks', and the great excitement of possibly setting eyes on eminent personages: 'the Prince is expected next week; if he does come ... it will be a matter for Conversation and afford us something to talk of the Remaining part of our Days'.[12]

Before long the doctors were recommending sea air and the drinking of sea water as a cure for almost every imaginable ailment – and a good alternative to a spa. From swallowing the sea water it was only a short step to immersing oneself in it. So the seaside holiday developed, starting with the fashionable eighteenth-century resorts of Scarborough and Weymouth, to be followed in time by Margate and Ramsgate, Brighton, Folkestone, Bournemouth and Eastbourne. A stay at a spa, or by the sea, need not be expensive, unless one travelled by private coach or hired post-chaise with a large family and several servants. (It cost about £100 and seven days of travelling to transport the Blois family from Suffolk to Dawlish in 1791.) The winter season in London could be extremely costly, however, if one travelled in style, rented a large house, saw all the sights, and did much entertaining. Lesser persons, like Squire Blundell of Crosby, in Lancashire, could do it much more cheaply by staying with friends and eating in taverns: his visit of fifteen weeks was managed for an outlay of only £25 3s 2d. By contrast, the stay between 13 January and 25 May 1735, of Sir Thomas Chester, Member for Gloucestershire, ran away with £371 for lodgings and housekeeping, while a further £384 was needed to meet the bills, such as those of the wine merchant (£51), the butcher (£31), the coal merchant (£15) and the candlemaker (£4 14s).[13]

Sir Thomas was not among the really big spenders, however. Members of the aristocracy, staying in their own houses with perhaps two score servants and entertaining on a lavish scale, reckoned the cost in thousands rather than hundreds. According to the jaundiced misanthrope, John Byng, it was the ladies who drove their husbands into the expenses of a London stay, 'urging the old motives of *education* for the girls and of stirring interest for the boys', and made them forgo their harmless country sports for the 'wicked idleness of London occupations'.[14] Apart from the round of theatres, balls, receptions, Ranelagh and Vauxhall, there were the purchases of wine and furniture to be shipped down to the country, while the ladies made a point of visiting the fashionable dressmakers and jewellers. The London season was the occasion for consulting one's lawyers and bankers, for having one's portrait painted, for ordering a new coach or a more fashionable peruke, for browsing in the bookshops and, if necessary, for chancing an operation by a noted London surgeon, perhaps the famous Sir William Cheseldon.

The spending could be vast, like the £1,000 lavished by the first Duke of Devonshire on a supper and masked ball, or relatively modest, like the 77 gallons of white wine bought by Lord Ashburnham for 38s 6d. Ashburnham's total expenditure was considerable, however, coming to nearly £26,000 for six years of London visits made between 1710 and 1716. A full-length portrait of his lordship by Mr Dahl cost £44 10s, but 'Mr Halley's Description of the Eclipse', with other pamphlets, only 2s. 'Music on my Lord's birthday' came to £5 7s 6d, and entertaining 'when Prince Eugene dined here' included £2 4s 3d for 2 pounds of Bohea tea and 1 pound of chocolate, and £3 15s for the confectioner's bill for sweetmeats. When not paying calls, being entertained or offering entertainment oneself, there were always commissions to be executed for relations and friends at home: Dudley North, Member for Suffolk, received in 1741 a letter from his bailiff to tell him his daughter was 'in perfect health, for she wares out a pair of Shoos in about a fortnight. She gives her humble Duty to y^r hon^r and hopes you will not forget her Quilted petty Coat'.[15]

Down in the country the village squire rarely left home to travel further than the nearby markets or occasionally to visit relations or a convenient spa. A stay in London was something to be indulged in perhaps only once in a lifetime, and to be remembered and talked about for years afterwards. But country life was not necessarily dull, except perhaps in the depths of winter when snow and mud made visiting impossible and outdoor sport unpleasant. Winter isolation was too often a bleak reality. In clayland areas especially, the lanes became dangerously churned up and rutted by farmers' carts and carriers' wagons, and by the drovers' beasts which left them 'so full of nastiness and stinking dirt that oft-times many persons who have occasion to come in or go out of town are forced to stop their noses to avoid the ill-smell'. The highly sociable Parson Woodforde infrequently ventured the 8 or 9 miles from his home to Norwich, and the Purefoys of Shalstone in Buckinghamshire were unluckily kept at home first by breaking an axle of their coach, which would 'hinder our coming to you this moon', then by their coachman's rheumatism, and once again by their coach's breaking an axle and overturning. If it was not broken axles it was smallpox: news of irruptions of the dread disease at places en route deterred timid travellers, while friends and relations came seeking refuge from outbreaks in their own neighbourhoods. Even at the close of the eighteenth century the hazards of winter travel kept gentlefolk at home, Wescomb Emerton of Thrumpton, barely six miles from Nottingham, writing:

> Consider the Country in which I live. Roads at any time but indifferent; neighbours at a distance, separated by Rivers as well as bad roads, which makes a visit to Dinner so late in the year almost an impossibility: you are confined, whilst here, within the walls of Thrumpton, without the least society for Mrs. W. and it is not in my power to make it more agreeable to her.[16]

In good weather a great deal of entertaining was done, dinners and cards with friends, and frequent visits made to nearby towns on market days or when there was a fair. And there were occasions when the squire or parson went out of his way to keep good relations with the less genteel members of the community. Parson Woodforde held an annual 'frolic' for the farmers of the parish when they came to pay him their tithe – apparently a time for boisterous drinking when the good parson's decanters were likely to be broken – while earlier in the eighteenth century Squire Nicholas Blundell was in the habit of throwing a party when the hard work of marling his land had been completed. In July 1712 he wrote:

> I had my Finishing Day for my Marling and abundance of my Neighbours and Tennants eat and drunk with me in yᵉ Afternoone. Severall of them had made presents to my wife of Sugar, Chickens, Butter etc: All my Marlers, spreaders, water-balys and carters dined here. We fetched home yᵉ Maypowl from the Pit and had Sword dansing and a Mery night in yᵉ Hall and in yᵉ Barne.[17]

There were also village wakes, which in Blundell's day were very numerous: in Northamptonshire, for instance, at least two of every three parishes held one. The most popular time for them was in late June or July, though a date in the autumn, especially about All Saints' Day, was also approved of. The wake usually began on a Sunday and went on for a few days, sometimes a whole week. There was music, dancing, sports and stalls, as at the town fairs, and the wake was an occasion for much entertaining of distant friends and relations. Gradually, however, the fairs declined and parish wakes fell into disuse, although a large number continued through the nineteenth century. Before then, however, the magistrates had come to frown upon fairs or wakes that had lost their original commercial functions and degenerated into mere opportunities for licentiousness. At Batheaston, for example, the revels were brought to an end in 1776, since, it was said, they were the occasion of

> idleness, drunkeness, riots, gaming and all manner of vice, immor-

ality and profaneness, amongst the lowest class of people, to the
evil example of others, and the great disturbance, damage, and
terror of the well disposed, as well as tending greatly to the increase
of the poor.

The magistrates coupled this step with a dire warning to those alehouse-
keepers who might be disposed to revive the celebrations, as also to 'all
fencers, bearwards, common players of interludes, minstrels, jugglers,
persons using any subtil craft to deceive or impose on His Majestie's
subjects, or playing or betting at any unlawful games or plays, all petty
chapmen and pedlars not duly licensed or otherwise by law, and other
idle and disorderly persons'.[18]

It was about this time that the movement against cruel sports began
to gather force, though its success was long in coming. It was not until
1835 that the law prohibited sports involving the baiting of animals,
and further years elapsed before the Act became effective. Village
pastimes gradually became more sober and respectable, though they
remained numerous and varied: it would be a mistake to think of leisure
activities as in decline. What was happening was a change in their
nature, with the more vulgar and brutal amusements prohibited or
falling into disuse, and an increase in those catering more for the income
and interests of the better-off. In East Anglia, for example, numerous
entertainers still perambulated a circuit of the county towns in the
1860s, performing in town halls, corn exchanges and assembly rooms,
and charging from 6d to 3s for admission – more than the majority of
country people could afford. At Beccles, the performances included
Hoffman's Organophonic Band, Mr Desarae's Equestrian Dogs and
Monkeys, the English Operetta, Veronu – 'the great original and only
Female Magician' – a Dramatic and Operatic Burlesque Company,
Nigger Minstrels, Mr Snowdon's Panorama: the American War and the
Overland Route to India, and Dr Shaw's Drawing Room Enter-
tainments ('extra-ordinary Magical Delusions ... Brilliant Chemical
Experiments'). In addition the town received visits by travelling
circuses, while sporting events included cricket and football, gymnas-
tics, archery and regattas. There were cheap excursions by train, and
Sunday School treats moved out from the grounds of one of the large
houses to go as far afield as Lowestoft, and even in 1862, to London
for the International Exhibition. The occasion of the marriage on 10
March 1863 of the Prince of Wales to Princess Alexandra saw a revival
of 'rural sports', events which harked back to an earlier age: steeple-
chases, a donkey race, a grand race with barrows, foot races for men
and boys, jumping in sacks, a jingling match, dipping for oranges, toad
in the basin and climbing a greasy pole for the prize of a new hat. In
the Beccles Assembly Room a 'Saturday night social meeting' included

chess, draughts and newspapers for the admission charge of only a 1d, with a cup of coffee for a further $\frac{1}{2}$d. Very popular in the winter were fortnightly penny readings which attracted between 300 and 400 people, although unfortunately some came only to disturb the proceedings with 'abominable cat-a-waulings, whistlings, etc.'. Among the readings extracts from Dickens were featured, as well as ones from Shakespeare and Macaulay's *Lays of Ancient Rome*. Other items included *The Charge of the Light Brigade*, Byron's *Prisoner of Chillon*, *The Ancient Mariner* and the fight from *Tom Brown's Schooldays*.[19]

Though well-intentioned parsons sometimes started similar readings in the villages, it must be doubted whether the fare was well suited to the majority of the rural community. Shut out from this modicum of middle-class culture by lack of education or want of interest, or by its sheer strangeness, ordinary villagers preferred simple country pastimes and the pleasures of the inn. Not usually the village's principal inn, however, since there labourers were too likely to encounter their superiors, the farmer, bailiff or parish overseer. Mostly they preferred the little hedge alehouse where they were free to say what they liked about the gaffer and make improper remarks about the girls. And at the alehouse they were apt to hear of things that interested them, the village gossip, news of the latest poaching affray, the dark dealings in stolen lambs, chickens and eggs. The alehouse was the centre of summer evening and Sunday diversions of duck-hunting, rabbit-netting and dog-fighting. And if the alehouse palled, within an hour's walk was a larger village or market town with a wide variety of pubs to patronize. Beccles, with a resident population of only 4,398 in 1851, boasted no fewer than twenty-six hotels, inns and taverns and fourteen beerhouses – one for just over every hundred of its men, women and children.[20]

Apart from drinking, gossiping and a little poaching, the village lads were attracted by any unusual opportunity for sport, and especially so in the years when cock-fighting, for instance, had been placed outside the law. Shrove Tuesday, a universal holiday, was the traditional day in some places for a robust game of football, when all the houses overlooking the green and main street had their windows protected by laths and bundles of straw. The game was played between several parties and might last for as long as four hours, the ball being 'kick'd about from one to t'other in the streets, by him that can get at it, and that is all the art of it', as a visitor tartly commented early in the eighteenth century. Also associated with Shrove Tuesday was the brutal game of cock-throwing, when the bird was placed in a pit and pelted with sticks and stones until a leg was broken or it was knocked unconscious. Sometimes the bird was suspended in an earthenware vessel with only the head and tail exposed. The players paid 2d for five shots, and the one who broke the pot could claim the bird as his prize.

All this was a far cry from the fashionable gatherings in the county town at the time of Quarter Sessions or the Assizes. In early nineteenth-century Lincoln the autumn was the season when the polite society of the county gathered for the Lincoln races, while other entertainments, hunts, plays, balls and assemblies, rounded out race week. The leading landowners were generally in the county at this time of year, and gentlemen from nearby estates, such as Lord Monson and the officials of the Burton hunt, helped organize the events and contributed to the purses offered for the races. The high point of the social calendar was the 'stuff', or colour, ball held in late October or early November, on a date when the revellers could get home by the light of a full moon. The patroness of the ball chose the colour of the year, and the purchase of woollen ball dresses was held to do much for the county's cloth trade. Moreover, the gathering of county notables was also a good opportunity for the holding of business meetings to discuss, for example, the projected county asylum, or suggestions for improving the assembly rooms.[21]

*   *   *

However, 'Merrie England' gradually ceased to be so merrie as the changing attitudes of the later eighteenth and early nineteenth centuries made themselves felt. While there were still many and varied diversions to brighten the lives of the gentry and middle class of countryside and country town, the lower orders, the farmers and their labourers, the craftspeople and ordinary villagers, found themselves increasingly restrained by the suppression of fairs and the prohibition of cruel sports – a ukase which excluded hunting – as well as by the growing influence of the Protestant work-ethic. Opportunities for sport and merry-making declined as former commons and waste lands were enclosed and the number of traditional holidays was reduced. Even ancient perquisites, gathering fuel from fallen branches in the woods, and gleaning, the gathering of the stray ears of corn after the reapers had finished, were increasingly frowned upon by farmers concerned with strict rights of property; and the men's daily allowance of beer or cider, as well as their harvest fare, were commuted into money payments, and eventually in 1887 the drink allowance was prohibited by law – if not effectively abolished – as the temperance movement took hold. Soon the only outlet for the drinking man (and woman) was the hedge alehouse or a Saturday night outing to the nearest town with its wider choice of inns and beershops.

On the surface deference remained, the labourer touching his cap to the squire, his wife curtseying to the squire's lady or parson's wife as they drove by. But below the apparent complaisance lurked envy, anger and bitterness, a frustrated desire for revenge which occasionally boiled over into positive action. Often this might be only the satisfaction to be gained from dropping an anonymous message through an employer's letterbox – its blood-curdling threats the more chilling because of their ungrammatical and ill-spelled directness. But such letters were only one expression of the 'counter-terror of the poor', as it has been called. Hunger, lack of work, poverty and injustice drove people to desperate measures, going far beyond mere threats. For the most part the measures were covert, cloaked in darkness – the theft or maiming of stock grazing in the pastures, the setting in the fields of iron spikes designed to wreck the farmer's cultivator or hay-tedder, the firing of barns and ricks, the disturbing of the family's slumber by a missile shattering a window. Farmers sat up at night with a gun to guard valuable stock and machinery, and unpopular magistrates, land agents, gamekeepers and Poor Law officials required not a little courage to venture out alone on dark nights. Many of the attacks on property and assaults on the person were the paying back of old scores, the revenge desired by people who considered themselves unfairly dismissed, wrongly turned out of their cottages, prosecuted for taking a pheasant or a rabbit or two, or summarily refused relief. The new police of the middle nineteenth century were also the target of private vengeance, victims being shot and maimed in the most brutal fashion. Such outrages had a long history and continued to disfigure at least the first forty years of Victoria's reign; but at times the crimes were more concentrated, as in the 1840s, when the night skies of East Anglia were very frequently illuminated by the flames of burning ricks.[22]

Private individual malevolence, concealed and anonymous (though with the perpetrator often guessed at, and sometimes caught and convicted), was a daily fact of life for country people in the south of England during the first six or seven decades of the nineteenth century. Its context was low wages and underemployment, resulting in poverty and the meagre relief of a begrudging Poor Law, the resentment flaring up strongly in years of particular tension, and particularly in the grain-growing districts of East Anglia. Conditions which sparked off unrest were associated with large-scale arable farming and a lack of alternative employment. Corn production required many hands in the busy seasons but many fewer in the winter. As the rural population grew, the pressure of numbers kept wages low, and there was insufficient year-round work to take up the extra hands. The labourers were mostly too poor and ignorant, too tied down by large families and the restrictions of the parochial basis of poor relief, to migrate to areas where work was more varied and more plentiful.

The same context fed also the large-scale and unconcealed forms of protest, especially those which flared up in 1816 and again in the 'last labourers' revolt' of 1830–1. The first half of the nineteenth century formed the turbulent close of a violent era when for long the aggrieved had thought it right to take matters into their own hands, and law-breakers pursued their illicit trades with near impunity. It was an era when the power of the mob (or 'crowd' as some historians prefer) could not be ignored, and the lack of adequate forces of the law made criminals dangerous and bold. Thus the Nottinghamshire magistrates, meeting at Mansfield to nominate men for service in the militia, found themselves menaced by a large crowd, members of which forced their way into the room, seized the papers and carried them triumphantly through the streets, ill-treating in the process Sir George Savile and other prominent gentlemen. The smugglers of the south coast intimidated customs officers, troops, townspeople and gentry alike. The infamous 'Hawk-hurst gang', who had a base at the Star and Eagle in Goudhurst, threatened on one occasion to burn down the village and kill the inhabitants, forcing the local gentry to organize their own militia to protect themselves. Another gang of twenty-four well-armed smugglers rode openly through the town of Rye, refreshed themselves at the Red Lion, and fired their guns several times to the terror of the populace. In Hampshire a Mr Wakeford, a landowner, woke one night to find robbers in his bedroom, one of them holding a carbine to his head and threatening to 'cut him to pieces' if he did not reveal where his money was kept; the gang made off with fourteen guineas, the silver plate and two silver watches, and dragged their unfortunate victim down the stairs and over the ground to their horses before releasing him. John Carrington, the Hertfordshire diarist, frequently recorded similar crimes in his part of the country. In September 1800, for instance, a Mr Limbury of Little Berkhamsted fought 'most desperately' with men caught stealing his geese, though he failed to catch the men or to prevent his geese from being killed; in the previous December the farmhouse of a Mr Camp was broken into by two ruffians who 'allmost killed Camp & his Wife and Robd them of all'; and in an earlier year a Mr Kent, a farmer of Bennington, was murdered by a family of robbers, the Clibbons, father and sons, who threw the victim 'into his cart and the horses brought him home'. Subsequently, one is not sorry to find, the patriarch of these homicidal footpads was killed in the middle of attacking another gentleman who, overpowered, 'calld for his man to shoot, which he Did and killd the old Roogue on the Spott'.[23]

Rural crime tended to centre on large 'open' villages where the property was divided among many small owners and there had developed a proliferation of inns and beerhouses as well as tradesmen's establishment and craftsmen's shops. Residents with a little spare capital ran up cheap cottages to attract newcomers, and open villages were the popular recourse of itinerant hawkers and pedlars, drovers and harvest gangs, along with bands of 'bankers', or drainage workers, and canal and railway navvies working in the vicinity. Bankers and navvies were notorious for hard drinking and violence, and they, together with vagrants and gypsies, were suspected of perpetrating much of the local crime. Often enough, however, a great many offences could be laid at the door of the permanent inhabitants, especially the casual labourers, the unmarried men and youths who were not infrequently addicted to drink, brawling and the cheap opium pills which could be readily obtained from country markets and shops.

Some villages, and within them certain families, gained a long-standing evil reputation for misbehaviour and crime. Such a village was Morton with Hanthorpe, in Lincolnshire, where, in the space of twenty months, ninety sheep were driven away or slaughtered on the ground, and gangs of armed thieves committed burglaries and robberies, keeping 'the public and private mind in constant alarm'. At Whaplode in the same county it was a 'common drunken frolic' to shoot into houses, break down doors and demolish windows – though the damage was usually paid for subsequently. And at Ruskington in the 1830s street fights were commonplace, with, on one occasion, two young women, stripped to the waist, indulging in fisticuffs in the yard of a public house.[24]

By contrast, the 'close' village was known for its sobriety and good behaviour – indeed, so much so that persons of independent disposition refused to live there and sneered at those who 'daren't blow their nose without the squire's permission'. In the close village the property was generally concentrated in the hands of few owners, perhaps only one, and there was often a resident squire who was careful to control the building and letting of inns and cottages in order to keep out unruly elements, families suspected of poaching or known for their heavy drinking. Such villages were typically small, and most of the limited number of residents gained their livelihood in the service of the squire or that of his principal tenants. Extra labour, when required, was hired from neighbouring villages, and one reason for restricting the population was to keep down the potential liability on the poor rates. The social structure was much tighter and more hierarchical than in the open village, and the influence of the church and parson much stronger. Social control often extended to political control, the farmers and other residents taking care not only to restrain their social habits and language but also their expression of opinions which might be deemed hostile to those of the squire and established church.

Nevertheless, the close village could not exist in total isolation, and its gamekeepers (and sometimes private police) could not always prevent poaching incursions, housebreakings and theft of livestock committed by vagrants, navvies working nearby or the inhabitants of a neighbouring open village. Consequently, landowners and farmers joined together to form local associations for the purpose of offering rewards and prosecuting suspected persons. Private police and game-keepers supplemented the old-style village constable, but they were not equipped to cope with serious crime, much less a riot, and the last resort, the calling out of the military, was only too likely to inflame a dangerous situation and lead to bloodshed. However, there was not always much enthusiasm for appointing new professional police forces when this was permitted by the Rural Police Act of 1839. The concern for local control and independence died hard, and by 1856 only about half the counties had established paid constabularies. In 1911 there were still more private gamekeepers than county policemen, indeed, more than twice as many. To a jaundiced eye the new police might be seen as providing publicly financed assistance in the continued war against poachers, a suspicion that was reinforced by the Night Poaching Act of 1862, which empowered the police to search persons suspected of poaching. By this time, however, the nature of rural crime was changing significantly. Cases of assault and stealing became much less common, while new offences, cruelty to animals and breaches of the Education and Highways Acts, mounted steeply in the later decades of the century. Drunkenness and disorderly conduct still accounted for many arrests, reflecting perhaps a lack of alternative outlets to brighten village life, and some villages still remained notorious for crime, whereas others were 'extraordinarily stable in a sea of discontent'.[25]

*   *   *

From the later seventeenth century a very common form of protest, especially in years of dearth and high prices, was the food riot. Angry crowds, often led by women, seized loads of grain on their way to large towns or ports, and sometimes sold off the corn at what they thought to be a 'fair' price, handing the proceeds over to the carrier. Occasion-ally, too, there were riots in marketplaces, and the magistrates inter-vened to raise voluntary funds for buying up grain and reselling it at a lower price. Those figures suspected of rigging the market, farmers, dealers and millers, were liable to be attacked by angry mobs, frequently made up of women and youths, and only rarely including agricultural workers. Investigation has revealed as many as seventy-four food riots in the years of high prices between 1795–6 and 1816–18, and they were particularly marked at centres of communication and points of shipment on the coast, rivers and canals, as well as at places near to major towns. This form of protest was beginning to die out, however, in the first decades of the nineteenth century as the dearness of food hit the more numerous industrial workers who had no access to land, the attacks on the corn trade being replaced by the industrial strike.[26]

Given the endemic violence and the weakness of the forces of the law, it is not surprising that the protests of the poor and hungry should sometimes turn to the use of threats backed by an array of rustic weapons. In 1740, for instance, a year of great scarcity, a group of men invaded the house of a grain exporter of Flint, drank his beer and wine, and menaced him and his family with pikes and a sword.[27] Both the East Anglian riots of 1816 and the more widespread Swing riots of 1830–1 saw peaceful demands for higher wages reinforced by machine-breaking and armed menaces which escalated into confrontations between the rioters and the military.

In 1816 a combination of adverse changes caused widespread distress among both industrial and farm labourers. Wages fell sharply at the end of the Napoleonic Wars, and East Anglia was a region of particularly low wages where farmworkers were paid only some 8–9s a week on average. While food prices generally fell from the near-famine levels of the closing years of the wars, the price of bread still fluctuated sharply and in 1816 was as dear as it had been during the worst scarcities of the previous years. The farmers, too, were severely affected. The changes in the markets and the collapse of easy wartime credit brought novel and unpleasant conditions. The farmers had got used to wheat prices which in the war years had occasionally topped 100s a quarter, in 1812 even more than 120s, but in 1815 had fallen to under 66s. They had got used also to paying much higher rents than before the wars, and their other outgoings had risen commensurately. The larger farmers, at least, had also much extended their operations by borrowing from local banks. Now they found it difficult to meet their commitments, especially as the banks called in their loans, refused new credit or failed altogether. Peace saw the farmhouses full of sheriff's officers. The farmers' reaction was to cut back, reduce their acreage and economize on wages and workforce. And lack of work among the labourers was intensified by demobilization and the casting of thousands of soldiers and sailors on to the labour market.

Norfolk was among the worst-hit counties. There the Board of Agriculture's inquiry of 1816 found substantial amounts of land unoccupied, rents reduced and the poor rates generally increased. Farmers were being sold up for the recovery of unpaid debts, and those who were solvent were obliged to sell their crops and stock for whatever they would fetch in order to repay the banks. 'Country-bank-paper has nearly retired from circulation, and agricultural credit has ceased to exist', wrote the well-informed John Moseley, farmer of Tofts in that county. Most universal, however, were the correspondents' reports of the sufferings of the poor: 'Greater distress than ever known'; 'Great want of employment: able hands 8d per day'; 'Very bad: 15s per week reduced to 9s'; 'In a most pitiable state'; 'The most alarming feature of this distressed period'.[28]

There had been rioting in Suffolk in 1815 when farm machinery was smashed, and in the following spring more incidents occurred in Essex and Huntingdonshire, and again in Suffolk. The May of 1816 saw the troubles concentrated in Norfolk. As in the past, corn merchants, millers and shopkeepers were the immediate objects of the labourers' ire. At Downham Market William Baldwin's flour mill was attacked, the crowd (which included industrial workers) helping themselves to his flour and meal. Next they turned their attention to the butchers' shops and a cooked-meat store, until the ultimate arrival of the yeomanry turned the marketplace into a battlefield and the mob was dispersed. At Littleport, 10 miles south on the road to Ely, money was demanded, and the crowd wrecked the home of the Revd Vachell before marching on to Ely armed with bludgeons, pitchforks and fowling-pieces. There the innkeepers were attacked, until at length the Royston Volunteer Cavalry put an end to the uproar. At the special Assizes held subsequently twenty-four of the rioters were sentenced to death, of whom five were executed. It was want which made the men desperate. 'Bread I want and bread I will have', was the cry of one of the rioters.[29]

The more extensive Swing riots of 1830–1 owed much to similar circumstances. Bread was as dear as it had ever been since the end of the wars, and the farmers were again laying off hands, following a poor harvest in 1829. Lack of work intensified the misery of the severe winter of 1829–30. Even when there was work average wages for men in East Anglia and the southern counties ran at only about 10–12s a week, and in the worst-paid areas under 9s. But there were also other factors involved. The threshing machine, introduced in Scotland and the north of England early in the wars, had reached the arable districts of southern counties and filled the labourers with the fear that their already reduced winter employment would be further curtailed. In launching destructive attacks on the threshing machine the labourers were tilting at a symbol rather than the root cause of their plight, but the machine was an obvious and easy target, and some 390 were broken in the course of the riots, mainly in Wiltshire, Berkshire, Hampshire, Kent and Norfolk. The machines usually adopted in the south were generally small and cheap, and not very efficient – which may help to explain why the farmers often did little to protect them. Indeed, they would sometimes put the machine in the yard ready for the rioters, and even provide hammers for its destruction and beer for refreshment. Perhaps they calculated that if they escaped with merely the loss of a small threshing machine, usually worth less than £50, and kept their barns, hay and livestock intact, they were getting off lightly enough.

Another factor that had some influence in the unrest was the screwing down of the poor relief provided for the able-bodied. Parish officials, alarmed by mounting poor rates, adopted degrading forms of relief

WE the undersigned Magistrates acting in and for the Hundred of Gallow, in the County of Norfolk, do promise to use our utmost Endeavours and Influence we may possess, to prevail upon the Occupiers of Land in the said Hundred,

To discontinue the use of Thrashing Machines, and to take them to pieces.

Dated this 29th. day of November, 1830.

CHAS. TOWNSHEND.
ROBERT NORRIS.
EDW. MARSHAM.

STEWARDSON AND SON. PRINTERS, FAKENHAM.

Figure 15 Attacks by labourers on the threshing machines which reduced their winter employment marked the Swing riots of 1830. Some magistrates, as in the Hundred of Gallow, in Norfolk, reacted by advising farmers to avoid trouble by setting aside and dismantling their machines, a measure which might have been followed with advantage elsewhere.

designed to reduce the financial burden and extract some return in labour from the paupers – the 'roundsman' system, the 'labour rate', the auctioning of paupers' labour to the highest bidders and the offering of work in parish road gangs. There was, too, something of a political element in the rioting, centring on the struggle for reform of Parliament. Protests were stirred up by the radicals among the better-educated and more politically conscious village craftsmen, no doubt helped by the inflammatory oratory and writings of William Cobbett, and perhaps by more distant sources in the turbulent industrial towns, and even abroad. The riots spread from one place to another along or near the line of the main roads, probably receiving stimulus in larger villages and towns where radical elements were active, and stirred to action as news of the unrest was spread by coachmen, travellers, drovers and carriers. It seems unlikely, however, that this was an organized revolt which had failed to get off the ground, even though the labourers' demands in different outbreaks were very similar and were supported by political arguments and intelligent contentions about the relevance to wages of rent levels and tithes. The majority of the rioters were untutored farmworkers, knowing little of politics or economics, easily influenced perhaps by more worldly men who could work upon their very real grievances. It was Cobbett himself who put his finger on the ultimate cause: 'They are people in *want*. They are people who have *nothing to lose*, except their lives.'

It was work and a higher wage, a wage a family could eke out a living on, that the labourers wanted: the threatening letters, riots, assaults, arson and attacks on machinery were all the by-product of these basic needs. And it is evident that many of them expected their ends would be achieved if only their plight was brought to the attention of their betters, to the employers, and to the gentry who, as magistrates and Members of Parliament, might be considered as having influence in high places. There were peaceful meetings at which the labourers, gathered in a dozen or so, or in hundreds strong, asked the farmers for an increase in pay: at Faversham and Boughton Street in East Kent a rise to 2s 6d a day. 'They are very quiet, and all they require is more wages', commented an eye-witness. And, as mentioned, the labourers seem to have appreciated that the farmers could pay them more only if their other outgoings were reduced: so the landlords were to be asked to reduce their rents, and the parsons their tithes – indeed there were some riots specifically over tithes, notably in East Anglia and East Sussex. In the middle of Kent, near Maidstone, large crowds on separate occasions confronted Sir John Filmer of East Sutton Park and the Revd James Gambier, Rector of neighbouring Langley. A spokesman described the sufferings of the poor, and hoped the gentlemen would support the men in getting the expenses of government reduced.[30]

Such parleying was, however, sometimes accompanied by threats, and mounting impatience and anger drove the more violent spirits to stronger action, to burn down haystacks and barns, break machines and assault unpopular figures in the neighbourhood. The incidents, violent or not, began in the late summer of 1830 in East Kent and spread northwards into East Anglia and westwards as far as Cornwall and Devon, and in a minor way to Monmouthshire and east Glamorgan. In all there were incidents in thirty-eight counties, but many of this number were affected only very marginally. As large a figure as 968 of the 1,475 incidents reported – two-thirds of the whole – occurred in only seven counties, in Hampshire, Wiltshire, Berkshire, Kent, Norfolk and East and West Sussex. The numbers of people involved are less easy to calculate but certainly ran into some thousands. However, the total of incidents exaggerates somewhat the extent of the troubles since it was common for a crowd from one village to make a circuit of the neighbourhood, pressing others to join them and destroying machines as they went; and every place where an incident occurred is counted separately.[31] There was apparently no organizing hand, and there is no hard evidence that Captain Swing ever existed, though well-dressed strangers were said to have been seen at various places. The subscription 'Swing', striking and evocative, served to round off the ninety-nine letters that were penned, a suitable subscription to such expressions as 'Your name is down amongst the Black Hearts in the Black Book ... make your Wills', 'Revenge for thee is on the Wing', and 'we will burn down your barns and you in them'.[32]

The reaction of the magistrates was at first mild, but as in the autumn the troubles spread the troops were eventually called out and there were a number of ugly incidents. Many hundreds were arrested as the riots died away, and almost 2,000 cases were tried at special Assizes. In the final account 252 were sentenced to death, of whom nineteen were executed, all but three of them for arson. As many as 481 were transported; 'wrenched from their families, and shipped 12,000 miles away with virtually no hope of ever returning to their homes. In the south of England, there were whole communities that, for a generation, were struck by the blow.' Over 600 other men were jailed, seven fined and one whipped; 800 were acquitted or bound over.[33]

The vengeance of the propertied was severe. It was also uneven – similar offences received dissimilar punishments – and much of the evidence on which people were convicted was flimsy. Numbers of the prisoners were immature youths, lacking any motives for their petty offences other than those of desiring to imitate, or having a little excitement when the worse for drink. George Steel, aged 18, was transported for taking 1s while in liquor, and William Sutton, another 18-year-old, was sentenced to death and subsequently transported for life for stealing 4d in a drunken frolic. But it is worth noticing that by no means all of the convicted were naïve or ignorant labourers: some were persons of superior status and education, wheelwrights, carpenters, joiners, smiths, bricklayers and shoemakers. That such individuals should be involved in riots over poverty and farm machinery was to the judges incomprehensible; and, as people who should have set an example, the judges deemed them as deserving of more severe punishment.[34]

*   *   *

In the aftermath of the riots the countryside of East Anglia and the south remained restless, the resentment now expressing itself mainly in arson, together with sporadic cattle maiming and assaults. The labourers were generally cowed but not entirely demoralized. Some increases in wages gained in 1830 were maintained; and the farmers were wary of installing new threshing machines, though subsequently they turned to hiring the large steam-driven threshers supplied by contractors, which were much more efficient than the machines destroyed in 1830. There were a number of strikes called in attempts to prevent wages from being reduced, and even, at Ramsbury in Wiltshire in 1831, a threat of making a march round other villages, as in 1830. More serious was the short-lived wave of protest against the introduction of the harsh Poor Law Amendment Act of 1834. Sometimes, as at Wroughton, in Wiltshire, the men expressed their hostility by walking out of church during the service and smoking their pipes in the cemetery. At Christian Malford a hundred people took possession of the church and prevented the overseers from entering it. Fifty men armed with sticks came from Worth and Ardingly in Sussex to threaten the Guardians at Cuckfield, while 150 rioted against the new law at Chertsey in Surrey. There were also attacks on workhouses and Poor Law officials, and attempts to call local strikes. But after 1834–5 the agitation died down and incendiarism remained the predominant form of protest. The deliberate conflagrations were widespread in the affected counties, especially in the years 1843–5, when an Act to amend the law regarding the burning of farm buildings was passed (and insurance companies sharply raised their premiums). Occasionally labourers who were drawn to the scene refused to help put out the fire, even cheered on the flames, obstructed attempts to douse the blaze, and in one instance 'actually lit their pipes by the burning corn stalks and deliberately smoked them in the farm-yard'.[35]

West Wales, too, had its disturbances, though the most serious of these were of a different kind. The 'Rebecca riots', which broke out on the border of Pembrokeshire and Carmarthenshire some ten years after 'Swing', were so called because the leaders of the small farmers and labourers involved disguised themselves in women's clothing. At first the target of the rioters' lethal anger was the newly erected turnpike gates and their keepers. Then the agitation turned to more general objects of dislike, displaying a strong current of anti-English feeling and degenerating into an instrument of private hate and vengeance. At first the rioters had the sympathy of the community, but this was lost as the nightly gatherings and outrages persisted, until eventually the use of the military and peaceful reform of the turnpikes restored quiet to this part of the Principality.

In England, the incendiarism continued into the 1850s, but by 1860 a change was evident. The glut of rural labour had been gradually reduced for some time by migration to towns and by emigration, and wages were slowly improving (although in the south-west they still averaged under 10s a week). Railway building and free trade helped stimulate the economy at large, and the New Poor Law had fallen far short of its objective of entirely abolishing outdoor relief for the able-bodied. Its main effects on the respectable poor were to create a horror of the workhouse, a fear of 'the house' which persisted down to recent times, and to discourage all but the helpless or desperate from looking to the authorities for relief. Poverty remained on a huge scale, but only a small proportion of even the abysmally poor sought help from the Poor Law.

The incendiarism, maiming and violence of the first half of the century died down as unemployment was lessened and the labourers gradually became a little more comfortable. Religion and education played some part. Primitive Methodism and other dissenting creeds were making converts in the former disaffected areas of the south and east, and in some degree diverted the labourers' energies and grievances. In the 'Swing' counties of the south the Primitive Methodists had by 1840 increased their circuits from the five of 1830 to as many as eighteen. It was not done without opposition from farmers, nor from men resenting the attacks on their drinking and their sports, who at first organized counter-attractions to defeat the work of the preachers. The new religion was something novel and unfamiliar, striking and compelling to those accustomed to the traditional drowsy service of a scholar-priest whose language and way of thinking clearly placed him among the upper classes of rural society. And the preaching itself was 'passionate, dramatic, and often hysterical', appearing to its listeners as visible glory, 'as a light', or 'as fire falling among people'.[36]

Ignorance, superstition, naïvety and a general lack of sophistication made the rural poor receptive to preachers of force and personality, using homely metaphors in accents that were familiar. The same naïvety was at the root of the extraordinary little rising which occurred in 1838 at Boughton under Blean, a village near Faversham in East Kent.

A deranged individual named John Tom, who came to live in the neighbourhood after his release from the county asylum, curried favour with some of the farmers and labouring families, using a variety of extravagant promises and pronouncements. Tom believed himself to be Sir William Courtenay, the rightful heir to the earldom of Devon, and his supposed status, his striking personality and strange oriental garb (complete with pistols and scimitar) gained him a messianic influence among the credulous poor. Believing his claim to be the risen Christ about to usher in the millennium, a band of some thirty men flocked to his banner. Following the waving emblem of the red lion, and bearing a pole with a loaf of bread impaled on it, they made a march round the countryside without gaining further adherents, and then retired to Bossenden Wood, near Boughton. When a brother of the messenger sent by the magistrates was murdered by 'Sir William', the authorities reacted by calling out the troops from Canterbury. There followed a short unequal fight, grandiloquently called 'The Battle of Bossenden Wood', in which 'Courtenay' and eight of his followers were killed. A street of modern houses, named Courtenay Road, has now been erected near the spot, a somewhat strange memorial to a deranged murderer. Nearby stand the school and church which the government ordered to be built following the riot, witnesses to the official belief that only a lack of education and absence of religion could explain the labourers' fanatical support of so outlandish a charlatan.[37]

Education, indeed, was seen as the panacea not only for unrest but also for poverty. The New Poor Law of 1834 had attempted to reduce pauperism by discouraging the able-bodied from seeking relief, thus forcing them back into the labour market. There was on the part of numbers of the well-to-do a rejection of private charity, especially charity that was unsystematic and casual, and the efforts of well-meaning clergymen and squires to help the poor by gifts of clothing, coal and food were derided by those who believed in the need to tackle the problem at its root, to *cure* poverty, rather than merely *treat* it. Education, it was held, would enable the poor to appreciate the merits of thrift, temperance and restraint, the advantages of hard work and putting by for illness and old age. The growth of benefit club membership in rural areas of the south came late in the history of the friendly society movement, mainly after 1845, but is perhaps evidence of the influence of the propounding of 'self-help', and of a changing way of life among the labourers. Of course, neither friendly societies nor schools could solve the fundamental cause of rural poverty, which was basically the lowness of wages, nor yet such ancillary factors as seasonal underemployment, large families, the slow decline of some ways of supplementing family earnings, and the illness, incapacity or early death of the husband. In any case, many village clubs were financially unsound and failed when claims on the funds became heavy; while education, though perhaps enabling some brighter and more ambitious pupils to rise above their parents' status, did not succeed in bringing about a labouring class that was rational, prudent, sober and thrifty. The schools, frequently entirely lacking in some parishes before the 1870s, could do little more than achieve among the young a degree of literacy, some smattering of arithmetic, history and geography, and perhaps some moderate skill in woodwork or needlework. In a few of their pupils they created, as in Hardy's Jude, an unfulfilled desire for superior knowledge and advancement; in the majority they instilled the ability to write an occasional letter to distant relations and to read – but what they read was seldom the kind of literature that the advocates of education had in mind; and a minority were left in a state of semi-literacy and ignorance that formed the basis for unkind Edwardian jokes about country bumpkins and rustic idiots.

7

THE COUNTRYSIDE IN DECLINE, 1870–1914

As noted in the previous chapter, education was seen as a means of instilling nineteenth-century middle-class morality into the labour force. Nevertheless, despite the riots, assaults, maiming, arson and poaching, the provision of the schools that were supposed to stem the unrest in the countryside lagged behind their growth in the towns. Before the 1870s many rural parishes had no church school, established by one or other of the two major voluntary societies, but only a makeshift substitute initiated and supported by the local parson, perhaps in a room in the vicarage or in a barn lent by a farmer. Many other parishes could boast only a 'Dame' school, a small private establishment held by an elderly lady in her front room or run as a part-time occupation by a village shopkeeper or tradesman, and in either case amounting to little more than a child-minding operation. Yet others, in certain parts of the south midlands and home counties, had only craft schools, where children acquired dexterity in a local trade, such as making pillow lace or straw plait, and were taught little else. And not a few country places had no school of any description.

The Act of 1870 followed on the report of the Newcastle Commission, which had revealed how defective was much of the country's elementary education. The Act imposed the building of a new school by an elected school board wherever the existing provision was inadequate, and in addition empowered the board, if it so decided, to enforce attendance and remit the fees of very poor children. Within a few years new schools had plugged the gaps in the old voluntary and private provision, although it took further legislation to raise by gradual steps the minimum school-leaving age and to abolish fees in publicly supported schools. The system of part-timers, children over 12 years of age who were permitted to attend school for part of the day and go to work for the rest of it, was done away with only in 1918, when the school-leaving age was also raised to 14 and fees were entirely abolished. The Education Acts, after that of 1870, were mainly concerned with raising the standards of elementary schooling, and were aimed primarily at heel-dragging town authorities and the educationally backward countryside in general.

Although nationally standards were gradually improved, the countryside always tended to lag behind. In the late nineteenth century, when the beginnings of secondary education for working-class children were being developed in the more progressive towns, nothing of that sort was to be found in the villages. Classes in technical subjects, evening classes and adult education were sparse or entirely lacking. The village elementary schools, too, were still often deficient in accommodation and the qualifications of the staff; and despite the employment of school attendance officers (possibly retired policemen or sergeant-majors) attendance frequently remained poor. The well-paid harvest work was a special problem for the school authorities, obliging some of them to adjust the school calendar to allow for such late crops as hops, potatoes or apples to be gathered in.

Of education designed to suit the environment and interests of country children there was little or none. Farmers complained of town-bred teachers who could not distinguish wheat from barley, nor yet a dock from a thistle, though the reasons for young people quitting the countryside went far beyond the academic nature of the schooling. Provision of specialized training in agriculture came in only slowly, and then mainly for the better-off sons of large farmers and landowners. Young boys continued, as ever, to learn farm skills on the job from their fathers or the old men. Back in the 1790s William Marshall, the agricultural writer, had put forward proposals for research establishments and the training of farmers, and he argued also for the proper training of pauper boys who were apprenticed to farmers as a means of relieving the ratepayers. But the only outcome of his enthusiasm was the creation of the first Board of Agriculture of 1793, a voluntary body supported by government grant, which was wound up after a rather undistinguished career in 1822. The Royal Agricultural College, founded at Cirencester in 1845, was the first establishment specifically concerned with agricultural education and was originally intended for the sons of farmers. Subsequently a number of British universities began to offer degrees in agriculture (though a Chair of Agriculture had been founded in Edinburgh as early as 1790). Courses offered by a few private colleges were supplemented in due course by publicly financed colleges of agriculture attached to universities, but before 1900 farm institutes, designed to give special training to the sons of small farmers and farmworkers, were to be found only in four counties, though their number had risen to sixteen by 1927. Major difficulties in the way of the poor country boy included not merely the cost of attending a farm institute but frequently the weakness of the basic education he had received at school, the failure of farmers to value employees who had acquired specialist qualifications, and the near impossibility of advancing up the farming ladder when suitable holdings and sufficient capital were both lacking.

Failure to train the workforce adequately was the more remarkable in view of the advance of machinery in British farming. Already by mid-century certain types of factory-made machines had become commonplace, and of course the threshing machine, gradually moving from its Scottish origins in the eighteenth century, was at the root of the riots of 1830. The new American reapers attracted attention at the Great Exhibition of 1851, and by the end of the century the self-binding reaper was making inroads into the troops of women and children who formerly followed the reaping gangs or mechanical reapers to bind and stook the sheaves. By 1910 even a mixed husbandry farm as small as 100 acres was held to require an iron roller, a horse hoe, a drill-harrow and two other kinds of harrow, a turnip drill, a mower and reaper and a horse rake – in addition to ploughs, carts and barn machinery. Large farmers needed, in addition to greater numbers of these implements, a grass-seed sowing machine, a turnip-scuffler, sheaf-binder, horse fork and potato-raiser.[1] In consequence many farmworkers were expected to be able to carry out simple maintenance and repairs to the machines as well as operate them. The very large and expensive items of equipment, such as steam-powered threshing machines and steam-powered rigs for cultivation, were hired out by contractors and operated by their own men, although the farmer's own hands helped in the work. Moreover, the era of 'high farming' in the years between the mid-1840s and the mid-1870s had seen the fields expensively drained by subsoil pipes or tiles, the application of new and costly fertilizers, the introduction of valuable pedigree stock and the reconstruction of farm buildings, even to creating specially designed 'model' farms.

It is a matter for surprise, therefore, that landlords and farmers who were prepared to lay out thousands of pounds on machinery, drainage, fertilizers, new stock and buildings should have done so little to improve the education and training of those who were to provide the labour for such farms. Many farmers, indeed, were hostile to the very idea of education, viewing the post-1870 Board schools as an unwelcome innovation which contributed to the migration of labour from the countryside. Improvements in the schools, and in technical training, came about despite the farmers' apathy or outright opposition; this was still true eighty years later of the introduction of secondary education into the countryside following the Act of 1944. In general, farmers wanted labour that above all was cheap, and so they showed hostility to anything which might tend to raise its cost. They were not as a rule much concerned about the quality of labour, unless it was the kind of quality which expressed itself in skill in the traditional tasks. They were deaf to the argument that better-paid labour was more productive and so cheaper in the end. Nor did they have the foresight to appreciate that in the not very distant future the farmworker would be as much a mechanic as untutored follower of the plough. It may be true, as was argued in the early years of this century, that many of the smaller farmers were operating on so narrow a margin of profit that any rise in labour costs was likely to bring about their collapse. And, despite the advent of machinery, the proportion of farm labour to acreage does not appear to have fallen greatly in the later nineteenth century. Only where uncompetitive arable farms were converted to grass did labour requirements fall at all sharply or where a new breed of economical tenants (often Scots who came south to take up dairying for the London market) dispensed with almost all hired labour. But even the larger farmers, whose enterprises were still profitable after the fall in grain prices, took the same shortsighted view of the matter, resisting all suggestions that might improve the level of wages, and opposing anything that made labour less plentiful, particularly the village school.

*   *   *

Neither education nor machinery was the greatest factor in the decline in the farm workforce which occurred in the fifty years before 1914. Between the censuses of 1871 and 1901 the numbers of males engaged in agriculture fell by 300,000, or nearly a third; the numbers of females by nearly 46,000, or a huge 79 per cent. (The numbers of both men and women employed showed modest increases in the following census of 1911, when agriculture was recovering from the depression of the late nineteenth century, only to fall again thereafter.)[2]

The fall in the numbers of women and girls reflects a variety of changes that were going on in the countryside. In particular, there was the mechanization of some tasks in which females had commonly been employed, such as the hoeing of root crops, haymaking and the binding and stooking of the sheaves behind the reapers. By the end of the century the troops of women who could once be seen helping on the farms had disappeared. Also significant were the widening opportunities for village girls outside farming, especially in domestic service, and in shops and factories in towns. As their husbands gradually became better off so there was a tendency for village wives to avoid the heavy ill-paid work on the farms and turn instead to cleaner and more convenient tasks in surroundings less exposed to the elements, in country crafts such as bone-lace-making, straw-plaiting, glove-making and the like; or perhaps taking in washing, keeping chickens and serving as part-time domestic help in the large houses of the neighbourhood.

The decline in male farmworkers also owed much to migration and expanding employment opportunities for able-bodied men of limited

Figure 16 A decline in the employment of women in farming was a feature of the later nineteenth century, so that eventually a woman working in the fields was said to be an uncommon sight. Hop-picking, however, remained a seasonal employment for whole families until a few years after the Second World War.

education and skills. They were able to find somewhat better paid and more regular work in the police force, the army, the railways and the post office – jobs which carried with them a uniform, often housing, and a small pension at the end of their working life. They were also attracted by town jobs associated with horses, such as coachmen, grooms and carters, and some found a niche in town gasworks or waterworks, or as hotel porters and council roadmen. It was said that many had simply followed the girls. Not a few were attracted to try a new life overseas, in America, Australia or New Zealand, and here the growing contacts with the wider world through education, the reading of newspapers and, not least, letters from friends and relations who had already emigrated, were influential. It was fortunate that the period offered new opportunities outside farming and an expansion of the means of moving to towns or overseas, for the labour demands of

Figure 17 A village scene in Mill Street, Fordingbridge, Hampshire, in the late nineteenth century. More and more village women chose to stay at home to look after their young children rather than take them with them to the farmyard or field.

agriculture itself were falling. The late nineteenth century saw a considerable growth of dairy farming, which was almost always a family operation, while many larger farmers were seeking to cut costs by employing fewer regular hands and relying more on casual labour. Further, the conversion of some 2 million acres of wheat and barley land to pasture between 1878 and 1903 must have reduced local labour demands substantially, and in total by probably some 70,000 or so.

One effect of the migration of people from the countryside was the relative shortage on the farms of workers in their prime, those between 20 and 45 years of age. Compared with many other occupations agriculture had always employed large numbers of boys and youths (farm servants were commonly in their teens, and farmers often preferred to employ day-labourers with sons old enough to be useful); at the other end of the age range, elderly men were kept on, perhaps for having some special skill, or merely out of charity, used only for light work

173

and helping out in the barns and stockyard. From a study of 262 rural parishes Charles Booth found that 55 per cent of persons over 65 could exist by their own earnings or means.[3]

The large outflow of young men must have exerted an upward pressure on farm wages, although this may have been offset in part by the decline in the arable acreage as grain prices fell, and by the farmers economizing in labour in order to cut costs. Money wages, though still varying widely from one region to another, and especially between the high-paid north and the low-paid south, advanced in the 1870s (when the first large-scale unions of farmworkers ran their brief course), but generally fell back slightly in the 1880s. Then, between the early 1890s and 1907, the rise was resumed, with some regions showing substantial gains, of as much as 2s or more a week. This sounds paltry enough, but in fact represented in the most affected areas (such as the west midlands, the south-west and the south-east) a rise of some 17–20 per cent.

But money wages have never told the full story. To the cash payments have to be added the value of such perquisites as a free or cheap cottage, free fuel, a potato patch and produce given away by the farmer or sold by him at a low customary price. In some districts the illegal allowance of a daily supply of beer or cider continued also. Further, many tasks might be performed at piece-rates rather than day-rates, to the advantage of the worker's earnings. In practice the value of the perquisites was less than might be supposed: the free cottage was all too often a tumbledown hovel, damp, dirty and insanitary; the free fuel might be only peat, furze or culm; the produce might be such that the farmer could not have hoped to find any purchasers for at the market. Then, again, farmworkers lost pay through illness and accidents, and were particularly liable to loss of earnings in bad weather, a large, if uncertain, proportion of farmers paying no wages when there was heavy frost, snow or rain. If allowance is made, so far as is possible, for the value of perquisites and other factors, the *earnings* of farmworkers were estimated at the end of the century to be some 20 per cent higher than their money wages. In 1867–70 earnings varied from as low as 12s 5d a week in the south-west to as high as 18s 9d in Northumberland and Durham, showing the influence of relatively well-paid alternative occupations in the north-east and the lack of them in the south-west. The average earnings for the whole of England and Wales in 1867–70 of 13s 9d had risen to 16s 0d by 1898, and to 17s 11d in 1907 – an increase over forty years of 4s 2d, or 30 per cent.[4]

Moreover, the rise in earnings was accompanied (at least to the end of the century) by a substantial fall in the prices of the things most heavily consumed by farmworkers and their families: food, clothing, boots and simple household necessities. This rise in real incomes was checked in the early years of the new century, but already by 1900 the

Figure 18 Cottage scene of the late nineteenth century. Father, with spade on shoulder, returns home.

Figure 19 Cottage scene of the late nineteenth century. A young gamekeeper imbibes the wisdom of a rustic elder. Although agriculture was in decline, the living standards of farmworkers were showing much needed improvement at this time.

change in living standards was widely remarked upon. The fall in food prices was the great boon, for farmworkers spent some 70 per cent of their earnings on food. As the quartern, or 4-pound, loaf fell from 7d or more to 4d or $4\frac{1}{2}$d, beef and mutton from 1s to 8d or less, tea to 2s a pound and sugar to 3d, so there was money to spend on improving the diet and on things other than food. By 1902 weekly purchases of beef, mutton and port had gone up to over 5 pounds a week in the midlands, and to nearly 4 pounds even in the low-paid eastern counties. Tea rose to half a pound a week as compared with 2 ounces forty years earlier, and the cottage saw foods formerly unknown, such as coffee and cocoa, canned meats, salmon and sardines, eggs, raisins and pickles.[5] A peep inside one of the better cottage homes on a Sunday morning would have revealed the labourer smoking his pipe, reading his weekly newspaper and perhaps even thinking of taking the family on an excursion to the seaside. There would have been mats on the floor and a stair-carpet, the furniture would appear quite respectable and might even have included a piano. Outside the cottage good linen, and not rags, would be seen drying on the clothes line, and the young men of the village noticed as sporting watches as they rode by on their bicycles. By this time paraffin lamps had replaced the old rushlights, making it possible to stay up beyond seven or eight o'clock, and the public houses were doing good business.[6]

Organization of farm labour had played a very minor role in this improvement. There had been minor local 'turn-outs' as early as the 1830s, and of course it was in 1834 that the celebrated incident of the 'Tolpuddle martyrs' occurred. The band of Dorset men attempting to form a union fell foul of an overbearing and vindictive squire, were prosecuted under an obscure statute and transported to Australia. Fortunately public opinion was aroused, and the men were eventually repatriated. Tolpuddle, however, did not bring an end to the occasional attempts at harvest strikes, nor to the demands for higher wages which sometimes achieved temporary success. By the beginning of the 1870s changing conditions in the countryside produced an environment more favourable to large-scale organization. There was the example of union successes in other occupations, while in the villages railways, newspapers, the penny post and the activities of emigration agents were breaking down rural ignorance and isolation. Union activity sprang up in a number of counties, and in 1872 a champion hedger and mower, and self-educated Methodist lay-preacher, Joseph Arch, worked to form a national body, 150,000 strong, out of the diverse local organizations. The main strength of the National Agricultural Labourers' Union lay in Lincolnshire and the low-wage counties south of the River Trent, and the movement owed much to men of Arch's stamp, self-educated men, quite a number of them Nonconformist lay-preachers, with a sprinkling of village teachers, shopkeepers and journalists. It is not surprising, therefore, that the union had a strong moral and intellectual aspect, with much emphasis placed on education and temperance; it assisted many thousands of people to emigrate, and it also supported radical political changes such as extension of the franchise and nationalization of the land.

Though some farmers and their landlords showed sympathy, many others were deeply shocked by the union's radicalism, and were alarmed by the sudden upsurge of demands for independence and advancement among workers who had always seemed to be nothing more than dull, complaisant drudges. By 1874 the employers were responding to union

Figure 20 Effective unions of farmworkers appeared in the 1870s but collapsed after a few years, to be successfully revived only after 1914. Here villagers at Milbourne St Andrew, Dorset, watch evictions carried out by incensed employers.

demands with measures concerted by their own farmer organizations. To defeat the union they resorted to lockouts, the use of blackleg labour and the eviction of union supporters from their cottages. Poor people without work and without homes could not carry on a long resistance: subscriptions could not be kept up and union membership fell. Farm-workers, being scattered in small units and living in the employers' cottages, had only a limited sense of solidarity and were peculiarly exposed to the masters' retaliation. They were all too often in situations where there were many workers willing to take their jobs, and no other employers to turn to. A fall in grain prices in 1875–6 further weakened their position as farmers looked for economies in labour. Lastly, the labourers' movement itself suffered from lack of unity, personal rivalries, organizational weaknesses and rapid exhaustion of funds. By 1879 little remained of the great enthusiasm of seven years before. The 'revolt of the field' had failed, and its leaders turned to political action for a new way forward.

When conditions improved in the late 1880s union feeling again sprang into life, only to flicker out once more in the depressed years of 1893 and 1894. The true foundations for a permanent organization were built only in the environment of rising prices and lagging wages in the years before 1914, but the new start was of minuscule proportions. True, the 7,000 members of 1911 more than quadrupled in the next three years, but even then they represented only a tiny proportion, less than 5 per cent, of the total numbers still toiling on the land. The First World War subsequently had the effect of strengthening agricultural unionism, but the numbers involved remained a minority of the total workforce. In the postwar era the union's main influence was exercised through the right to nominate representatives on such bodies as the County Wages Committees and Central Wages Board, and through protecting members in cases of eviction from tied cottages, recovery of arrears of wages and compensation under the Workmen's Compensation Act. In the years after the First World War the official regulation of farmworkers' wages had far more effect on their incomes than the unions had ever been able to achieve.

Although some farmworkers were still able to earn money for years after town-dwellers had been obliged to give up their trades, for country people, nevertheless, old age had its terrors. The farmworker's large family was an uncertain security when sons and daughters migrated to towns or moved away overseas, and village benefit clubs could also prove unreliable. That there were any benefit clubs in the villages speaks volumes for the country-dweller's capacity for thrift and self-denial, as does also the existence of savings clubs, emigration clubs, coal, boot and clothing clubs, pig clubs and the like. The benefit clubs were all too often actuarially unsound and easily shaken by a blast of heavy claims. Instances were reported of people having subscribed their 1s 6d a month for as long as thirty-five years only to see it disappear overnight. Failing the help of relations, a friendly society or kindly employer, only the workhouse loomed at the end of the road.

True, by the end of the century the workhouse regime was a little less harsh than it had been seventy years before, but an aura of strict regulation and grim frugality still clung to it. No doubt it was clean and hygienic when workers' homes were dirty and insanitary, there was the certainty of food and shelter, and medical assistance was to hand; by now, indeed, the workhouse even offered comforts unknown to the poor cottage – an allowance of tobacco for the aged, for instance. The old people hated leaving their familiar homes, however, with their few pieces of worthless but highly treasured furniture and ornaments, their habitual discomfort and unnoticed squalor; we know from the reports of Medical Officers of Health that there were many old people who refused 'the house' and died at home from accidents, starvation and neglect. There was an old couple at Brentwood, in Essex, who 'crouched round a fire, in great need of a wash', and who 'would rather die than leave' their home; a woman of 85 of High Ongar, partly paralysed, who lived for many years in a caravan and refused to enter the workhouse infirmary; a Boreham man of 73 who had lived twenty years as a hermit, and who was found on Christmas Eve 1898, 'quite naked, on bundle of rags, very weak, cottage most filthy; no furniture'; and a Writtle woman of 89 found dead on her bedstead on a bundle of rubbish: 'next day, rats had gnawed chin and hand, were all over the place, stench very bad'.[7]

*   *   *

Though in the years after 1870 earnings and real incomes increased substantially, many farmworkers were still appallingly housed. Conditions varied greatly, however, and local building traditions, stone and slate in the north, brick in the midlands, mud and stud in the south-west and tile-hung brick and timber-framed cottages in the south, affected in various ways size, dryness and warmth, at least in the older houses. On some of the large estates conscientious landowners had gone in for replacing the worst of their old cottages with new ones that were much roomier, and they took care to let the cottages directly to the farmworkers rather than with the farms, the farmers having a bad reputation in respect of the rents charged and repairs left undone. Some big owners, such as the tenth Duke of Bedford, had in mid-century undertaken building on a large scale, using a small number of sensible designs and employing mass-production methods in order to keep down the costs. He was followed in later years by other proprietors, such as the Duke of Manchester, Lord Leconfield, the Earl of Stradbroke in Suffolk, the Duke of Rutland and Lord Dacre in Cambridgeshire, and

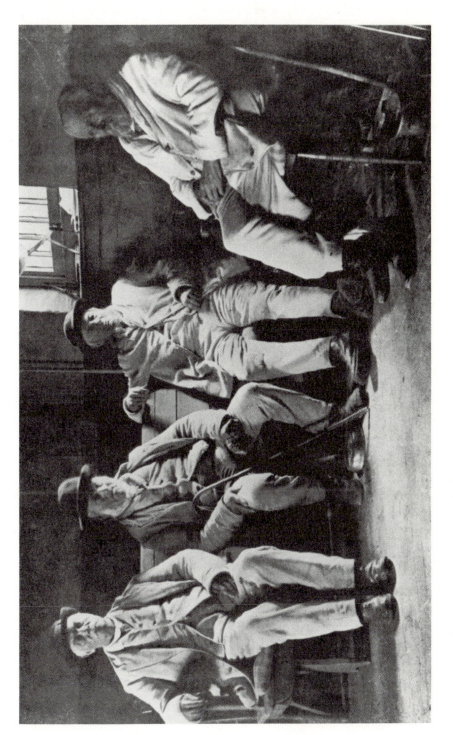

Figure 21 The workhouse – clean and hygienic, but also frugal and regulated – was the much-feared last resort of the aged country-dweller.

in Northumberland the Duke of Northumberland and Earl Grey – to mention a few of the more distinguished. They raised standards with new homes of more ample dimensions and often with substantial gardens. Gardens were important to farmworkers, and especially so where vegetable allotments were unavailable, a survey carried out by the Land Agents' Society in 1914 showing that on landed estates nearly three-quarters of the cottages had gardens of over an eighth of an acre.

The difficulty was that cottage building, as the Duke of Bedford remarked, was 'a bad investment of money'. It simply was not possible to let a large, well-built cottage to a farmworker at a rent that would provide a moderate return on the capital and an allowance for repairs. The Duke pointed out that landowners should not expect to invest in improved farm buildings for the farmers while leaving the cottages unimproved. (He might have added that there was the consideration that good cottages attracted a better class of worker, while the better tenants in turn might be drawn to the estate by the existence of a superior workforce.) There were also other aspects of the question: to provide the labouring class with 'the means of greater cleanliness, health, and comfort, in their own homes, to extend education, and thus raise the social and moral habits of these most valuable members of the community, are among the first duties, and ought to be among the finest pleasures, of every landlord'.[8]

Some landlords, unfortunately, had made their new cottages less convenient than they might have been by designing them in the fashionable gothic style, which meant loss of useful space and cramped and dark interiors; or by attempting to achieve a quaint or romantic effect by using tiny leaded windows and thatched roofs with huge overhanging eaves. Others did not have the money or the incentive to improve their cottages at all, while yet others preferred to improve only those situated near the entrance to their private park, where they were likely to catch the eye of visitors. A survey of cottages on the famous Holkham estate, carried out in 1851, showed that neglect had brought many of them to a desperate state. Of a total of 224 cottages let directly by the estate, 64 were classed as in 'good' repair, and another 64 as 'bad', while among those not categorized at all there was one with two bedrooms and eleven inhabitants described as 'very filthy and unwholesome', another as 'a most wretched cottage unfit to be inhabited', yet another with only one small bedroom and five inhabitants, 'a house quite unfit for a family to live in', one with no privy, and four cottages with only one privy between them. Of the cottages let with the farms some were reported as good, others fair and a few as unsuitable. The last sort included at Castle Acre 'three very small poor cottages, originally sheds, but turned into dwellings for which they are quite unfit', one at West Lexham with 'two bedrooms, small and poor, wretched state, rain comes in', and at Sparham 'one very wretched. Quite unfit to be repaired.'[9]

If such conditions could be found on one of the most famous estates in the country, it is not surprising that the general standard was low. Even so, it could be said that estate cottages, if often old and dilapidated, were usually let at very moderate rents, and that much higher rents had to be paid for badly built and ill-maintained cottages run up very cheaply by unscrupulous farmers, or by petty speculators in the market towns and larger villages. Often the 'houses' were in fact converted barns, sheds or outhouses, or an old farmhouse divided into tenements. Just as there were estates with good, well-maintained cottages let cheaply at £2 10s or £3 10s a year (1s to 1s 4d a week), as on the estates of the Duke of Grafton, the Marquis of Bristol and Lord Cadogan, so some of the farmers' cottages were equally good and cheap. At Ixworth Thorpe, in Suffolk, a Mr Manfield's cottages were of brick with tile or slate roofs, containing a large sitting-room, three bedrooms, and pantry, scullery and bakehouse, together with an outhouse, a closet, a well and a garden of a quarter of an acre. Some of the occupiers were able to pay the £3 a year rent out of the profits they made from their fruit trees in the gardens.[10]

By contrast, the cottages put up by small tradesmen in open villages were often deplorable. The owners had often mortgaged the property and had not the means to improve it even if they wished to do so. The 'one object is to get as high a rent as possible'. Many of the bedrooms let in rain and wind, and sometimes the ceilings were so low, only a little over 5 ft 6 in, that it was impossible to stand upright. Staircases were steep and dangerous, windows were often only a foot or two square, and one of the two bedrooms was little better than a passage; 'many have no light or ventilation except through the door of the adjoining apartment'. Gardens, where they existed, were very small, and often a back door or shed was lacking, meaning that all the washing and cooking had to be done in the living-room. Frequently one or two closets served for several cottages. A labourer at Barrow stated: 'I have to shift my bedstead to stop the rain. My room is 7 ft 6 in by 6 ft 9 in. There are two bedrooms both this size. It is hardly a prisoner's cell. Twenty-one people go to one closet.'[11]

Even many of the estate cottages had only two bedrooms, though they might be as large as 15 feet by 10 feet 6 inches, 12 feet by 11 feet or 12 feet by 9 feet 6 inches. Such accommodation became very cramped where the family was large, and where, on occasion, a lodger was taken in. A report on the Earl of Stradbroke's estate, made in 1874, showed that in some of the cottages with two bedrooms of the size mentioned, there were such families as, in one case, the parents, two youths of 16 and 19 and a girl of 8; in another, the parents, two youths of 14 and 19 and a girl of 13; and in a third, the parents, two boys aged 6 and 10 and five girls of 1, 4, 9, 12 and 13 years.[12] It was this kind of over-crowding that aroused fears not only of the dangers to health, but even more of those to morals.

Fed by these concerns, investigations of rural housing mounted towards the end of the nineteenth century. Reformers showed that country housing could be just as insanitary as the worst town slum, if it was less extensive in area. Public opinion was aroused by a number of full-length studies as well as by newspaper articles, such as that which appeared in the *Daily News* of 9 October 1891, reporting on conditions in Quainton, Buckinghamshire: its rustic cottages, flowery gardens and laden orchards concealed homes 'alive with vermin' and a village site that was 'literally saturated with sewage'. Alarm over the flight from the countryside of strong, able-bodied men was heightened by the consideration that a large proportion of the regular army and of the Metropolitan police force was recruited from country lads, and by the revelation that in industrial cities of the north about half of the men volunteering for the army in the South African War had been rejected as physically unfit. If the country's reservoir of healthy manhood was being drained away, where was the army of future wars to be obtained?

Housing legislation made little impact on the countryside. The Housing Act of 1890 was largely ignored by Rural District Councils, and the subsequent Housing and Town Planning Act of 1909, which empowered the Councils to acquire land and build cottages, was also of little effect. The inspections required to be carried out by Medical Officers of Health had resulted in relatively few improvements to existing houses or closures of insanitary ones, the difficulty being to persuade the Councils to act against property owners, and, further, the obvious inhumanity of forcing inhabitants out of insanitary homes when they had nowhere else to go. The Land Enquiry Committee, an unofficial body of Liberal persuasion, investigated in 1912 a sample of 2,759 parishes in England and Wales and found in just over half of them a shortage of cottages. It was estimated that over the whole country a total of 120,000 new cottages was needed to meet the shortage and to replace homes not fit for human habitation – a figure equal to a tenth of the existing stock of country homes. It was found also that in 45 per cent of villages no new cottages at all had been built during the previous five years. Private enterprise in building was deterred by the impossibility of letting new houses at a commercial rent, and by the difficulty and high cost of obtaining land. The failure of the District Councils to act was attributed partly to the scepticism of local councillors that any shortage existed, and partly to the fundamental drawback that building council homes would mean an additional burden on the rates.[13]

For good measure, the Land Enquiry Committee gathered many reports of defective housing. Dampness, as a result of leaking roofs, walls only one brick thick, lack of guttering and absence of dampcourses, was a frequent complaint; 'it is impossible to keep the paper on the walls for any period of time, and I have seen cases where the pictures are quite rotten'. Brick floors, too, were often damp and the rooms unceiled and low; 'in one old lady's pantry the floor bricks are raised with mud and fungus coming through'. There was a report of three cottages using one open privy and a cesspit within four feet of a back door: 'the drainage of the village street of 113 houses falls into the stream. In dry weather the stench is vile.' Only a curtain divided a bedroom where parents and six children of both sexes slept, and in one instance a man of 80, his daughter of 50, granddaughter of 26 and grandson of 17 shared a one-bedroom home with a lodger.[14]

In 1916 the Land Agents' Society published its riposte to the report of the Land Enquiry Committee. The Society conceded that the housing question was 'admittedly a serious social problem', but argued that the national statistics showed that the shortage of houses was in fact much more severe in the towns, and that the recent decline in new building was most serious there. Overcrowding in the country was greatest where mining or other industries competed with agriculture for the available homes, and it was pointed out that mining districts (especially in Wales) were largely responsible for the high average number of illegitimate births recorded in country areas. 'In respect of crimes and mis-demeanours, the record of the agricultural population in proportion to numbers occupied is markedly superior to that of the general population of England and Wales.'

Evidence was collected to show that the shortage of homes for agricultural workers arose in large part from their being taken up by workers in other occupations, including the employees of the Post Office and the railways, police officers, road-workers and a variety of other non-agricultural workers. It was estimated that as high a proportion as two out of every five cottages originally intended for farmworkers was thus occupied. Landowners, it was true, had probably cut back on their cottage-building: they had been hit by increased taxation and were deterred by the low rate of return on the investment. At the same time the demand for country homes had been intensified by the introduction in 1908 of the Old Age Pension, which enabled many elderly people to continue in occupation of farmworkers' cottages, while the rising standard of sanitary requirements had caused the closing or demolition of many houses 'which forty years ago were regarded as adequate and satisfactory'.[15]

The rural housing question was therefore complicated and disputable, but it is clear that although in the long term the decline of the farm labour force must have had the effect of reducing the demand for country homes, the opposing factors mentioned by the Land Agents' Society were operating to create conditions of continuing shortage. Further, it seems likely that young people's standards were rising, and they were no longer willing to start married life in the kind of primitive hovel which their parents had accepted. It was not merely an absolute shortage of homes, but one of decent homes, which influenced the young farmworkers' decision to quit the land.

*   *   *

Labour and housing were only two of the questions which plagued landlords and their tenants in the closing decades of the nineteenth century. These and other problems were the more troublesome, however, since they came at a time when the political uncertainties surrounding the land and its owners were greater than at any time in the recent past. The first reform of Parliament in 1832 had done little to weaken the grip that landowners had on Parliament and government. Regarded at the time as a 'fatal precedent', it merely restored the size of the electorate to what it had been at the beginning of the eighteenth century, removed the long-standing scandal of rotten boroughs and enfranchised newly expanded industrial towns. It left the old domination of county and country-town representation virtually intact, and the constitution remained undeniably aristocratic. Between 1830 and 1868 two-thirds of ministers came from the ranks of landowners, and before 1900 peers were only rarely outnumbered in the Cabinet.[16] The real threat to the political pre-eminence of land lay in the later extensions of the franchise in 1867 and 1884 and in the Secret Ballot of 1872 – although the watchful eye of landowners' agents made that novel institution less secret than might be supposed.

Meanwhile, the repeal of the Corn Laws in 1846 had put an end to an age-old policy of regulating the overseas trade in grain, and, more immediately, abolished the protective sliding-scale of corn duties first brought in by the Act of 1828, and modified by a subsequent Act of 1842. A succession of urgent problems – the terrible famine in Ireland together with the Malthusian fatalism of the government's Irish policy, the poor harvest of 1845 at home and the pressure exerted by the Anti-Corn Law League – combined to force the hand of Peel, despite the continued enthusiasm for protection of the mass of country gentry. But Peel was driven to reform by other and wider issues. Like many of his party, he saw the attack on the Corn Laws as a constitutional issue. The protection of grain production had to be sacrificed in order to hold back for a while the rising tide of industrial democracy. The Corn Laws were abandoned in order to remove a focus for a renewed assault on the political power of the landed interest, against the limited franchise and the control of seats on which that power rested.

Peel saw, too, that the Corn Laws were not economically essential, at least for those landlords and farmers who marched with the times and directed their farming towards meeting changing market trends that favoured meat and dairy products at the expense of wheat. An improving landlord himself, he believed that farming could survive, and indeed prosper, if it were efficient – and repeal had coupled with it the offer of cheap government loans to help farming meet the challenge. Under-drainage, together with the adoption of new kinds of fertilizers and improved breeds of livestock, would enable farming to withstand the cold winds of increased overseas competition. And, for a lengthy period, he was right. After a short post-repeal depression, markets improved as an expanding and better-off home market absorbed both home production and rising quantities of imports. Prices for livestock products rose substantially, and even the price of wheat was favourable. Taken as a whole, the years between the repeal and the end of the 1870s did not produce wheat prices very markedly lower than in the decade preceding repeal.

In this third quarter of the century, indeed, landowners enjoyed their Indian summer. Rentals were higher than they had ever been, were actually more than twice as high as a century before, and were still rising. Tenants were prosperous, and the lauded techniques of 'high farming' made the capitalist agriculture of England and Scotland a model for the world. Fashionable society still revolved around the great houses with their hunts and shoots, their garden parties and balls, their political weekends and literary *soirées*. While the great families still dominated in Cabinet and at court, the gentry continued to run county affairs despite the apparent upstart democracy of Poor Law Boards, Highways Boards and School Boards. And younger sons still proliferated in the church, the army and the law.

But the evident ability to survive was in fact misleading. This apparently stable and serene world, its niceties of rank and etiquette mirrored for us in the pages of Trollope, was nearing the precipice, the edge of a slope of continuous decline. The new reforms in the franchise and elections, in education, in county government and, not least, in death duties, ushered in a period of more rapid and definite change. And economic forces undermined the very basis of landownership by making land less profitable as a productive asset; in the worst areas, indeed, making it totally unprofitable. The opening of vast new areas of productive farmland across the world, together with more efficient and cheaper means of transport, enabled distant areas to compete in the British market, not merely in wheat and non-perishable commodities like wool, but also in meat. Dairy products had long come in from Ireland and from Denmark and other near parts of the Continent; now they were supplemented by imports of fruit, vegetables, poultry, even hay. Only liquid milk stayed completely out of the range of overseas competition, and British dairy farmers were pushed into that limited specialism by the growing competition from imported butter and cheese, as well as from margarine.

Areas which concentrated on wheat-growing were particularly badly hit. Wheat, which averaged about 51s a quarter in the 1870s, fell in the 1880s to some 37s, and in the 1890s to under 29s; in 1894 and 1895 it averaged less than 23s. This was in fact the nadir – at least until after 1922; it was fortunate that wheat-growers and their landlords could not see that far into the future. In the worst-affected corn districts landlords found it hard to re-let their farms when tenants gave up, bankrupted, or emigrated. Indeed, they were often lucky to get any net return at all when rents sank to near the level of the outgoings. Some districts, like the Essex claylands, went over to grass, occupied by a new race of thrifty Scottish tenants attracted south by the cheapness of the land and the easy access by rail to the expanding London milk market.

Pasture areas in the north and west of the country were better off, and especially so if they were near large towns or not much over 100 miles from the capital – the economic limit for transporting liquid milk. Livestock enterprises were actually helped by the fall in grain prices, which meant for them lower costs of fodder. Where there were good rail services to expanding urban markets some farmers could do well by going in for market-gardening, potatoes, poultry and fruit – especially when the second-quality produce could be sold to nearby outlets in the developing commercial jam-making industry. However, pasture and grain areas, market-gardeners and fruit-growers alike, suffered in some years from extreme weather conditions. There were excessively wet seasons in 1879–82, years which saw flooded fields, ruined crops and many thousands of livestock struck by disease; in the Cherwell Valley, as George Dew, a local Relieving Officer of the Bicester Poor Law Union recorded, some meadows could not be mown, and in others the hay was swept away by the floods.[17] Then there succeeded years of damaging droughts and severe frosts, with ferocious blizzards in January 1881 and March 1891 causing severe losses of stock, even sheep blown over cliffs; the summers of both 1892 and 1893 were marked by ruinous droughts, when there was little or no grass for haymaking, while the winter of 1894–5 brought prolonged frost and weeks of snow-covered ground.

Although the 'depression' was patchy, both chronologically and in geographical terms, the combination of growing foreign competition with falling prices and some extraordinarily bad seasons spread gloom in country mansions and farmhouses alike. In many areas, it was true, farmers had been little affected, or, by shifting to products favoured by rising urban demand, had managed to weather the storm. But Rider Haggard, the landowner-novelist, traversing the country on a protracted agricultural tour at the beginning of the new century, found few land agents or farmers without some complaint. Over and over again they told him of the threats they saw in the continued lack of protection, in the inequitable treatment of farmers by legislature and railways, the loss of skilled hands to other occupations and the adverse effects of educational reform on the rural labour supply. Some said they should have given up years before. But Haggard perceived that the main burden of the depression was being shouldered by the landlords, whose rents, and consequently the value of their land, had not infrequently plummeted.

Nevertheless, it was often difficult to see much change in the life of many estate owners. Some houses, it was true, had been let out to urban plutocrats, together with the sporting amenities. Some owners, indeed, had been obliged to part with land, especially outlying properties, and a number had found additional resources by selling off their pictures or libraries – a Holbein owned by the Duke of Norfolk fetched in 1909 the then considerable sum of £72,000, and in 1892 the Spencers' Althorp library went to Manchester to found the new John Rylands Library, bringing the fifth Earl the very useful windfall of £210,000. In arable England landed incomes were much reduced. The Duke of Bedford published rentals which showed his estates at Woburn and Thorney to be losing money at the rate of £7,000 a year – and this after an expenditure on them of nearly £4.25 million since 1816.[18] In Lincolnshire Lord Ancaster found in 1893 that his estates were producing a mere 2.2 per cent return on the million pounds he had laid out in improvements over the previous twenty years, while Edmund Turnor's 21,000 acres yielded a net income of £16,000, a fall of over 40 per cent on the £28,000 he had received in 1878. In Essex the Strutt family had over 4,000 acres in hand by 1896, and a few years later had become involved in the London retail milk trade with shops and vehicles bearing the legend 'Lord Rayleigh's Dairies'.[19]

The large landowners, however, usually had scattered estates, which was an advantage during the depression since it was unlikely that their rentals would tell a tale of universal gloom. The Duke of Bedford, for instance, had more prosperous lands in the West Country; and furthermore, numbers of owners had large sources of income from industrial enterprises, or valuable urban properties in expanding seaside resorts or London's West End, as did the Dukes of Westminster. But urban properties could take time to become fruitful: witness Lord Scarbrough's investment in his new 'model Watering Place' of Skegness, which in 1896 produced less than £3,000 a year – a poor return indeed.[20] Prudent owners had taken care to diversify out of land into stocks and shares, or were busily doing so. Thus the second Lord Leicester, with his Holkham estate rentals fallen by half by 1895, had been putting substantial sums into a variety of railway, brewery and other shares at home and abroad. His overseas holdings included, for example, shares in the Sind, Delta and Punjab Railway, the Buenos Aires and Pacific Railway, the Illinois Central and the Canadian Pacific. In 1890 his investment income amounted to £11,000, although this represented only a quarter of that year's revenue from rents.[21]

While the greater landowners, with their varied and extensive resources, could meet the economic storms of the period without coming to grief, this was not so with the less fortunately placed gentry owners, gentleman farmers and country parsons. The smaller owners frequently held estates which were unified and compact, and if situated in a corn-growing region, suffered severely from the price fall. Mortgages still had to be paid, and if it was thought necessary to realize land, it could often be sold only at a heavy loss: East Firsby in Lincolnshire, a property of 534 acres, was sold in 1899 for £6,700, only £12 10s an acre; it had changed hands about 1852 for £17,000, or near £32 an acre. Country clergy suffered reduced circumstances as the value of the tithes (on which their incomes were based) plummeted, while their glebe tenants fell into arrears and the cost of repairs to rambling rectories mounted. One Lincolnshire parson, who had five children to educate, was summoned for non-payment of rates; another, whose problems were exacerbated by drink, left his creditors a mere 3s in the pound when he died in 1900.[22]

The change in conditions broke down the traditions of the old rural community. The severely straitened gentlefolk cut down on hospitality; some, indeed, let their homes to strangers and went off to live more cheaply at an agreeable seaside resort or continental spa. Non-residence weakened the political and social hegemony of the landed class. Parsons and leading farmers, too, lost status as it became rumoured round the neighbourhood that their debts were mounting and they were 'in trouble'. Former ties of mutual interest and respect between landlord and tenant were fatally loosened when the older generation of farmers retired, emigrated or went bankrupt, replaced by strangers from Scotland or the West Country – careful, prudent people who understood dairying, and who understood also how to run a farm with the minimum of hands. By economizing, by catering more closely for the needs of urban consumers, and sometimes by supporting their farm income with sidelines in trade, the new farmers could thrive where the old ones had sunk. Indeed, some went on to rent additional lands or buy up smallholdings cheaply to amass substantial bundles of property.

Such people felt little loyalty to the old-established landed families, however grand they once had been. They perceived clearly enough that other things had changed besides prices, rents and land values. They saw that the landowners' hold on Parliament and local government was slipping, and it was no use looking to them to come to the rescue of agriculture. Government measures, such as the Ground Game Act of 1881, the new Agricultural Holdings Act of 1883 and the repeal of the unpopular malt tax were all welcome; but they hardly met the central problems of foreign competition and low prices. New farming organizations, the Farmers' Alliance of 1879 and Lord Winchilsea's National Agricultural Union of the 1890s, failed to hold the farmers' allegiance. They showed more enthusiasm for specialist associations, such as those specifically concerned with the interests of dairy farmers, hop-growers and fruit-growers. In the end the farmers broke away completely from landowner tutelage to establish their own organization, the National Farmers' Union (NFU), an independent body founded in 1910, following the initiative of the Lincolnshire farmers a few years earlier. Henceforth, the farmers moved gradually towards the advancement of a powerful pressure group, one devoted solely to the interests of producers, leaving the landowners obliged to abandon any pretence of being able any longer to dominate the national policies for agriculture.

Landowners could not, however, escape receiving much of the blame for what critics saw as their neglect of the land and the welfare of those who worked on it. The labourers' 'flight from the land', the farmers' complaints and the bad condition of many farms were heaped at their door. The migration from the land was deplored as intensifying pressures on jobs and houses in the towns, and threatening the survival of the main reservoir of able-bodied manpower from which the army was recruited. The plight of the farmers, evident in the decline of the arable acreage, in neglected pastures, overgrown hedgerows and dilapidated farmhouses, made the country dangerously dependent on imported food, and hence on the navy's continued mastery of the seas. The countryside was in decline, and if additional evidence were required it was necessary only to take a glance at the obvious decay of many country towns, their trades and crafts. Town populations had fallen, markets and coach services had been discontinued, mills, workshops and even public houses were closed. But, as R. J. Olney remarks of Lincolnshire, appearances might obscure the decline: the towns of 1900 'looked cleaner and less "rural" than they had thirty years before'; they were in general better drained, paved and lit, with respectable artisans' terraces or semi-detached cottages.[23]

The attack on the landowners came from many quarters. Jesse Collings, a Liberal Member of Parliament and associate of Joseph Arch, proposed a new measure which would call upon state aid to restore land to the 'class of yeoman farmers and peasant proprietors which in former times were such valued elements in our rural economy'. The writer F. E. Green attacked in his *Tyranny of the Countryside* the neglect and indifference which had emptied the countryside and threatened the loss of 'our bold peasantry ... and with it our virility as a race'; William Savage, Medical Officer of Health for Somerset, enlarged on the much-discussed problem of rural housing, and advocated strengthened legislation, higher agricultural wages and state assistance in the building of cottages; and Seebohm Rowntree in *How the Labourer Lives* studied farmworkers' wages and living costs, finding that average earnings were below his 'poverty line' (20s 6d a week for a family of five) in every county of England and Wales bar five – Northumberland, Durham, Westmorland, Lancashire and Derbyshire.[24] Historians, too, like J.L. and Barbara Hammond, and the German scholars Hasbach and Levy, delved back into the past to find the origins of the decline of the peasantry in the era of 'agricultural revolution' and parliamentary enclosure before 1830. Enclosure, bluntly stated the Hammonds, 'was fatal to three classes: the small farmer, the cottager, and the squatter'. The agricultural revolution, wrote Hermann Levy in 1911, involved the sacrifice of the small farm and cottage holding: 'the industrious small agriculturist had to give way to the large farmer possessed of capital and education', leading to 'the development of the antagonism of class-interests on the land as it exists at the present day'.[25]

What was probably the most sustained and detailed attack on conditions in the countryside was launched in *The Land*, the Report of the Land Enquiry Committee, an unofficial group of Members of Parliament and others, chaired by A. H. Dyke Acland, and including Seebohm Rowntree. Volume I of the Report, dealing with rural problems, appeared in 1913 and ranged over agricultural labour and wages, housing, allotments, smallholdings, game preservation, farmers' security of tenure, rates, co-operation, credit, transport and education. Perhaps the most radical recommendations were those for state aid to help tenants purchase their farms and to stimulate 'peasant proprietorship', and the institution of a land court to stand between landowner and tenant to ensure security of tenure and the setting of 'fair rents'. The Report was based on official sources together with answers to a questionnaire collected from some 3,600 individuals of all social classes across England and Wales. Statistics and opinions were marshalled to support arguments for bringing in a legal minimum wage, the building of cottages by Rural District Councils, the subjecting of all cottage lettings to a minimum notice of six months, measures to increase the availability of allotments and smallholdings, and to entitle tenant farmers to take or destroy ground game freely and receive compensation for damage done to crops.[26]

When the Land Agents' Society replied in 1916 it was conceded that all was not well with the countryside, that wages in some districts were lower than they ought to be, that there was in some areas a shortage of cottages, that more produce might be raised from the land and that the recent break-up of estates had created a new sense of insecurity among tenant farmers. It held, nevertheless, that the Land Enquiry Committee had produced 'an inaccurate and partial picture of agricultural conditions', and that its remedies were 'calculated to deteriorate rather than improve the general position of agricultural labourers', and would 'check rather than promote the progress of agriculture'.

Facts about Land went systematically over the subjects covered by *The Land*, producing alternative statistics and criticizing the recommendations of the latter Report. On wages, for example, it was argued that the figures used in *The Land* were biased and outdated, and could not be taken as showing the true picture for 1913; on housing, it was pointed out that overcrowding was less intense in rural districts than in urban ones, and that the shortage of cottages for agricultural workers would not exist at all if owners were prepared to give notice to quit to all those non-agricultural workers who were in occupation of country homes; and on allotments, that the figures produced in *The Land* were many years out of date and 'ludicrously insufficient'.[27]

It was inevitable in a period of rapid change, and in so complex and regionally varied an industry, that contradictory 'facts' and opinions should be put forward. But at heart the division of opinion was based on fundamental differences in ideology: between radicals who distrusted the system of private enterprise and looked to the state to redress grievances, and conservatives who held that the solution to admitted problems could and should be found within the traditional framework of private relations between landowner, tenant farmer and farmworker. For example, land courts, it was stated by the Land Agents' Society, had been asked for 'by no class in the industry which is directly interested' – meaning landowners and farmers – and 'would destroy the personal goodwill and kindly feeling which, as the Enquirers admit, at present exist between landlord and tenant and constitute valuable national assets'.[28]

Meanwhile, the attack on landowners had taken a fiscal turn. Lloyd George's Budget of 1909 raised income tax from 1s to 1s 2d in the pound and proposed a new 'super-tax' on incomes above £3,000. This was bad enough in a peacetime Budget (although in fact the income tax favoured agricultural incomes, and the art of tax avoidance was already well advanced). But two measures were aimed more specifically at landowners: one was a steep increase in death duties designed to raise an extra £4.4 million, more than the newly increased yield of income tax and the super-tax put together; and the land value duties, a levy of 20 per cent on the unearned increment of land value, to be paid whenever land changed hands, together with a duty of a halfpenny in the pound on the capital value of undeveloped land and minerals. The new land value duties followed the ideas of Henry George, the American economist, who had proposed a 'single tax' on land which would cover the full cost of government. Lloyd George's innovations were more restrained, and what his new duties would have produced had they been carried out as intended is uncertain. Their political menace lay in the necessity of making a complete valuation of the land of Great Britain, a proposal to which landowners, led by the peers, objected most strongly. A 'new inquisitorial machinery' was to be set up presaging swingeing cuts in the windfall profits of mineral lands and urban ground rents which now played a key role in supporting the lifestyles of many aristocrats. Soon, owners were faced with the notorious Form 4, a detailed questionnaire, to be jointly filled in by owner and government valuer, a document replete with such arcane distinctions as 'gross value', 'total value', 'full site value' and 'assessable site value'.[29]

The political consequences of the Budget are well known – the conservative hostility, the obstinacy of the Lords, the two general elections of 1910 and the subsequent restriction of the Lords' power of veto. The landowners fought back in a variety of ways, with the Land Union, a pressure group intended to obstruct the working of the new taxes; and by seeking to oppose 'single chamber tyranny' by encouraging Ulster Protestantism in order to frustrate the Liberal policy of Irish Home Rule. The Ulster question became a main response of the landowners to Lloyd George. From the furore which surrounded the Budget and the subsequent party manoeuvring, Professor Spring has concluded that the landed interest was not prepared to give up its traditional power without a struggle: 'the aristocracy's appetite for political leadership – in other words, their will to govern – had not vanished'.[30] But within a very few years of the Budget and all its clamour the issues were overshadowed by the intervention of world war: 1914 marked the end of this chapter, as it did for so many others.

The countryside of 1914 was split by constitutional reform and political controversy, by cries for state intervention in farm wages, housing and tenures, by fears of new tax burdens of unknown extent, by new alignments of landowners and farmers, each group seeking their own interests. Yet agriculture was now more prosperous than it had been for more than a decade. Wheat – at this point, it is true, a much less important crop – had risen a little since the turn of the century, the average price of 1910–14 being some 4s higher than in 1896–1900. More

The Street. Stockbridge.

Figure 22 Stockbridge, Hampshire, as it appeared in the late nineteenth century. With farming and many village crafts in decline, and the landowners and farmers in retreat, country towns became backwaters increasingly remote from the mainstream of English life.

important to many farmers, the prices of competing imports of fresh meat, butter and cheese, and hides had all risen since 1900, the last two substantially, while the price of exported British wool had doubled. A leading agriculturist, Sir Daniel Hall, saw much evidence of improvement in his travels round the country. The derelict Essex, not long since the archetype of agricultural ruin, had disappeared. Land there might not be kept 'so clean as formerly' but it was yielding a living. And other districts so miserable in the 1890s were now 'reasonably prosperous', with vacant farms quickly taken, while the small owners benefited from mortgagees who sensibly declined to levy the full burden of debt.[31]

In the village itself there were different kinds of evidence to be noticed, both good and bad. George Bourne, the pen-name of George Sturt, writing in 1912 of life about his Surrey home near Farnham, observed that women fieldworkers were diminishing rapidly, though some still went out to earn 1s a day at haymaking and harvest, in the hop-gardens, or at trimming swedes and collecting newly dug potatoes. In the lanes they could be seen carrying home on their backs prodigious

195

Figures 23 and 24 Village life was never without its diversions, even in the depression years of the late nineteenth century. In Figure 23 travelling entertainers bring out the inhabitants at Taplow, Buckinghamshire. In the fields the tractor was starting to make its appearance in the years before the First World War, but traditional ploughing methods, if with improved ploughs, still held undisputed sway.

faggots of dead wood or unwieldy sacks of fir cones. A few still took in washing for townspeople, though the new steam laundries had greatly reduced the possibilities of this sideline. Charwomen could get twice as much as fieldworkers – 2s a day and at least one good meal, a major consideration when money for feeding the family was short – and a small number of village housewives still earned a little at needlework. Such sources of income were irregular, however, and were lacking when most needed, when there was a new baby or small children to care for, and moreover the work involved neglect of the home and perhaps of the woman's own health.

As for the men, laborious and monotonous tasks, long hours of daily exposure to the elements and little hope of improvement were their common lot. Their wages had risen, but so had the prices of the things they had to buy. They had received education, but it had failed to start them on the path to learning; it opened no view, no vista, 'no inkling of the infinities of time and space, or of the riches of human thought'. They lacked the confidence to do much to help themselves, and remained dependent on, while deeply suspicious of, the better-educated classes set above them. In the political sphere they lacked understanding and initiative, and waited apathetically to see what the educated might do for them. Government was viewed as a sort of benevolent tyranny, their own parliamentary representative as a kind of self-interested quack doctor, arguing for occult remedies, who in time might possibly do them some good. Some men put value on education, getting their children to teach them in the evenings what they had learnt at school during the day. But generally their ignorance was profound. Contemporary nostrums like Tariff Reform were not understandable, even the newspapers hardly comprehensible in their language and ideas.[32]

Thus the English countryside on the eve of the First World War: the tractor just starting to make its appearance in the fields; the village more and more invaded by newcomers from the towns, strangers in speech and standards; the old inhabitants still enmeshed in lives surrounded by continuing, if declining, tradition, much ignorance and lingering superstition from the past.

8

THE COUNTRYSIDE IN WAR AND PEACE

The First World War opened without immediate effects on agriculture, except that the needs of the army soon began to weaken the industry's resources. Skilled farmworkers, together with estate workers and village blacksmiths, wheelwrights and carpenters, were allowed, indeed encouraged, to join up, and horses were taken from the stables of manor houses and farms to satisfy the demand for remounts and haulage animals. It was not until almost the end of 1916 that indiscriminate recruiting was seen to be a mistake, and the urgency of expanding home production of food was appreciated. The harvest in North America proved to be a poor one that year, but a more immediate problem was the effect of the shipping losses that threatened to starve the country of food and essential war supplies. At the outbreak of the war Britain had imported four-fifths of its cereals, two-fifths of its meat and three-quarters of its fruit, to say nothing of all its sugar and colonial produce and large proportions of other foodstuffs. The German U-boats found the slow, unarmed merchant vessels easy targets, and although the belated introduction of convoys guarded by warships – a system used to counter the depredations of French privateers in the Napoleonic Wars – reduced the losses, shortages of food, fuel and other vital imports became critical to the fighting of the war.

The government had already set up in each county a War Agricultural Committee to organize the supply of farm labour, machinery and imported fertilizers and feeding stuffs. These bodies were now used to enforce on farmers a major shift in production, the ploughing-up of pasture for grain and potatoes, thus attempting to reverse in a matter of months the process that had taken place over the previous forty years, that is, the gradual expansion of grass at the expense of arable. It was calculated that 100 acres of pasture would feed only nine persons if used for fattening, and forty-one persons if devoted to dairying; ploughed up, that same 100 acres would maintain 172 persons if planted with oats, 208 if planted with wheat and 418 if planted with potatoes.[1] But it takes time to bring about major changes in agricultural

199

production. The ploughing-up campaign added only marginally to the harvest of 1917: a few thousand acres of wheat, 117,000 acres of barley, 225,000 acres of oats and nearly 100,000 acres of potatoes – increases ranging from only 0.2 per cent for the wheat acreage to 8 per cent for that of barley, 7 per cent for oats and 18 per cent for potatoes. The effects of the 1918 harvest were much more substantial, with the acreages of wheat and oats up by a third over those of 1916, and potatoes up by a quarter. By 1918 the total area of permanent pasture had fallen by 9 per cent, bringing it back to the acreage of 1890.

These changes, rather modest as they may seem, could only be achieved with much effort and ingenuity, and with a certain amount of compulsion. Farmers who all their lives had known only the handling of livestock and the production of milk had to be ordered to part with prized stock and take the plough to their stretches of carefully maintained pasture. They, like other farmers, had to follow the directions of the Agricultural Committees, make do with the help of unskilled and female labour, and accept in lieu of plough-teams the loan of strange machines called tractors – the tractor being at this time very much 'a new, untried and rather distrusted implement'.[2]

Labour was a major problem, obliging the intervention of the government to supply what Lord Ernle, the President of the Board of Agriculture, described as 'blackleg labour on a massive scale'. By 1916 the conventional labour force had fallen to 91 per cent of the pre-war level, and subsequently declined to 89 per cent. The shortfall was intensified, of course, by the ploughing-up policy, since arable required considerably more labour for a given acreage than pasture. The army made an attempt to release those soldiers who could plough, and with others (some of whom were trained for ploughing) the number of soldiers on the land rose to as many as 84,000 by the November of 1918. By this time, too, prisoners of war were heavily used on the land, 30,000 out of a total prisoner workforce of 50,000. These workers, however, were not very productive, their efficiency limited by inadequate food, poor supervision and a lack of financial incentive. The Women's Land Army, formed in January 1917, provided a mobile force of fit young women trained for farmwork. Its numbers were small – only 7,000 at the end of 1917, 16,000 at the peak in September 1918. It was, however, a 'highly motivated and comparatively well-educated labour force', produced by careful selection of recruits, and supported by free transport, uniform and footwear, with a minimum wage set above the rate paid for village women. Farmers found the Women's Land Army 'plucky, patriotic and keen', and the girls were invaluable for some essential tasks, such as milking.[3]

Village women formed the largest source of replacement labour not provided by the government. There were 300,000 women working on

Figure 25 German prisoners of war helping with the hay harvest in Hertfordshire in 1918. The expansion of wartime food production ran into problems of labour shortages and some 30,000 of a total of 50,000 prisoners were employed on the land.

the land in 1918, the great majority part-time, and although the pre-war figure for women working in agriculture is uncertain, the wartime increase may have been of the order of over 200,000. Rather surprisingly perhaps, village women were apparently not much valued by the farmers: they were unskilled and untrained, and indeed unused to farmwork, the old tradition of helping on the farms having declined in most parts of the country long before the war. The second largest group of non-government replacement workers consisted of schoolchildren. Education authorities rapidly responded to the crisis by passing by-laws to enable children to work on farms during school terms as well as holidays, and some 15,000 children were employed by the autumn of 1916. In the summer they were reinforced by camps of public-school boys organized to assist with the harvests of 1917 and 1918. The sum of these miscellaneous kinds of workers did not make good the whole of the deficiency of conventional workers, but provided additional labour which, given the low level of wages in agriculture, free market forces could not have supplied; and given, too, the limited power of agricultural trade unionism – though much expanded since its revival in 1906 by George Edwards – there was no effective resistance by the conventional labour force to the dilution of labour which the emergency involved.[4]

The policy of compulsory ploughing-up of pasture was made more palatable to farmers by government guarantees of minimum prices for wheat, oats and potatoes, and this protection was extended into peacetime by the Agriculture Act of 1920, which appeared to inaugurate a new era of government-regulated farming. Two other wartime measures, the establishment of a Wages Board to set local minimum wages for farmworkers, and a virtual guarantee of security of tenure for tenant farmers (they could be ejected only for bad farming, a condition difficult to prove), were also incorporated into the new post-war policy. Wage regulation, together with the labour shortages, pushed up farm wages during the war and immediately after, the average minimum for men rising from 30s 6d in 1918–19 to 46s 10½d in 1920–1, as compared with an average of 16s 9d per week in 1914. The number of hours worked for this minimum wage fell from fifty-eight in 1914 to fifty-two in 1918–19, making a further improvement in conditions. In real terms, however, the minimum wage of 1918–19 represented a deterioration, and that of 1920–1 only a modest improvement, when the much increased cost of living is taken into account.

Farm profits certainly rose during the war, though adequate figures are lacking. If we may judge from prices, the improvement must have been considerable, for wheat, barley and oats had all doubled their pre-war prices by 1917, and fat cattle had nearly done so. The index for all agricultural products had considerably more than doubled by the end

Figure 26 The Women's Land Army was formed in January 1917 to supplement other kinds of temporary wartime labour used on the land in the First World War. By September 1918 its numbers had risen to 16,000.

of the war.[5] Farmers' costs, it is true, had risen also, and apparently at a faster rate than prices in the last two years of the war, while the working of farms was made more difficult and output reduced by shortages of skilled farmworkers as well as of blacksmiths and other village craftsmen. Furthermore, feed and fertilizers were in short supply and farm equipment became hard to obtain as agricultural machinery factories turned over to making munitions. Rents, however, rose little, and by various devices farmers were able to eat well when the rest of the population had to live on a restricted diet. A source of grievance in the countryside was the ease with which the sons of farmers could be kept safely at home, their presence claimed to be essential to the working of the farm, while the sons of landowners and other country people volunteered or were called up to fight.

The wartime losses of young men were perhaps more evident in small communities where the families were all known to one another. Not so evident, no doubt, as in the villages of France, where even tiny places were able to record long lists of names on their post-war memorials; but still grievous enough. Bereaved wives and mothers proudly displayed the official letter in cottage windows, but sometimes disillusion set in: 'I prayed for my boy morning and night, and now he is killed, what was the use of my praying', said a mother. Death touched the mansion, too. Even as early as the end of 1914, with the war less than six months old, the dead included at least three peers and fifty-two sons of peers, as well as large numbers of baronets and their sons. In all, of the peers and their sons under the age of 50 who served, almost one in five was killed.[6]

The loss of heirs was a factor in the large number of country properties coming on to the market from 1917, though low returns from rentals, increased taxes and the mounting cost and difficulty of running estates also contributed to the decision to sell land. But, generally, landowners took the lead in bringing patriotic initiatives into the countryside. Country houses were offered for hospitals and convalescent homes, rifle ranges were constructed so that village men could learn how to shoot, and servants dispensed with so that they might be free to join up. 'Have you a man preserving your game who should be helping to preserve your Country?' demanded *Country Life* early in 1915. Many owners had already responded by joining up themselves and by taking numbers of their workpeople with them, sometimes guaranteeing their dependants half the men's wages or their cottages rent-free for as long as the war lasted. Colonel Borton of Cheveney, in Kent, though too old to serve himself, took his cowman, footman and butler to the Maidstone recruiting office within three weeks of war being declared. But field sports were carried on much as before, or at least as much as wartime conditions would allow, the hunt occasionally boasting a lady MFH and sometimes swollen by officers from regiments stationed nearby or on leave. Lord Lonsdale, in particular, used his own money to keep the Cottesmore going, arguing: 'What on earth are officers home from the front to do with their time if there's no hunting for them?'[7]

*   *   *

At the end of the war farmers were prosperous and farmworkers somewhat better paid. But landowners were still feeling the pinch of rising expenses and inflexible incomes, ruefully attempting to balance their books and continuing, or contemplating, the sale of ancestral acres. Agriculture had expanded and the country was a little less dependent on imports, with home production now capable of feeding the population for 155 days in the year instead of the 125 days when war broke out. And, moreover, the Agriculture Act of 1920 – though attacked by the leaders of both the farmers and the farmworkers – seemed to promise a peacetime era of greater stability and prosperity than the countryside had known since the 1870s.

However, hardly was the ink dry on the new Act than grain prices began to collapse from the high post-war levels. All over the world farm production and means of transport were returning to normal peacetime operation, and a flood of imports brought British prices down with a fearful crash. Wheat had fetched over 80s a quarter in 1920 (a price not exceeded since the Napoleonic Wars), and was still over 70s in 1921. By 1922 it was down to less than 48s. The government saw that the guaranteed prices enshrined in the 1920 Act would cost far more than it had bargained for. It took the NFU and Workers' Union at their word, repealed the Act, and left both farmers' prices and farmworkers' wages to find their own market levels. Soon the decline turned into a rout: in 1923 the price of wheat was under 43s, and was to be only a little above that figure for the next four years. Subsequently it was to fall even further, to reach the nadir of 20s 9d a quarter in 1934, a price lower than any during the past 150 years for which records had been kept. The average price for the whole of the 1930s was only 27s 1d, which was worse than the lowest 10 years of the so-called 'Great Depression' of the late nineteenth century. It is true that wheat was now only a minor crop, but barley and oats also fell, if not quite so badly; while livestock prices, though holding up better, also fell, and in 1935 fat cattle reached only a little over a third of the 1920 figure. Nevertheless, agricultural prices in general were higher than those ruling before 1914. The problem was that costs were higher, especially wages, which now accounted for a quarter or more of total expenses, and although farmers cut their labour requirements they were usually unable to make much reduction in their total wages bill.

Even dairy farmers, who were usually so small as to employ no

205

labour outside the family, faced hard times. Milk, the most important single product of the land, was desperately low in some years, even obliging some owners of pedigree herds to cease registering their stock since they could not afford the fees. It was a hard task to keep going at all on such prices as the $4\frac{1}{2}$d per gallon for summer and $8\frac{1}{2}$d for winter that the Kettering Co-operative Society offered local producers in 1931. The farmworkers suffered along with their masters. Union membership, over 200,000 strong in 1920, collapsed to only a quarter of this figure. The average minimum wage, which had been nearly 47s a week in 1920–1, was rapidly driven down when the underpinning of the Wages Board was removed. It fell to only 28s in 1922–4, and even less in some areas, although the fall in real wages was much less steep as the cost of living fell also. Further, the skilled men – mainly those employed in handling livestock, a large proportion of the whole – were paid wages substantially above the minimum level. Subsequently, after wage regulation had been restored in 1924, the average minimum hovered at about 31s, rising in the later 1930s to reach 34s 8d in 1938–9.[8]

It was not surprising that, as before the war, men abandoned the farms to try and find better-paid work elsewhere – the average wages in manufacturing were some 60s, and building labourers got over 50s, in the years after 1924. The farmers simply could not afford to begin to bridge this gap, and were indeed themselves hard pressed to survive, cutting back on paid help and neglecting all but essential tasks. In consequence, the numbers of regular full-time males in farming shrank by 172,000 over the seventeen years after 1921, a drop of a quarter, while part-time and seasonal workers fell by a half. The losses would have been even greater if more farmers had commanded the capital to invest in labour-saving machinery, but the depression, especially in the arable areas, had reduced farmers' reserves to very low levels. Farmers were sometimes bankrupted, and some of them emigrated, as they had done in the Great Depression, but from the late 1920s conditions in the traditional goals of British emigrants, Australia, New Zealand and Canada, were themselves so bad that more people were returning home than were leaving.

Landowners, many of them having experienced long years of difficulty, found their problems now intensified. During the war they had generally refrained from taking advantage of conditions to put rents up sharply, though they had seen the post-war boom as an opportunity for making up lost ground. Now rents had to fall again in sympathy with prices, and by 1936 they were below the levels reached in the worst years of the Great Depression, perhaps lower than they had been for well over a century. Income tax, which before 1914 never exceeded 1s 4d in the pound, was afterwards never less than 4s. Super-tax was increased and began to operate on incomes as low as £2,000. Death duties, too, had mounted, and in the Budget of 1919 were raised to 40 per cent on estates valued at over £2 million, with pernicious effects on the survival of properties whose owners or heirs had been killed in the war, the deaths leading to rapid successions and more frequent liability to death duties. And, not least, the cost of domestic servants made the staffing of country houses on anything like the old scale out of the question – and such houses had been designed to be serviced by cheap and plentiful labour and could not be run on an economy basis.

'Land gives one position, and prevents one from keeping it up', Oscar Wilde had made one of his characters remark. If the aphorism was true of Wilde's day, it was even more valid later, and more and more owners were forced to the view that the cost of living as a country gentleman was simply too high. Estates had been coming on to the market more rapidly since the Great Depression, but the flow increased during the war and rose to a flood in the post-war years. As early as March 1919 the *Estates Gazette* spoke of a 'revolution in landowning', and *The Times*, in the following May, pronounced that 'England is changing hands'. Among the great owners who flooded the land market at this time was the Duke of Sutherland, one of the very wealthiest, who sold nearly a quarter of a million acres in Scotland in 1918, and offered a further 144 square miles of the Highlands in the following year, together with Dornoch Castle and his Shropshire seat of Lilleshall House. Other sellers included the enormously wealthy Duke of Westminster, and Lords Aberdeen, Aylesford, Beauchamp, Cathcart, Middleton, Northampton, Petre, Tollmache and Yarborough. Land totalling something over a million acres was sold during 1919, and in 1920 the more prestigious sellers included the Duke of Beaufort, the Marquess of Bath and the Duke of Rutland, who parted with about a half of his Belvoir estate for £1.5 million.[9]

The boom collapsed in 1921 although land sales were still very large by pre-war standards. As the depression bit deeper, purchasers became more cautious, especially the farmers, who were frightened off by the withdrawal of government guarantees and the rapid decline of agricultural prices. After a revival in 1924 and 1925 selling largely ceased, and those who were still prepared to speculate in land deals found farms could be disposed of at only about a third of the price they fetched in the good years. The consequence of the few years of hectic sales was a dramatic change in the structure of landownership. Farmers occupying their own land had accounted for only a little over a tenth of the total acreage in the years between the later nineteenth century and 1914: at that time nearly 90 per cent of the land belonged to private owners of estates and such institutions as the Crown and church, the great London hospitals and Oxford and Cambridge colleges. Between 1918 and 1921 some 6 or 8 million acres changed hands. However, not all of the land was bought by its occupiers; large quantities were acquired by existing landed families and by wealthy newcomers from the world of business. But 'the overwhelming mass of purchasers' consisted of sitting tenants, many of whom became mortgagees of their old landlords, or of the syndicates which acted as middlemen in the purchase and disposal of estates. The new owner-occupiers then paid interest of 5 per cent in lieu of finding the whole of the purchase money. For the seller, if he was the former landowner, this represented a beneficial change: he enjoyed a fixed and more certain return instead of a fluctuating rental which was heavily diminished by all the expenses of maintenance and management. For the former tenant, now entering on a period of severe difficulty, whether an inflexible mortgage was to be preferred to a more flexible rent payment was less certain. The new owner-occupiers, burdened by a fixed mortgage charge, and without a landlord to shield them from the full effect of low prices, formed perhaps the worst affected of any section of the agricultural community in the depression years. At all events, by 1927 owner-occupiers held 36 per cent of the country's land, a much larger figure, probably, than at any time over the previous 200 years.[10]

The terms on which death duties and income and super-taxes were levied contributed to the owner's decision to sell. Since farm rents at the end of the war were unrealistically low, it paid landowners to sell land at the current high prices and take the untaxed capital gain, rather than to raise rents which were liable to income tax and super-tax. Further, if the landowner's immediate priority was to find money to pay death duties, it was better to sell land rather than other assets, the more so as after the 1919 Budget land was valued for the purpose of death duties at its market value, which was considerably higher than the capitalized value of the rental income. Moreover, the cost of running an estate, in expenses of maintenance, management and making improvements, had risen sharply since 1914, biting deeply into rental revenue. Then it absorbed about a third of the rental; by 1921 some three-fifths.

But fiscal and income considerations apart, the underlying factor in the great land sales of 1918–21 was the unfavourable balance between, on the one hand, the cost of owning land in terms of low and uncertain returns and high expenses, and on the other, the traditional gain of land's political influence and social prestige. The former had been weakened, and almost eviscerated, by the long-drawn-out process of parliamentary reform and extension of the franchise; the latter by the rise of new and greater sources of wealth in the business world and by changes in the ways in which the country was governed. Locally, in the village, the squire was still spoken of with respect, and even with some degree of awe, as representing ancient wealth and a tradition of political and social domination. But the reality of that domination had largely disappeared, and, increasingly, village affairs were managed without the squire's approval or intervention, just as national and county government had become mainly, if not entirely, independent of the influence of landed families. Further, the economic logic of the situation was compelling: it made sense to get rid of a troublesome low-yielding asset while the market was good, and to use the proceeds to pay off debt or buy securities which produced twice as much and involved many fewer problems.[11]

The change was visible in a variety of ways: in neglected mansions and parks, in Mayfair residences pulled down or converted to flats, hotels or offices, in hunts controlled by new Masters of Foxhounds who came from unheard-of families of new wealth – *The Field* noting sadly that the 'last remains of the old squirearchy' could no longer afford to hunt.[12] But the effects should not be exaggerated. The social structure of the countryside was not transformed. Many old families were still in residence in their country seats, if presiding over shrunken territories, and perhaps with no London house to be thrown open for the season. Their incomes from farm rents and urban ground rents were much reduced, many of the ground rents having gone the same way as the farmland. It is true also that in the later 1920s and the 1930s incomes from mineral rights and other industrial activities, already hit hard by taxation, fell further as a consequence of industrial depression, as did also the returns from shareholdings. On the other hand, the property sales had enabled heavily indebted families to pay off burdensome liabilities, as well as survive death duties, where these had been incurred at this time. Prudent reinvestment policies had increased the net return on their remaining assets, and family finances were often healthier than they had been for generations. Nevertheless, it remains the case that total incomes were lowered, with obvious implications for the upkeep of the remaining estates and the country-house way of life. The Duke of Portland, surveying the scene in the middle 1930s, noted the decline of the great London houses, replaced by 'restaurants, cabarets and night-clubs', the breaking up of large estates, 'and the houses attached to them sold to individuals most of whom have had little or no con-nexion with the land ... When I first lived at Welbeck, the great neighbouring houses, such as Clumber, Thoresby and Rufford were all inhabited by their owners, who ... employed large staffs ... Now not one ... is so occupied, except for a few days in the year, and the shooting attached to them is either let or abandoned.'[13]

The incomes of farmers suffered also in the depression years. Where soils were suitable and markets were easily available there was some relief to be gained by abandoning grain and turning to other specialized crops. Market-gardening, fruit, poultry and eggs, pigs, potatoes and

Figure 27 Farming was severely depressed in the inter-war years, and village crafts suffered too. Some traditional skills, however, managed to survive, as illustrated by Mr Frost, an elderly ladder-maker of Biddenden, in Kent, photographed in 1925.

flowers might be more profitable in a period when living standards were improving, and the numbers of consumers of what were still semi-luxuries were expanding. Vegetables were increasingly grown by farmers as field crops, and hens, formerly neglected, were kept in large numbers in old buses and other makeshift housing. But even in some of these markets there was foreign competition. To the 60 per cent of cereals that were imported at the end of the 1920s, and the 50 per cent of meat and 80 per cent of butter and cheese, have to be added the 50 per cent of eggs and egg products, the 12 per cent of potatoes and even the 5 per cent of liquid milk, as well as substantial proportions of fruit and vegetables. In practice there were very few farm products not subject to some considerable degree of overseas competition, while for liquid milk, the largest item that was almost entirely home-produced, competition between dairy farmers and between milk distributors, together with a slow-growing market, kept prices uncomfortably low. In most areas farmers responded by cutting down on their own household expenses. Numbers, managing on an income only about equivalent to that of a skilled worker, shared in the work alongside their men. Gone were the tennis parties and new cars on which some had blown their wartime gains, gone too were the leisurely days of sport and riding with the local hunt. The farmers' support of hunting was now held to be 'all the more commendable and unselfish in view of the fact that fewer and ever fewer of their number can afford to hunt'.[14]

By 1937–8 only a minority of farmers could show an average income of more than £480 a year, about the bottom level of the earnings of professional people. In the inter-war years both farm wages and farmers' incomes remained at about three-fifths of comparable non-agricultural incomes. The east of England was on the whole the worst affected by the depression because of the concentration there of large arable farms. In the west the prevalence of grass meant that there had always been specialization in fattening or dairying, and many of the farms were family concerns employing few, if any, hired workers. The large eastern arable farms were badly hit by the low prices of grain and sheep, and by heavy and inflexible labour bills. Farmers there ran down their capital and exhausted their credit until the debts owed to banks and corn merchants mounted to the point where the creditors were sometimes obliged to call a halt. Accumulated losses, along with the more immediate effects of two very low years accounted for the peak of 600 bankruptcies recorded across the whole country in 1932, a figure which may be compared with an average of 322 a year in 1911–13 and only forty-three in 1917–19. Still, 600 bankrupts was a very small proportion of the 200,000 holdings of over 20 acres which were being farmed, a mere 0.3 per cent, reflecting the ability of tenacious farmers to cling on through the economic blizzard, and also the reluctance of creditors to force a sale which might gain them very little.[15]

The ascertaining of net farm incomes, of course, has always been difficult, since the commodities finally marketed were the product of a variety of inputs, of which the costs might be spread over a period of years. On small farms little cash was used, except perhaps for paying the one or two hired hands, the sale of the corn paying for purchases of seeds and feeds, and the receipts from the fat bullocks squaring the outstanding account for the same beasts bought as stores. Much of the labour was uncosted, consisting as it did of that of the farmer himself, his wife, teenage children and very frequently a relation living on the farm. And a good deal of the family's food came from the farm itself, in meat and poultry, milk, eggs, fruit and vegetables – but rarely butter or cheese, for most dairy farmers had by now ceased to trouble themselves with anything other than liquid milk. And the cost of leisure activities – horse-riding, rabbit-shooting, ploughing matches, village fairs and county shows – were absorbed into the general running expenses of the farm. The arrival of the motor car produced a variety of changes, adding to the mobility of the farmer and his family and making it possible to visit friends and nearby towns more frequently; it also made it easier for agricultural extension advisers and marketing board officials to reach a larger number of farms. On the other hand, the motor car brought into the countryside the careless town picnickers, who left gates open for cattle to stray and allowed their dogs to chase the sheep. And further, motor transport was associated with increased thefts of game and stock: cattle from distant pastures, sheep from the hills, turkeys from the barn at Christmas, even Christmas trees from plantations and holly from the hedgerows.[16]

Despite the low incomes, lack of capital and often a limited education, many farmers were able to achieve some progress in both their farm output and their techniques of production during the depression years. Between 1930 and 1937, for example, the total value at constant prices of agricultural output rose overall by 17 per cent, with some increase in crops, large but erratic rises in fruit and vegetables, and a steady growth in livestock and livestock products. With a fall in both the cultivated area and the number of farmworkers, there was thus a considerable rise in productivity per acre and per person. In dairying, for example, cows that gave a remarkable 2,000 gallons of milk per lactation had already arrived, and more attention was being given to milk recording in order to weed out the low-producing animals, as well as to scientific feeding and the importance of producing pure, tuberculosis-free, milk.[17]

Many farms were handicapped by their legacy of antiquated and unsuitable buildings and by the lack of a mains electricity supply.

Landowners had not been able, or willing, to spend large sums on updating their farms, and many owner-occupiers, burdened by large interest payments, lacked the wherewithal to do so. Mechanization was costly and its benefits uncertain. Early tractors, for instance, were beset by serious technical weaknesses, including the lack of suitable implements to be used with them, and, often enough, the need to remove hedges and widen entries to give access to roads and yards. Further, it was not self-evident that the cost of using a tractor was less than that of horses. In 1935 a new Fordson cost about the same or more as a pair of good horses, but the horses had a working life of about twice as long. Before the invention in the middle 1930s of the heavy-treaded pneumatic tyre the uses of a tractor were quite severely circumscribed, and in fieldwork the machine was liable to bog down in heavy soils. Nevertheless, the numbers of tractors grew, reaching nearly 16,000 in 1930 and some 38,500 by 1938, when the majority of farms with a substantial acreage of arable employed one or more. But many farmers continued to use only horses, or combined the tractor with horses, reserving the machine for the heavy work. The 885,000 horses kept for agricultural use before the war had fallen to 563,000 in 1935–9, showing that although in decline, the horse still remained an important source of power and traction on farms at the outbreak of the Second World War.[18]

Economy, the principle of 'do not spend', which governed many farmers during the depression applied also to the slow spread of machine milking. Here again technical problems, particularly the rapid perishing of the rubber parts under sterilization, made the early machines unsuitable. Even when this problem was overcome, the advantage of adopting the machine lay in increasing the total number of cows that could be milked. Costs might actually be increased, especially with the need to provide new or converted milking-parlours, cooling-rooms and separate housing for the oil engine, but the output of milk rose even more. By the end of the 1930s, with good hand-milkers becoming more expensive and less easy to find, the improved milking machine began to come into its own. About 20,000 machines were in use in 1939, but the great majority of dairy farmers were still milking by hand.

By this time a few leading farmers were experimenting with American combine harvesters, although the problems of using them in British conditions were considerable; for potato harvesting patient experimentation was showing how mechanized methods could reduce the numbers of both hands and horses that were needed. The logic of mechanization, especially with the limitations of the tractor for carting fodder and dung, pointed to a future in which the old mixed farming would decline, a future of grain farms without stock and of dairy farms

213

without crops, but few farmers of the 1930s were ready to go along this route, even if they had the means of doing so.[19]

The farmworkers, unlike the farmers, diminished in numbers during the inter-war years. The 685,000 regular male workers of 1921 had fallen to 511,000 by 1939, the consequence of farmers' reduced demand for labour, low wages and the attractions of better pay and conditions elsewhere. Among the various categories of farmworkers it is not surprising to find that between 1921 and 1931 bailiffs and foremen were reduced by a quarter, and workers with horses down by nearly two-fifths, while workers with cattle increased somewhat and the number of shepherds fell only slightly. To low wages and diminished numbers of jobs was added an increase in hours. By 1932 an increase, generally of two hours a week, had been instituted in fifteen English and Welsh counties, and in eight counties the minimum weekly wage for the general farmworker had fallen below £1 10s.[20]

But it was not only the miserable wages and the long, indeed increased, hours that made work on farms unattractive. Housing, or more accurately the lack of cheap, decent houses, was another aspect of farmworkers' conditions which was often, in fact, the decisive issue in whether a family chose to leave the countryside. The nub of the farmworkers' housing problems was still, as it had long been, the inability of low-paid workers to pay a rent that made it worthwhile for landowners or farmers to build cottages for them. Moreover, there was considerable competition for the existing cottages. Many were occupied by other rural workers engaged in industrial or other non-farming occupations, or by people who chose to live in the country and commute to work in the towns; the supply of homes was further reduced by the purchase of cottages by townspeople seeking weekend retreats, as well as by the demolition of those old and insanitary homes deemed no longer fit to live in.

It was estimated in 1937 that two of every five houses occupied by agricultural workers, some 200,000 out of 500,000, were tied cottages, the remainder consisting of private houses (250,000) and council houses (50,000). The sum fixed by the Agricultural Wages Board as the maximum rent that could be deducted from a man's wages for a tied cottage was 3s. In interest alone this sum could have paid only for a cottage with a capital value as low as some £150; and in 1935–6 it cost £310 to build a very simple new cottage. The main attraction of the tied cottage for the farmworker was indeed its cheapness. Other kinds of cottages might be much more costly, and indeed in 1930 subsidized council houses built under the Act of 1924 carried rents varying between 4s and 7s a week. The latter figure, it must be remarked, represented nearly a quarter of the average minimum wage of that time.[21]

Another advantage of the tied cottage was that it was usually situated very near the place of work, often just across the lane from the farmyard. There were no long walks to work in winter dark through rain and snow, and the time so saved could be spent on the vegetable garden or allotment. The great disadvantage was that the man's independence was greatly reduced and he felt a lack of security. The loss of the job meant the loss of the home as well – and when he finally got too old to work where could he go? The occupier of a tied cottage was frequently afraid to ask for better wages, or for repairs to be made, for fear of dismissal; the same fear, justified or not, lay behind his unwillingness to take a free part in elections or in trade union work. The landowners and farmers, on the other hand, argued that the tied cottage was essential for the efficient operation of the farm. Stockmen, especially, needed to live very near their charges to give them continuous attention, and it might be difficult, or even impossible, to find a new hand if there were no cottage to offer him. There was here an irreconcilable clash of points of view. As the Liberal Land Committee remarked in 1925: 'The case for the tied cottage is economic. The case for freedom in the home is human.'[22]

Housing legislation of the period failed to resolve the problem, since, with rural councils controlled by landowners and farmers anxious to keep down expenditure, it resulted in the building of relatively few new council houses in the countryside. Some 30,000 were built in rural areas under the Act of 1924, but only a third of these were let to agricultural workers. A special effort to produce new homes for low-paid rural workers under the Act of 1931 fell victim to the deep slump of 1931–3, and in the event very few were built. Again, in the middle and later 1930s further legislation provided subsidies for agricultural cottages, but the effects before the outbreak of the Second World War were small. However, rural electrification brought improved living to farms and cottages, and there developed a programme for the demolition of unfit houses: in 1937, 51,080 houses were reported as unfit. Houses that were dilapidated but not near to being condemned were entitled to grants designed to encourage the owners to recondition them, and after 1927 an average of something over a thousand a year were improved with grant aid. Again the results were meagre in relation to the size of the problem. Ignorance of the existence of the legislation played some part in this, but the major factor was the apathy of landlords who lacked the capital, and, perhaps, the interest in their estates and confidence in the future, to devote scarce funds to cottage improvement.[23]

The cottages which farmworkers inhabited were likely to be without a good water supply or modern sanitation. In 1939, despite progress made over the previous twenty years, there were still more than 3,000 parishes without piped water, and not a few homes that relied on rainwater, the families having to purchase water by the bucket from a water-cart in times of shortage. Droughts and outbreaks of typhoid gave some stimulus to the improvement of rural sanitation during the years before 1933, but the slump then caused a heavy reduction in expenditure on sewerage schemes. Where the refuse found its way into a river or stream a drought brought conditions that at best were unpleasant and at worst highly dangerous. Small populations scattered over large districts made both piped water and sanitation expensive to provide, and hence the well and rainwater tub remained, as did the old earth closet and midden and cesspool; and indeed many rural areas still lack main drainage at the present day.[24]

It remained true, however, that the health and physique of country people were generally superior to those of townspeople, although inter-war evidence suggested that the margin between them was declining. The physical condition of rural schoolchildren caused concern in the 1920s, when medical officers pointed to the ill-effects of a number of adverse factors: the migration of the most healthy to the towns, bad housing, insufficient wholesome food, inter-marriage and large families. Later investigations in 1935 showed there to be little or no difference between urban and rural children, the urban child, apparently, having improved in physique relative to the rural child.

As before, expectation of life at birth was still greater in rural than in urban areas, although occupational mortality in agriculture was not so favourable in 1930–2 as it had been in 1921–3. The standard mortality rate for agricultural labourers in 1930–2 was slightly superior to that for farmers and their relatives, and indeed both groups were inferior only to building workers, bank and insurance officials, workers in chemical processes, teachers, Anglican (but not other) clergymen, and officers of the Civil Service and local authorities. The death-rate of stevedores was three times, and of tin- and copper-mine workers nearly five times, that of agricultural workers. Country life and work were thus shown to be healthy, despite 'the unfavourable effects of lower income levels and inferior housing', as the official report put it. As for causes of death, the farmers were more likely to die from diseases associated with good living and overnutrition, their workpeople from causes usually associated with malnutrition and poor living conditions (such as tuberculosis, bronchitis and pneumonia). But mortality figures could never tell the whole story. Long-lived farmworkers might reach a great age, but were seldom hale and hearty; they were often subject to painful forms of rheumatism and their backs were crooked and stooping. Their children, too, often showed signs of undernutrition and poor physique, as well as damage caused by long hours of heavy work at too early an age. Differences in income might have little effect on longevity but inevitably showed themselves in other ways. As a member of the Wages Board of 1917–21 once remarked, there was a noticeable contrast between the well-fed farmers' delegates who sat on one side of the table and the lean representatives of the workers on the other side.[25]

*   *   *

The repeal of the Agriculture Act in 1921 seemed at the time to bring to an end a brief, isolated chapter of government intervention which had begun with the measures to deal with the wartime emergency. In the event the retreat to conditions of *laissez-faire* continued for only a little over a decade, and in that decade there appeared a few piecemeal measures designed to help various elements of the agricultural community. As early as 1919 the Forestry Commission had been set up to make good the heavy wartime fellings. It continued its work after 1921, using its powers of buying or leasing land for planting and of assisting private owners who wished to make or extend plantations. By 1939 about one million acres had been acquired by the Commission, and private woodlands had become a useful sideline for owners of estates.

In 1919, 1926 and again in 1931, new legislation was passed to encourage smallholdings by providing central government subsidies to the county councils for the purchase of land. However, the policy, though costly, did little to stem the decline of smallholdings; indeed, the statistics reveal a considerable drop. The number of holdings of less than 5 acres stood at about 90,000 on the eve of the First World War; in 1925 they were down to 75,000, and in 1935 to 67,000. Holdings of between 5 and 20 acres also fell: from some 120,000 before the war to 110,000 in 1925, and 97,000 in 1935. In fact, as large holdings of over 300 acres were also declining in this period, the only category to show an increase, albeit a modest one, was that of holdings of between 50 and 100 acres.[26]

In 1923 tenant farmers were given by statute freedom of cropping and greater security of tenure (since again they could be evicted only for bad husbandry) – another nail in the coffin of landlord control and the old system of managing landed estates. And in 1928 farmers received a direct financial benefit when all agricultural land and buildings were relieved of paying local rates. Attempts in this same year to provide farmers with long-term mortgage loans and more generous credit facilities, making any farm assets eligible as security for the loans, foundered on the farmers' unwillingness to saddle themselves with mortgages in a period of great uncertainty; the more so as the depression became more intense just as the measures were coming into force.

But the most important government intervention in the 1920s was the use of subsidies to create a beet sugar industry. Sugar beet had been grown on the Continent for many years, but without a subsidy there was no possibility of producing beet sugar in Britain at a price that could compete with the cheap imported cane sugar. Experiments had shown that British conditions were suitable for the crop, and that the land would benefit from the deep cultivation and heavy manuring, while the pulp could be used as feed for livestock. In 1925 the subsidy was introduced, and the sugar beet acreage rose from virtually nothing to well over 350,000 acres in the 1930s, providing employment for 32,000 workers in agriculture as well as other jobs in the factories. Already in 1930 8.4 million hundredweight of sugar was being produced, equivalent to nearly a third of the total imported, and seventeen sugar-beet factories were at work. The cost, however, was substantial: £30 million in subsidies for the ten years 1925–34, together with the £10 million forgone in abatement of excise duty.

The farmers did not look solely to the government to help them out of their difficulties. There were some attempts at self-help, in the form of voluntary producers' organizations and co-operative societies, but these made little headway in the depression years. Most of the farmers' co-operatives were purchasing societies organized to buy in cheaply requirements such as feeding-stuffs and seed; others packed and sold specialized products, eggs, dairy produce, meat and fruit. Agricultural co-operation and farmers' credit societies never took strong root in Britain, as they did in other countries, perhaps because of the wide differences in the scale of the farms and the limited degree of regional concentration, or perhaps because of the farmers' variety of interests and their strong sense of individualism.[27]

The conditions in agriculture deteriorated further in the early 1930s as world stocks of cereals mounted and prices sank even lower. But it was the very severity of the world economic crisis, and especially its effects in swelling the already large numbers of the industrial unemployed, that ultimately brought relief. In 1931 the government abolished free trade altogether, having already made some notable gestures in this direction since the war. With full industrial protection finally conceded, there were no grounds left for opposing the protection of farming also. Between 1931 and 1933 large sections of British agriculture became highly protected, organized and subsidized. One complication was the principle of 'Imperial Preference', favourable terms for the import of Commonwealth products, which was enshrined in the Ottawa agreements of 1932. The effect of Imperial Preference, however, was limited by trade agreements made subsequently with non-Commonwealth countries. By these additional agreements Britain conceded quotas for the import of meat, butter and other natural products in return for similar concessions for British exports, notably coal. In this way the bargaining power of the tariff was used to reduce the value of the import privileges won by the Dominions at Ottawa.

The idea of introducing marketing boards into sectors of British agriculture where a two-thirds majority of the producers were in favour, was inherited from the Labour government's Agricultural Marketing Act of 1931, but it was vigorously implemented by Walter Elliot, the Minister of Agriculture in the new national government. Marketing boards, their powers made more effective by the control of imports after 1932, were instituted in milk, pigs, bacon, potatoes and hops. Producers of eggs and poultry rejected a marketing scheme but were protected by quotas and import duties, while import duties also protected the growers of fruit, flowers and vegetables. The fishing industry was not neglected, British fishermen being helped by the imposition of quotas for imports of foreign-caught fish. It did not prove possible to protect livestock farmers from imports of meat coming from the Dominions, but they were assisted by a subsidy, first introduced in 1934.

Wheat-growers, too, were subsidized from 1932 by a 'deficiency payment' designed to bridge the gap between the market price of wheat (down to 5s 11d per hundredweight in 1932) and a guaranteed price of 10s. Ten shillings in fact represented a return to what had been the lowest of the prices that ruled in the 1920s. As a result of better returns, by 1937 the wheat area had increased by half a million acres or over 40 per cent, and output by 10 million hundredweight or a third. Nevertheless, some three-quarters of Britain's annual consumption of wheat still came from abroad. Apart from the deficiency payment (financed by a tax levied on the milling of wheat), a low duty was imposed on foreign wheat imports, as on imported barley also, while growers of barley and oats received in addition an acreage subsidy.

Of the marketing boards – really producers' cartels – the largest and best known was the Milk Marketing Board, inaugurated in 1933. Its objectives were to raise and stabilize the price of milk paid to producers, to expand consumption and to improve standards of production, especially in regard to hygiene and the elimination of bovine tuberculosis in the herds. In none of these objectives was the Board entirely successful in the years to 1939, although progress was made. The dairy farmers, now obliged to sell their milk through the Board, received a 'pool price' which was roughly halfway between the higher price of liquid milk intended for the doorstep, and the lower price of milk sold for manufacture into butter, cheese, condensed milk, cream and items of plastic (including umbrella handles). The returns for the dairy farmer improved somewhat, especially for small producers remote from large markets, although overproduction remained a problem. Attempts to expand consumption met with only slight success, despite the subsidies found by the government to provide cheap milk for mothers living in depressed areas, and for schoolchildren. Problems were also met in maintaining the price of manufactured milk, which had to be supported by levies on imports of dairy produce.

The cost of government assistance to agriculture was estimated to have risen from £45 million a year in 1934 to as much as £100 million in 1939 (if the additional costs of raising at home food that could have been imported more cheaply are taken into account). This costly policy gave some relief to hard-pressed farmers and, fortunately, did so without injuring the consumer by raising prices in the shops. The continued cheapness of food was due in part to the low prices of primary products the world over, and also to the lowering of prices by foreign exporters in order to offset the protection given to British and Dominion foodstuffs. The 1930s was indeed a very cheap period for food, a saving which enabled more and more families to purchase more of the manufactured goods and luxuries appearing on the High Street, and to spend more on amusements and leisure. The index number of retail food prices, with 1914 as 100, was 131 in 1931, 120 in 1933 and 130 in 1936.[28]

In economic terms the policy of intervention hardly made sense. Despite the protection and subsidies, in 1937–9 agricultural prices, taken as a whole, were still below the level of 1927–9, though admittedly a little higher than the disastrous ones of 1933–4. Strategic considerations played no part in initiating the policy, and it was not until 1937 that the importance of an enlarged food production in a possible future war began to be planned for in legislation of 1937 and 1939. International relations were certainly not improved by the introduction of import duties and quotas, and in particular, the interests of Denmark, long a major supplier of the British market, were hurt by the Bacon Marketing Board's restriction of total supplies. It was nonsense, furthermore, to suppose that it was possible simultaneously to help the British farmers as well as the Dominion ones, whose interests were supposed to be guaranteed under the Ottawa agreements.

It is true that agricultural output rose in the middle 1930s to above the pre-war level, though some of the additional output was that of inefficient producers who were kept in business by subsidies and protection. Productivity rose also as the labour force declined and marginal land went out of production. Mechanization was progressing, as we have seen, and yields, pest control and farm management were improved, advances which owed much to the great expansion of government-supported agricultural research. Nevertheless, farming did not become so profitable in the 1930s as to yield many on the land a fair return on their capital or a good living wage. Although the numbers of farmers and members of their families working on farms fell but little, the workers' flight from the land continued, the loss of young men being particularly marked, with the number of young males employed on the land falling by 44 per cent between 1921–4 and 1938.[29]

The 1930s policy of intervention, therefore, was only marginally successful. Agriculture was still depressed, its labour force still shrinking, and the pre-war trend for grass to expand at the expense of arable still very evident. Indeed, the proportion of land under grass remained about as high as before 1914. But all over the advanced world government intervention in agriculture was increasing, and it was politically impossible, after Britain's return to protection in 1931, to allow British farmers alone to bear unsupported the brunt of a massive world oversupply of foodstuffs. Intervention in the 1930s did not result, as it was to do subsequently, in the conflict between the interests of producers of food and those of its consumers, a conflict which has proved so difficult to resolve in contemporary Europe.

*   *   *

The landscape of 1938 assumed, as contemporary observation noted, 'a neglected and unkempt appearance'. One saw 'derelict fields, rank with coarse matted grass, thistles, weeds and brambles', choked ditches, overgrown hedges, dilapidated buildings, farm roads, gates and fences left unrepaired.[30] Yet not all was in decay. New council houses brought new standards into rural housing, country buses, together with cars, motorcycles and bicycles, made it easier for people to get into towns – most villages had never had a railway station – and the radio broke down the sense of isolation and made country people realize they were part of a wider community. Village halls were regularly buzzing with dances, social evenings and whist drives, and the 5,000 Women's Institutes, dating from 1915, offered advice on housewifely matters as well as cultural and educational activities. Local football elevens and cricket teams brought cheer to Saturday afternoons, and traditional events, the flower shows, fêtes and bazaars held in the grounds of the rectory or manor house, brought people together and made them feel part of a real living community.[31]

In the winter visiting lecturers, provided by the Workers' Educational Association or the extra-mural departments of universities, journeyed out from the towns to discourse on economic problems, politics or village history. The village, with its small, scattered and educationally diverse population, presented a special challenge to adult education. Nevertheless, in 1931–2 there were as many as 428 village classes, and in the mid-North Riding area in 1939 over 30 per cent of the adult population were students. The popularity of the classes, and their social composition, varied greatly from one type of village to another, and the proportion of students who were paid agricultural workers might be a remarkable 10 per cent or, by contrast, a disappointing 1 per cent.[32]

Influential figures supported the preservation movement, which was fostered particularly by aristocratic landowners and leading Fabians concerned with passing on an unspoilt rural heritage and enlarging social justice through planning measures. One of the most influential was Patrick Abercrombie, a founder of the Council for the Preservation of Rural England. He strongly advocated such measures as the restriction of ribbon development and the institution of green belts to keep urban sprawl from extending its ugly tentacles further into the countryside, while the creation of national parks was urged to protect the most beautiful areas – a movement which had begun more than half a century earlier in America. In the nation at large country life became a special interest, a kind of escapist cult. There were talks on the radio and country features in the papers, while readers devoured J. W. Robertson Scott's *Countryman* and the easily digested books of A. G. Street and S. L. Bensusan.

Country writers liked to dwell on the unruffled round of days and seasons, the annual rise and waning of crops, flowers and hedgerow plants, the old traditions and quaint customs, the intriguingly eccentric rustics who supposedly populated the villages and, above all, the deep peace of country life. In reality, of course, many strains and frictions lay beneath the apparently placid surface, sometimes breaking through to create little disturbances that might even reach the pages of the press: drought-hit people buying their water by the pail; villages cut off by snow or floods in winter, and livestock lost; a farmworker's family evicted from a tied cottage, their few pathetic belongings scattered across the road. There was also the deep, persistent poverty which helped feed the rural exodus. That exodus owed much, too, as we have seen, to deficient housing and bad living conditions. And in the early 1920s the scrapping of the Agricultural Wages Board caused a bitter conflict between farmers and their workers as wages were forced down to well below 30s a week. The crisis came to a head in Norfolk, where the farmworkers were most strongly organized. In the February of 1923 the farmers there proposed a reduction of wages to under 25s for a week that was to be increased to 54 hours and, most serious, the abandonment of the guaranteed weekly wage, with no payment for days lost through bad weather. The farmers apparently hoped to force the government into assisting them with a tariff or subsidy; the farmworkers, for their part, feared a return to the conditions prevailing before the war and believed that the outcome in Norfolk would be decisive for other counties. Negotiations broke down and some 5,000 farmworkers went on strike. Flying pickets on cycles tried to prevent the use of non-union labour, police were drafted in from neighbouring counties, tempers rose, and at the 'Battle of Holly Heath Farm' pickets were fired on by an incensed employer, though fortunately without casualties. Ultimately the intervention of Ramsay MacDonald, then Leader of the Opposition, led to a settlement at the former conditions of 25s for a 50-hour week, with the guaranteed week retained. Afterwards there were recriminations over the interpretation of the agreed 'no victimization' clause, workers were left unemployed and homeless, and although the union claimed a victory it was realized that any hope of effective progress lay in the re-establishment of a statutory wages board. In the following year the new Labour government did restore the wage-fixing machinery.[33]

Apart from the lowness of incomes, the general conditions of life for country people lagged behind those in the towns. Women, in particular, had a hard struggle to feed and clothe a family – often a large one – on something like £1 a week or little more. Many still had to get all the water from a well, and do their cooking on a combination range, which meant continually laying the fire, carrying the coal and clearing the ashes. The milkman, baker and frequently a butcher, came round the village, but all the groceries and other necessities usually had to be fetched from the village shop, which might easily be more than a mile away. To obtain a better choice of goods, and cheaper ones, meant an expedition to a nearby town, expensive in terms of fares and time. There might be chickens and a pig to be looked after, and perhaps some help given to the husband in the vegetable garden or allotment. The few hours of leisure revolved around the family, if its members had not moved away, around the events of the village hall, the Women's Institute and the pub. Not usually the church: that had ceased to be important in most villagers' lives for years past.

Holiday excursions were few and far between. As late as 1937 many farmworkers still had no weekly half-day holiday. At that date three of the county wages committees had failed to take any step in this direction, and elsewhere some farmers preferred to pay overtime rates and keep their employees at work. Where livestock was kept it was difficult to arrange a regular weekly holiday unless the farmer himself were prepared to do the work, and this same problem existed with public holidays. Even after the Holidays with Pay Act of 1938 the agricultural workers were singled out for discrimination, since the wages committees could direct that the seven days with pay that the Act enforced must be split, no employee being allowed to take more than three of the days consecutively.[34]

When country bus services and private means of transport enabled villagers to get about more easily there was a gain in terms of wider opportunities for leisure but a loss in the decline of support for village clubs – other than the strongly entrenched Women's Institutes. Organizations which had been able to flourish when supported by a wealthy patron, and when they offered one of the few alternatives to the village pub, lost members now that people could go further afield and find counter-attractions, not least the town cinema. The church suffered also, although the waning of the support for this goes much further back. Rural parsons often lacked intelligence and character, complained Robertson Scott, and they proved unable to stimulate interest in a faith that fewer and fewer people really believed in. In not a few villages, he went on, the church was to all intents and purposes dead; in many it was dying. A committee appointed by the Archbishop of Canterbury had already reported in 1920 that people accused the rural clergy of want of energy, spirit and initiative. In many parishes, it was stated, 'they have ceased to have any influence'. One cause of this decline was the detachment of the parsons from the day-to-day problems of the people, and the tendency for the clergy to side with, or at least be associated with, the 'local representatives of wealth and social influence'.[35]

There were, however, some new and growing organizations in the countryside. Perhaps the most notable of these was the Young Farmers' Club, which first appeared in 1922 following the initiative of Lord Northcliffe, proprietor of the *Daily Mail*, and was supported by the United Dairies Company. In 1925 the Ministry of Agriculture stepped in, and subsequently there was further financial help from the Carnegie Trust, the King George Jubilee Trust, the County Councils and the National Farmers' Union. By 1939 the thirteen clubs of 1925 had increased to 400, with a membership of 17,000. Practical training in agriculture, including the keeping of livestock, was a main feature of the clubs, but there were also wider educational and social activities. The clubs' weakness was that they tended to become local cliques, consisting largely of farmers' children, who had an obvious advantage in facilities for keeping stock of their own, and consequently 'a great amount of educational effort' was concentrated 'on a very small number of youngsters'.[36]

Sports clubs appealed to the widest circle of villagers, and many people who never took part in a game, or even watched it, felt pride in the clubs' successes. Farmworkers were often effectively barred from taking an active part by lack of free Saturday afternoons, though occasionally a farmer would encourage a man who was a good player to take the afternoon off while he attended to the farm and milked the cows in his place. But many clubs suffered from the increased mobility of young people, and this, together with the exodus of young people from the countryside, had the effect of weakening the clubs and making it difficult for some of them to continue.

Finally, the county Rural Community Councils, built up from 1921, played a valuable part by offering assistance in promoting the social welfare of the countryside, concentrating on educational and recreational activities, health concerns, and the development of agriculture and rural industries. In particular, the Councils encouraged existing organizations, such as drama groups, music societies and Young Farmers' Clubs, and helped to promote playing-fields and village halls. Demand was stimulated for public libraries and lectures, and the Councils also fostered interest in housing and sanitation as well as helping to revive rural crafts. Since the Councils worked entirely through voluntary co-operation, their activities necessarily grew slowly, with much depending on acceptance of their help by local communities. It was noticeable that the Councils were much less popular in the north of England than in the south.[37]

In practice social activities in the villages were generated by the initiative and enthusiasm of a few dedicated individuals. The majority of the residents stood apart, satisfied with their evenings in the pub, or with their own fireside and the radio. This apathy resulted in part from natural reserve or diffidence, exaggerated by the familiarity of a small community in which every person knew every other. But there were also highly relevant practical causes. Poverty made it difficult for the poorer people to pay subscriptions or meet membership expenses, while farmworkers and smallholders and their families worked late in the evenings and did not have a half-holiday. Further, the scattered nature of many villages meant an unattractively long walk through dark, muddy lanes in rain and cold to attend a meeting or a class after a hard day's work. And as the radio and cinema raised people's standards, the term 'amateur' became one of contempt, and local performances of drama societies, concerts and lectures no longer exerted their former magic. Inevitably, the combination of all these factors made it difficult to start or sustain village activities.

Another practical reason for apathy was poor education. Many villagers felt themselves to be inferior and likely to be embarrassed if they joined a society or evening class. The village schools had always tended to lag behind those of the towns. Many of the buildings were now old and were still cramped, poorly ventilated and inadequately heated. Few schools had more than one classroom, playgrounds and playing-fields were small, unsuitable or non-existent, piped water was often lacking, and the toilets nothing more than neglected earth closets. The general standard of rural teachers was lower than those of the towns, as had always been the case, and the country ones were paid less. In 1933–4 over 70 per cent of all uncertified teachers and nearly 90 per cent of supplementary teachers were to be found in country schools. Even the headmistress might be unqualified. Many of the teachers were of local origin, with little experience of the wider world, while others were former town teachers, broken in health, who had sought out a quieter post in the country; others were married women unable to get work in the towns; and only a small number were countryside enthusiasts who put up with a lower salary in order to live in their chosen environment.

Often the parents, lacking much education themselves, took little interest in their children's schooling, and there were reports of a noticeable lack of ambition in schools dominated by the children of farm-workers. Only an occasional, exceptional child could win a scholarship place in a town grammar school. Distance was still a problem. True, by the 1930s many counties were transporting children by bus, and others supplied pupils with bicycles, capes and leggings; in 1932 East Suffolk provided 750 cycles. But these schemes usually applied only where children had to go more than 2 miles to school, and even 1 or nearly 2 miles in wet or snow, twice a day, was a deterrent to regular attendance.

A major change to affect the schools derived from the Hadow Report of 1926. This recommended the institution of senior schools, where they were lacking, for all children over 11 years of age, thus introducing the concept of 'secondary education for all'. Numbers of authorities adopted the reform, though in many rural areas it was left to the Education Act of 1944 to implement it: in 1936 only 35 per cent of rural children were in reorganized schools, as compared with 74 per cent of urban children. Where 'Hadow reorganization' was introduced rural children benefited greatly from the translation to a larger central institution with improved facilities, a wider range of subjects and more specialized teaching. The children could now be educated more nearly according to their interests and abilities, they could play team games, and more-over, their mixing with a wider range of children of their own age was itself educational. There were some drawbacks, of course, notably the long journeys of the older children to a distant senior school, and the enforced closing of some village primary schools where reorganization had too drastically reduced the numbers.[38]

Much discussed among educationalists was the question of technical education in agriculture. Many country children, it was argued, had no need of the kind of elementary rural lessons that village schools could give – rather, they needed to be taught about the wider world, and that this world was larger than the farm or the village. But the lack of more advanced technical training was increasingly felt as agriculture became more scientific, more mechanized, more specialized. The old practices, based on tradition, rule of thumb and the ignorance described as experience, had to give way to more informed knowledge, precise measurement and an understanding of scientific processes. By 1939 courses in agriculture were offered by nine British universities, and additional educational facilities were provided by forty-three farm institutes and experimental stations, not overlooking the help given to farmers by officers of fourteen regional advisory centres across the country. Nevertheless, it was estimated that not more than one in twelve of British farmers had any institutional training, while the number of formally trained farmworkers was negligible. The lack of sufficient opportunities for agricultural workers to obtain technical training was most serious. Farmers could, if they wished, keep up to date by reading the agricultural press and journals of breed societies, by attending shows, inspecting prize stock and examining the latest advances in farm equipment. But little of this knowledge reached the farmworkers, though if it had, it might have made them more efficient, and possibly have given them greater interest in their work and more reason for staying on the farm. The material and social gap between farmer and farmworker had also its dimension of knowledge.[39]

On the eve of the Second World War there was indeed much amiss with the countryside: depression among the farmers, rootlessness among the younger workers, deficiencies in the conditions of life, in social relations, in education. Some writers still pressed for farm output to be expanded, and raised again the old nostrum of a revival of smallholdings – despite the obvious economic weaknesses of the arguments.[40] Others looked on the countryside with a critical eye, attacking the circumscribed imagination, the inertia, the innate conservatism of the country-dweller.[41] Farmers, it was said, were seldom people of wide experience or enlarged minds. Further, there was little real democracy in the village, affairs being dominated, much as ever, by an unholy alliance of squire, large farmer and parson. This triumvirate managed to block any improvement schemes that, however desirable, might result in raising the rates, and resisted also all improvements to the village school. There had been an increase in people's mobility, but it was severely limited: the majority of villages in Devon, for example, were isolated after six o'clock in the evening so far as public transport was concerned; once a week a late bus ran from the town. And a 1s bus fare made a big hole in the tight budget of an agricultural worker.

Many of the social organizations, it was also argued, were not the natural flowering of a vibrant village community but artificial growths, depending heavily on the initiative of some individuals from outside, who might have little or no connection with the village itself. Adult education, for instance, was coming to depend on the enthusiasm of a specially appointed tutor-organizer, financed by a university or the Board of Education. In any case, adult classes, like other social programmes, were merely ameliorating the life of the countryside; they were doing nothing to reconstruct it, to give country people an adequate standard of life. Many branches of the Women's Institute, similarly, depended on leaders who were 'ladies', who moved in elevated county circles and were part of the governing group. It could not be expected

Figure 28 Women's organizations played their part in the efforts to revive village life in the 1930s. Here is shown the National Federation of Women's Institutes stall at Bath in 1936, the first stall to be taken to agricultural shows and exhibitions.

that Women's Institutes would ever be radical: 'They will struggle to encourage District Nursing Associations, and they will attack the occasional Mrs Gamps that survive. They will not, however, encourage dissatisfaction with the prevailing agricultural wage rate.'[42]

To the great majority of the nation's people, those who lived in towns, few of these issues seemed relevant or important, even if they had heard of them. To them the village was somewhere to go on a weekend excursion, to admire the quaint black and white cottages, the rustic churches and stately manor houses, to take a drop of 'real country ale' in a village pub that in truth was rather dirty and uncomfortable. To them, as to G. K. Chesterton, addressing the Council for the Preservation of Rural England in 1931, the village 'was a relic: it was even a marvellous relic, like the relic of a great saint. It was something that would not be replaced. They were guarding not stones but jewels.' Chesterton had recently visited America, and, he went on, such villages could not be found in all the vast spaces of that country, nor such inns. 'The village inn was also something unique, like the whole of the English village.'[43]

Thus spoke the romantic, the traditionalist who overlooked the long history of struggle and change that had produced the village of 1931, who thought, in fact, of only one sort of village and forgot the many other plain or ugly ones; and who ignored, too, the reality of material deprivation and unremitting toil that lay beneath even the most enchanting of hamlets, and praised the peacefulness which in truth was mere stagnant tedium. A jewel perhaps, but one that was sadly flawed.

NOTES

1 LORD AND PEASANT

1 Christopher Taylor, *Village and Farmstead: a history of rural settlement in England*, London, 1983, p. 227.
2 R. Fieldhouse and B. Jennings, *A History of Richmond and Swaledale*, London, 1978, pp. 52–3.
3 Taylor, op. cit., pp. 167–70.
4 Fieldhouse and Jennings, op. cit., p. 58.
5 Bernard Jennings, ed., *A History of Nidderdale*, 2nd edn, London, 1983, p. 89.
6 Fieldhouse and Jennings, op. cit., pp. 54–5.
7 Christopher Dyer, 'Deserted medieval villages in the west midlands', *Economic History Review*, 2nd ser., XXXV, 1982, pp. 20, 23–4, 31–3.
8 Taylor, op. cit., esp. pp. 130–1; Edward Miller and John Hatcher, *Medieval England – rural society and economic change 1086–1348*, London, 1978, p. 36.
9 Taylor, op. cit., pp. 130–1.
10 This paragraph is based on material in Joan Thirsk, *England's Agricultural Regions and Agrarian History, 1500–1750*, London, 1987.
11 M. W. Beresford and J. K. S. St Joseph, *Medieval England: an aerial survey*, 2nd edn, Cambridge, 1979, pp. 23–4; Joan Thirsk, 'The common fields', *Past and Present*, XXIX, 1964, pp. 9–10.
12 Beresford and St Joseph, op. cit., pp. 24–5.
13 Ibid., pp. 24–5.
14 Alan R. H. Baker and Robin A. Butlin, eds, *Studies of Field Systems in the British Isles*, Cambridge, 1973, pp. 257–61.
15 Ibid., pp. 287–9, 304–5, 387–9.
16 John Hatcher, 'English serfdom and villeinage: towards a reassessment', *Past and Present*, 90, 1981, pp. 5, 9–10.
17 R. H. Hilton, *A Medieval Society: the west midlands at the end of the thirteenth century*, London, 1966, p. 230.
18 Miller and Hatcher, op. cit., pp. 130, 235–9. R. H. Hilton, *The Economic Development of some Leicestershire Estates in the Fourteenth and Fifteenth Centuries*, Oxford, 1947, p. 15.
19 Miller and Hatcher, op. cit., pp. 148–54, 215–18.
20 John Hatcher, *Rural Economy and Society in the Duchy of Cornwall*, Cambridge, 1970, pp. 101, 119.
21 F. R. H. Du Boulay, 'Who were farming the English demesnes at the end of the Middle Ages?', *Economic History Review*, 2nd ser., XVII, 1964, pp. 443–55; Barbara Harvey, 'The leasing of the Abbot of Westminster's demesnes in the later Middle Ages', *Economic History Review*, XXII, 1969, pp. 20–1.

22 T. H. Swales, 'The redistribution of the monastic lands in Norfolk at the Dissolution', *Norfolk Archaeology*, XXIV, 1966, p. 43.

23 Beresford and St Joseph, op. cit., pp. 142–3.

24 Hilton, *Economic Development of some Leicestershire Estates*, p. 4.

25 A. Hamilton Thompson, 'The English house', in Geoffrey Barraclough, ed., *Social Life in Early England*, London, 1960, pp. 140–5, 150–1.

26 L. F. Salzman, *English Life in the Middle Ages*, Oxford, 1926, pp. 94–5.

27 Quoted by Miller and Hatcher, op. cit., p. 156.

28 M. W. Barley in Joan Thirsk, ed., *Agrarian History of England and Wales*, IV, *1500–1640*, Cambridge, 1967, pp. 713–14, 735, 737, 749, 755.

29 Maurice Keen, *The Outlaws of Medieval Legend*, rev. edn, London, 1977, Introduction.

2 THE PROGRESS OF THE PLOUGH

1 John Hatcher, 'English serfdom and villeinage: towards a reassessment', *Past and Present*, 90, 1981, pp. 5, 10–13, 15, 26, 38.

2 Ibid., pp. 6, 13, 25.

3 Robert Trow-Smith, *English Husbandry*, London, 1951, p. 62.

4 Ibid., p. 65.

5 M. E. Seebohm, *The Evolution of the English Farm*, 2nd edn, London, 1976, pp. 156–7; Andrew Jones, 'Harvest customs and labourers' perquisites in southern England, 1150–1350: the hay harvest', *Agricultural History Review*, XXV, 1977, pp. 98–101.

6 Seebohm, op. cit., pp. 158–60.

7 Andrew Jones, 'Harvest customs and labourers' perquisites in southern England: the corn harvest', *Agricultural History Review*, XXV, 1977, pp. 14–18.

8 Trow-Smith, op. cit., pp. 66–7.

9 Seebohm, op. cit., pp. 130–7.

10 Ibid., pp. 160–3.

11 See G. E. Mingay, *The Gentry*, London, 1976, p. 57.

12 E. Kerridge, *The Agricultural Revolution*, London, 1967, pp. 40, 328.

13 R. B. Outhwaite, 'Progress and backwardness in English agriculture, 1500–1650', *Economic History Review*, 2nd ser., XXXIX, 1986, pp. 1–18.

14 Quoted by Outhwaite, op. cit., p. 7.

15 Ibid., pp. 9–12.

16 Ibid., pp. 13–16.

17 Peter Bowden, 'Agricultural prices, wages, farm profits and rents', in Joan Thirsk, ed., *Agrarian History of England and Wales*, V–II, *1640–1750*, Cambridge, 1985, pp. 1, 12.

18 Ibid., p. 13.

19 Christopher Morris, ed., *The Journeys of Celia Fiennes*, London, 1947, pp. 83, 96, 187.

20 Daniel Defoe, *A Tour through England and Wales*, Everyman edn, London, 1928, I, pp. 59–60, 65, 82–3, 289; II, pp. 199, 284.

21 Joan Thirsk, ed., *Agrarian History of England and Wales*, V–I, *1640–1750*, Cambridge, 1985, p. xix.

22 Ibid., pp. xxiii, xxvi–xxix; Defoe, op. cit., I, pp. 128–9; Morris, op. cit., p. 31.

23 Bowden, op. cit., pp. 9–11.

24 *Kalm's Account of his Visit to England*, London, 1892, p. 341.

25 A. Young, *General View of Oxfordshire*, London, 1809, p. 102.

26 Nottingham University Archives, Manvers Collection, Survey of Hanslope 1763;

J. A. Yelling, in R. A. Dodgshon and R. A. Butlin, eds, *An Historical Geography of England and Wales*, London, 1978, p. 153.

27 W. G. Hoskins, *The Midland Peasant: the economic and social history of a Leicestershire village*, London, 1957, pp. 233, 238.

28 See J. D. Chambers and G. E. Mingay, *The Agricultural Revolution 1750–1850*, London, 1966, p. 50.

29 Berkshire RO, D/EPb E3–5.

30 See G. E. Mingay, *English Landed Society in the Eighteenth Century*, London, 1963, pp. 54–6, 178.

31 R. Fieldhouse and B. Jennings, *A History of Richmond and Swaledale*, London, 1978, pp. 136, 152–3.

32 Philip A. J. Pettit, *The Royal Forests of Northamptonshire: a study in their economy 1558–1714*, Northants Records Society Publication XXIII, 1968, p. 142.

33 Vanessa S. Doe, ed., *The Diary of James Clegg of Chapel-en-le-Frith 1708–1755*, *Part I*, Derbyshire Record Society, Matlock, 1978, p. xxv.

34 Thirsk, op. cit., *Agrarian History*, V–I, pp. 372–4.

35 See Anthony Wrigley, 'Urban growth and agricultural change: England and the Continent in the early modern period', in Robert I. Rotberg and Theodore K. Rabb, eds, *Population and History: from the traditional to the modern world*, Cambridge, 1986, pp. 135–45; H. J. Habakkuk, 'The agrarian history of England and Wales: regional farming systems and agrarian change, 1640–1750', *Economic History Review*, 2nd ser., XL, 1987, pp. 283–7.

3 IN SICKNESS AND IN HEALTH: DISEASE AND FAMINE

1 Charles Creighton, *A History of Epidemics in Britain*, 2nd edn, Cass, 1965, I, pp. 32, 48.

2 Ian Kershaw, 'The Great Famine and agrarian crisis in England 1315–1322', *Past and Present*, 59, 1973, pp. 6–9, 11–14, 50; Creighton, op. cit., p. 48.

3 W. G. Hoskins, 'Harvest fluctuations and English economic history, 1620–1759', *Agricultural History Review*, XVI, 1968, pp. 15–23.

4 Andrew B. Appleby, 'Disease or famine? Mortality in Cumberland and Westmorland 1580–1640', *Economic History Review*, 2nd ser., XXVI, 1973, pp. 419, 429.

5 Quoted by Creighton, op. cit., I, p. 358.

6 Creighton, op. cit., II, pp. 23, 47, 78–9.

7 Ibid., II, pp. 73, 79.

8 Ibid., I, pp. 52, 57–8.

9 Ibid., I, pp. 24, 63, 72, 87, 97–8, 110.

10 David Van Zwanenberg, 'The last epidemic of plague in England? Suffolk 1906–1918', *Medical History*, XIV, 1970, p. 72; F. F. Cartwright, *A Social History of Medicine*, London, 1977, pp. 72–4.

11 Appleby, op. cit., pp. 404–5.

12 Ibid., pp. 404–5.

13 A. R. Bridbury, 'The Black Death', *Economic History Review*, 2nd ser., XXVI, 1974, pp. 577–92.

14 Creighton, op. cit., II, p. 456.

15 Ibid., pp. 317, 367–8.

16 Ibid., p. 317.

17 Daniel Defoe, *A Tour through England and Wales*, Everyman edn, London, 1928, I, p. 13.

18 J. Beresford, ed., *Woodforde*, London, 1935, p. 172.

19 Margaret C. Barnet, 'The barber-surgeons of York', *Medical History*, XII, 1968, p. 25; H. D. Chalke, 'The impact of tuberculosis on history, literature and art', *Medical History*, VI, 1962, pp. 303–5.

20 Barnet, op. cit., pp. 22–3, 25.

21 Irvine Loudon, 'The nature of provincial medical practice in eighteenth-century England', *Medical History*, XXIX, 1985, pp. 2, 7–9, 11, 15, 25.

22 Vanessa S. Doe, ed., *The Diary of James Clegg of Chapel-en-le-Frith 1708–1755*, Part I, Derbyshire Record Society, Matlock, 1978, pp. xlii, xliv-xlvi, 15, 17, 18.

23 M. Blundell, ed., *Blundell's Diary and Letter Book 1702–28*, Liverpool, 1952, pp. 66–7; C. H. C. and M. I. Baker, *The Life and Circumstances of James Brydges, first Duke of Chandos*, Oxford, 1949, p. 424; Virginia Berridge and Griffith Edwards, *Opium and the People*, London, 1981, pp. 21–48.

24 Beresford, op. cit., pp. 102, 321, 378.

25 Vicars Bell, *To Meet Mr Ellis: Little Gaddesden in the eighteenth century*, London, 1941, pp. 35, 38, 41–4.

26 Private communication by Dr J. Whyman; P. S. Brown, 'Medicines advertised in eighteenth-century Bath newspapers', *Medical History*, 1976, pp. 154–62.

27 Creighton, op. cit., II, p. 560.

28 Sir D'Arcy Power, in A. S. Turberville, ed., *Johnson's England*, Oxford, 1952, II, pp. 275–6.

29 E. S. Turner, *Call the Doctor: a social history of medical men*, London, 1958, pp. 110–11.

30 G. E. Mingay, 'Thrumpton: a Nottinghamshire estate in the eighteenth century', *Transactions of the Thoroton Society*, LXI, 1957, p. 54.

31 Lady Holland, *A Memoir of the Rev. Sydney Smith*, London, 1855, pp. 55, 230.

32 William Brockbank, 'Country practice in days gone by', *Medical History*, VI, 1962, pp. 181–3.

33 Wayland D. Hand, 'Folk medical inhalants in respiratory disorders', *Medical History*, XII, 1968, pp. 153–8.

34 Quoted by F. F. Cartwright, *A Social History of Medicine*, London, 1977, p. 80.

35 Creighton, op. cit., II, pp. 495–8.

36 Beresford, op. cit., p. 320.

37 P. E. Razzell, 'Population change in eighteenth-century England. A reinterpretation', *Economic History Review*, 2nd ser., XVIII, 1965, pp. 315–26; 'Edward Jenner: the history of a medical myth', *Medical History*, VIII, 1965, pp. 216–29.

38 Creighton, op. cit., II, pp. 558–67.

39 Edwin Chadwick, *Sanitary Condition of the Labouring Population*, 1842, new edn, Edinburgh, 1965, pp. 82–7.

40 W. A. Armstrong, in G. E. Mingay, ed., *Agrarian History of England and Wales*, VI, *1750–1850*, Cambridge, 1989, p. 815.

41 Anne Digby, *Pauper Palaces*, London, 1978, pp. 169–75; Pamela Horn, *Labouring Life in the Victorian Countryside*, Dublin, 1976, pp. 188–9.

42 B. M. Willmott Dobbie, *An English Rural Community: Batheaston with St. Catherine*, Bath, 1969, pp. 67–71.

43 Horn, op. cit., pp. 189–90.

44 C. B. Andrews, ed., *The Torrington Diaries*, London, 1954, p. 395.

4 PLENTY AND WANT

1 Peter and Jennifer Clark, 'The social economy of the Canterbury suburbs: evidence of the census of 1563', in Alec Detsicas and Nigel Yates, eds, *Studies in Modern Kentish History*, Maidstone, 1983, pp. 69–70.

2 David Levine, 'The demographic implications of rural industrialization: a family reconstitution study of Shepshed, Leicestershire, 1600–1851', *Social History*, I, 1976, p. 186.

3 George Ewart Evans, *The Horse in the Furrow*, London, 1960, p. 89.

4 Alan Everitt, 'Farm labourers', in Joan Thirsk, ed., *Agrarian History of England and Wales*, IV, *1500–1640*, Cambridge, 1967, p. 421.

5 J. P. P. Horn, 'Wealth distribution in the Vale of Berkeley', *Southern History*, III, 1981, pp. 93, 101.

6 Dennis Baker, 'A sixteenth-century farmer of Goodnestone-next-Faversham', unpublished paper.

7 Dennis Clarke and Anthony Stoyel, *Otford in Kent: a history*, Otford, 1975, p. 160.

8 Everitt, op. cit., pp. 401–5.

9 W. Cobbett, *Rural Rides*, Everyman edn, London 1912, I, pp. 248, 294.

10 A. Young, *General View of the Agriculture of Norfolk*, London, 1804, pp. 91, 94–5, 102, 107, 125, 133, 135, 147, 161.

11 Christopher Morris, ed., *The Journeys of Celia Fiennes*, London, 1947, p. 101; Cobbett, op. cit., II, p. 30.

12 Clarke and Stoyel, op. cit., p. 205.

13 B. M. Willmott Dobbie, *An English Rural Community: Batheaston with St. Catherine*, Bath, 1969, p. 63.

14 See Ann Kussmaul, *Servants in Husbandry in Early Modern England*, Cambridge, 1981.

15 Cobbett, op. cit., I, pp. 265–6.

16 Kussmaul, op. cit., pp. 39, 81–2.

17 Donald Woodward, 'Wage rates and living standards in pre-industrial England', *Past and Present*, XCL, 1981, pp. 39, 41.

18 Everitt, op. cit., p. 435.

19 Ibid., p. 436.

20 Ibid., p. 437.

21 A. Young, *A Six Months Tour through the North of England*, London, 1770, IV, pp. 445–9.

22 Ibid., p. 441.

23 J. Caird, *English Agriculture in 1850–51*, London, 1852, p. 512.

24 Pamela Horn, 'Child workers in the pillow lace and straw plait trades of Victorian Buckinghamshire and Bedfordshire', *Historical Journal*, XVII, 1974, p. 796.

25 For details see Alan Everitt, 'Country carriers in the nineteenth century', *Journal of Transport History*, n.s., III, 1976, pp. 179–202.

26 William Cobbett, *Cottage Economy*, London, 1926, p. 103.

27 Mary Chamberlain, *Fenwomen: a portrait of women in an English village*, London, 1983, pp. 29, 35.

28 M. W. Barley, 'Rural building in England', in Joan Thirsk, ed., *Agrarian History of England and Wales*, V–I, *1640–1750*, Cambridge, 1984, pp. 591, 597, 599, 653.

29 Ibid., pp. 654–5, 657, 678, 682.

30 Morris, op. cit., p. 207.

31 M. Grosley, *A Tour to London or New Observations on England and its Inhabitants*, English trans. 1772, p. 17.

32 Vicars Bell, *To Meet Mr Ellis: Little Gaddesden in the eighteenth century*, London, 1956, pp. 19–20, 50–1.

33 W. A. Armstrong, 'The influence of demographic factors on the position of the agricultural labourer in England and Wales c. 1750–1914', *Agricultural History Review*, XXIX, 1981, pp. 71–6.

34 F. E. Green, *The Tyranny of the Countryside*, London, 1913, pp. 155–7.

35 Nick Lyons, ed., *The Courts and Yards of Brigg*, Scunthorpe, 1983, pp. 17–19.
36 Dobbie, op. cit., pp. 73–4; Clarke and Stoyel, op. cit., p. 230.
37 G. E. and K. R. Fussell, *The English Countrywoman*, New York, 1971, pp. 31, 34, 60.
38 Bell, op. cit., pp. 23–5.
39 Ibid., pp. 25–7
40 Cobbett, *Rural Rides*, I, p. 179.

5 LANDED SOCIETY AND RURAL CULTURE

1 See J. V. Beckett, *The Aristocracy in England 1660–1914*, Oxford, 1986, p. 332.
2 Jill Franklin, *The Gentleman's Country House and its Plan, 1835–1914*, London, 1981, ch. 3–4.
3 John Beresford, ed., *Woodforde*, London, 1935, pp. 389–90; Rider Haggard, *Rural England*, London, 1902, Preface.
4 Christopher Morris, ed., *The Journeys of Celia Fiennes*, London, 1947, p. 100.
5 F. M. L. Thompson, *English Landed Society in the Nineteenth Century*, London, 1963, p. 93; Jill Franklin, 'The Victorian country house', in G. E. Mingay, ed., *The Victorian Countryside*, London, 1981, II, pp. 403–4.
6 G. E. Mingay, *English Landed Society in the Eighteenth Century*, London, 1963, pp. 227–30.
7 Merlin Waterson, *The Servant's Hall: a domestic history of Erddig*, London, 1980, pp. 2, 24, 30–1, 56, 57, 58, 59, 78, 101, 170, 228.
8 J. Marchand, ed., *A Frenchman in England 1784*, Cambridge, 1933, pp. 28–31, 34, 44.
9 Arthur J. Rees, *Old Sussex and her Diarists*, London, 1929, pp. 110–12.
10 Ibid., pp. 46, 89.
11 H. S. Bennett, *Life on the English Manor*, Cambridge, 1960, pp. 329–33.
12 Ibid., p. 29; C. G. Coulton, *The Medieval Scene*, Cambridge, 1959, pp. 44–5.
13 Rosalind Mitchinson, 'Pluralists and the poorer benefices in eighteenth-century England', *Historical Journal*, V, 1962, pp. 188–90.
14 W. Cobbett, *Rural Rides*, Everyman edn, London, 1912, I, p. 226; II, p. 67.
15 W. Addison, *The English Country Parson*, London, 1947, pp. 141, 144.
16 Ibid., p. 85; David Davies, *The Cast of the Labourer in Husbandry*, 1795.
17 See G. E. Mingay, *The Gentry*, London, 1976, pp. 127–8.
18 C. P. Fendall and E. A. Crutchley, eds, *The Diary of Benjamin Newton, Rector of Wath, 1816–1818*, Cambridge, 1933, pp. 34, 80.
19 David W. Howell, *The Gentry of South-West Wales in the Eighteenth Century*, Cardiff, 1986, p. 209; Bernard Jennings, ed., *A History of Nidderdale*, 2nd edn, 1983, pp. 433–7.
20 See Eric J. Evans, *The Contentious Tithe: the tithe problem and English agriculture 1750–1850*, London, 1976; David W. Howell, *Land and People in Nineteenth-Century Wales*, London, 1977, pp. 83–5; G. E. Mingay, *Rural Life in Victorian England*, London, 1977, pp. 150–1.
21 See J. Obelkevich, *Religion and Rural Society: South Lindsey 1825–1875*, Oxford, 1976.
22 Christina Hole, *Witchcraft in Toner's Puddle*, Dorchester, 1964, pp. 3–4.
23 See Samuel Pyeatt Menefee, *Wives for Sale*, Oxford, 1981, esp. pp. 31–40, 50–5, 160, 167.
24 Edwin Grey, *Cottage Life in a Hertfordshire Village*, Harpenden, 1977, pp. 176–80.

25 David Cressy, 'Levels of illiteracy in England 1530–1730', *Historical Journal*, XX, 1977, p. 5.

26 Lawrence Stone, 'Literacy and education in England 1640–1900', *Past and Present*, 42, 1969, pp. 101–3, 120.

27 Ibid., p. 112; R. Hume, 'Educational provision for the Kentish poor, 1660–1811: fluctuations and trends', *Southern History*, IV, 1982, pp. 126–7, 132.

28 Stone, op. cit., p. 112.

29 Howell, op. cit., p. 206.

30 R. J. Olney, *Rural Society and County Government in Nineteenth-Century Lincolnshire*, Lincoln, 1979, pp. 66–7, 93–4.

31 Jennings, op. cit., pp. 459–61.

32 M. K. Ashby, *Joseph Ashby of Tysoe*, Cambridge, 1961, p. 18.

33 Jennings, op. cit., pp. 463–5.

34 Mingay, *The Gentry*, pp. 153–63.

35 J. A. Sharpe, 'The history of crime in late medieval and early modern England: a review of the field', *Social History*, VII, 1982, pp. 195–200; Henry Summerson, 'Crime and society in medieval Cumberland', *Transactions of the Cumberland and Westmorland Archaeological and Antiquarian Society*, LXXXII, 1982, pp. 111, 116.

36 J. M. Beattie, 'The pattern of crime in England 1660–1800', *Past and Present*, 62, 1974, p. 87.

37 E. P. Thompson, 'The moral economy of the English crowd in the eighteenth century', *Past and Present*, 50, 1971, p. 112.

38 W. Branch Johnson, ed., *'Memorandums For ...': the Carrington Diary*, London, 1973, pp. 133–4.

39 See A. J. Peacock, *Bread or Blood: a study of the agrarian riots in East Anglia in 1816*, London, 1965.

40 Olney, op. cit., pp. 75–7.

41 D. J. V. Jones, 'The new police, crime and people in England and Wales, 1829–1888', *Transactions of the Royal Historical Society*, 5th ser., XXXIII, 1983, pp. 156–8, 161, 167.

6 THE TWO FACES OF THE COUNTRYSIDE

1 A. L. Poole, ed., *Medieval England*, Oxford, 1958, I, pp. 611–13, 625–31; Joyce Godber, *History of Bedfordshire, 1066–1886*, Bedford, 1969, p. 181.

2 Gloucestershire RO, D 23.

3 Florence Maris Turner, ed., *The Diary of Thomas Turner of East Hoathly (1754–1765)*, London, 1925, p. 19.

4 BL Add. MSS 35, 127, fo. 63.

5 E. W. Bovill, *English Country Life 1780–1830*, London, 1962, pp. 201–7; R. J. Olney, *Rural Society and County Government in Nineteenth-Century Lincolnshire*, Lincoln, 1979, pp. 35–6.

6 Bovill, op. cit., pp. 124–6; Christopher Sykes, *Four Studies in Loyalty*, London, 1946, pp. 12–14; E. Wingfield-Stratford, *The Squire and his Relations*, London, 1956, p. 253; E. D. Cumming, ed., *Squire Osbaldeston: his autobiography*, London, 1926, pp. vii–viii, 3, 312.

7 Bovill, op. cit., p. 65.

8 W. Branch Johnson, ed., *'Memorandums For ...': the Carrington Diary*, London, 1973, pp. 76–7, 148, 172.

9 William Salt Library, Stafford, Salt MSS 2/41/42.

10 Turner, op. cit., pp. 30–1, 33.

11 Christopher Morris, ed., *The Journeys of Celia Fiennes*, London, 1947, pp. 16, 31–2.

12 Gloucestershire RO, D 214 F 1/61.

13 M. Blundell, ed., *Blundell's Diary and Letter Book, 1702–28*, Liverpool, 1952, p. 158; Gloucestershire RO, D 674a E21a.

14 C. B. Andrews, ed., *The Torrington Diaries*, London, 1954, pp. 474–5.

15 G. Scott Thomson, *The Russells in Bloomsbury 1669–1771*, London, 1940, pp. 238–9; E. Sussex RO, Ashburnham MSS 3000; E. Suffolk RO, North MSS 331.

16 G. Eland, ed., *Purefoy Letters, 1735–1753*, London, 1931, II, pp. 332, 377–8; Nottinghamshire RO, DD SY 160/xxxviii, 169/xxx.

17 J. Beresford, ed., *Woodforde*, London, 1935, p. 158; Blundell, op. cit., p. 138.

18 B. M. Willmott Dobbie, *An English Rural Community: Batheaston with St. Catherine*, Bath, 1969, p. 66; Robert W. Malcolmson, *Popular Recreations in English Society 1700–1850*, Cambridge, 1973, pp. 124–6.

19 E. A. Goodwyn, *A Suffolk Town in Mid-Victorian England: Beccles in the 1860s*, Beccles, 1965, pp. 25–7.

20 Ibid., p. 29.

21 Olney, op. cit., pp. 13–15.

22 David Jones, 'Rural crime and protest', in G. E. Mingay, ed., *The Victorian Countryside*, London, 1981, II, pp. 571–2; David Jones, 'Thomas Campbell Foster and the rural labourers: incendiarism in East Anglia in the 1840s', *Social History*, I, 1976, pp. 19–20.

23 Cal Winslow, 'Sussex smugglers', in Douglas Hay *et al.*, *Albion's Fatal Tree: crime and society in eighteenth-century England*, London, 1975, pp. 130–3; Branch Johnson, op. cit., pp. 28, 43, 52.

24 Olney, op. cit., pp. 75–7.

25 F. M. L. Thompson, 'Landowners and the rural comunity', in G. E. Mingay, ed., *The Victorian Countryside*, London, 1981, II, p. 459; David Jones, 'Rural crime and protest', in G. E. Mingay, ed., *The Victorian Countryside*, London, 1981, II, pp. 568, 573.

26 John Stevenson, 'Food riots in England, 1792–1818', in John Stevenson and Roland Quinault, eds, *Popular Protest and Public Order: six studies in British history, 1790–1920*, London, 1974, pp. 35, 43–6, 48, 62–3.

27 E. P. Thompson, 'The moral economy of the English crowd in the eighteenth century', *Past and Present*, 50, 1971, p. 121.

28 Board of Agriculture, *The Agricultural State of the Kingdom, 1816*, new edn, Bath, 1970, pp. 185–227.

29 See A. J. Peacock, *Bread or Blood: a study of the agrarian riots in East Anglia in 1816*, London, 1965.

30 E. J. Hobsbawm and George Rudé, *Captain Swing*, Penguin edn, Harmondsworth, 1973, pp. 76–7.

31 Ibid., Appendix I.

32 Ibid., pp. 173, 175, 177.

33 Ibid., pp. 224–5.

34 J. L. and B. Hammond, *The Village Labourer*, new edn, London, 1978, pp. 207, 209.

35 Hobsbawm and Rudé, op. cit., pp. 243–7.

36 Ibid., pp. 250–1.

37 See P. G. Rogers, *Battle in Bossenden Wood: the strange story of Sir William Courtenay*, Oxford, 1961.

7 THE COUNTRYSIDE IN DECLINE, 1870–1914

1 E. J. T. Collins, 'The age of machinery', in G. E. Mingay, ed., *The Victorian Country-side*, London, 1981, I, p. 212.
2 W. A. Armstrong, 'The workfolk', in G. E. Mingay, ed., *The Victorian Countryside*, London, 1981, II, p. 494.
3 Quoted by Armstrong, ibid., p. 499.
4 Ibid., p. 499.
5 John Burnett, 'Country diet', in G. E. Mingay, ed., *The Victorian Countryside*, London, 1981, II, pp. 562–3.
6 Armstrong, op. cit., p. 499.
7 George Cuttle, *The Legacy of the Rural Guardians*, Cambridge, 1934, Appendix VIII.
8 Tenth Duke of Bedford, in the *Journal of the Royal Agricultural Society of England*, X, 1849, pp. 190–1.
9 Susanna Wade Martins, *A Great Estate at Work: the Holkham Estate and its inhabitants in the nineteenth century*, Cambridge, 1980, Appendix 5, pp. 275–82.
10 BPP 1893, R. C. on Labour XXXV, pp. 35–6, quoted in Joan Thirsk and Jean Imray, eds, *Suffolk Farming in the Nineteenth Century*, Suffolk RO, Ipswich, 1958, p. 125.
11 Ibid., p. 126.
12 Ibid., pp. 121–4.
13 Land Enquiry Committee, *The Land: the report of the Land Enquiry Committee*, London, 1913, pp. 84–5, 117, 123.
14 Ibid., pp. 93, 95, 96, 98, 100.
15 Land Agents' Society, *Facts About Land: a reply to 'The Land', the Report of the Unofficial Land Enquiry Committee*, London, 1916, pp. 71, 73–5, 81, 82–3, 89.
16 J. V. Beckett, *The Aristocracy in England 1660–1914*, Oxford, 1986, p. 408.
17 Pamela Horn, *Oxfordshire Village Life: the diaries of George James Dew*, Abingdon, 1983, p. 92.
18 David Spring, 'Land and politics in Edwardian England', *Agricultural History*, 58, 1984, pp. 18–19, 24–5, 27.
19 R. J. Olney, *Rural Society and Country Government in Nineteenth-Century Lincoln-shire*, Lincoln, 1979, p. 179; W. Gavin, *Ninety Years of Family Farming: the story of Lord Rayleigh's and Strutt and Parker farms*, London, 1967, pp. 83, 113.
20 T. W. Beastall, *A North Country Estate: the Lumleys and Saundersons as landowners, 1600–1900*, London, pp. 190, 197–9.
21 Wade Martins, op. cit. pp. 64, 267–9.
22 Olney, op. cit., pp. 179–81.
23 Ibid., p. 172.
24 Jesse Collings, *Land Reform: occupying ownership, peasant proprietary and rural education*, London, 1908, p. ix; F. E. Green, *The Tyranny of the Countryside*, London, 1913, p. 32; William G. Savage, *Rural Housing*, London, 1915, ch. X; B. Seebohm Rowntree and May Kendall, *How the Labourer Lives: a study of the rural labour problem*, London, 1913, pp. 30–1.
25 J. L. and B. Hammond, *The Village Labourer*, new edn, London, 1978, p. 58; W. Hasbach, *History of the English Agricultural Labourer*, 1894, English edn, London, 1908; Hermann Levy, *Large and Small Holdings: a study of English agricultural economics*, Cambridge, 1911, p. 44.
26 Land Enquiry Committee, op. cit., pp. xv–xvi, 67, 135, 153, 189–90, 229, 281–2, 323, 352–3, 356.
27 Land Agents' Society, op. cit., pp. iv–v, 11–14, 72, 83, 144.
28 Ibid., p. 298.

29 Spring, op. cit., pp. 30–1.

30 Ibid., pp. 32–42.

31 J. H. Clapham, *An Economic History of Modern Britain*, III, Cambridge, 1938, pp. 94–5.

32 George Bourne, *Change in the Village*, London, 1912, pp. 23, 54–5, 150–1, 172–4.

8 THE COUNTRYSIDE IN WAR AND PEACE

1 G. P. Jones and A. G. Pool, *A Hundred Years of Economic Development*, London, 1959, ch. 16.

2 Quoted by Sidney Pollard, *The Development of the British Economy 1914–50*, London, 1962, p. 59.

3 P. E. Dewey, 'Government provision of farm labour in England and Wales, 1914–18', *Agricultural History Review*, XXVII, 1979, pp. 111–16.

4 Ibid., pp. 116–20.

5 Ministry of Agriculture, *A Century of Agricultural Statistics: Great Britain 1866–1966*, London, 1968, pp. 82–5.

6 Quoted by Pamela Horn, *Rural Life in England in the First World War*, New York, 1984, pp. 40, 184.

7 Ibid., pp. 27–9.

8 *Ministry of Agriculture*, op. cit., p. 65; Jonathan Brown, *Agriculture in England: a survey of farming, 1870–1947*, Manchester, 1987, pp. 80–4; G. E. Mingay, *British Friesians*, Rickmansworth, 1982, p. 56.

9 F. M. L. Thompson, *English Landed Society in the Nineteenth Century*, London, 1963, pp. 329–31.

10 Ibid., pp. 331–4.

11 Ibid., pp. 334–5, 338–9.

12 Raymond Carr, *English Fox Hunting: a history*, London, 1976, p. 233.

13 Thompson, op. cit., pp. 338–40.

14 Carr, op. cit., p. 233.

15 Edith H. Whetham, *The Agrarian History of England and Wales*, VIII, *1914–1939*, Cambridge, 1978, pp. 238–9, 315.

16 Ibid., pp. 58, 257, 271–2, 282.

17 Ibid., pp. 314–15; Mingay, op. cit., pp. 57–9.

18 Whetham, op. cit., pp. 205–10.

19 Ibid., pp. 205, 208, 267–9.

20 Ibid., pp. 213–39.

21 W. H. Pedley, *Labour on the Land*, London, 1942, pp. 72–3.

22 Ibid., pp. 73, 76.

23 Ibid., pp. 80–3, 85–8.

24 Ibid., pp. 94–100.

25 Ibid., pp. 101–11.

26 Ministry of Agriculture, op. cit., p. 19.

27 Pollard, op. cit., pp. 136–8.

28 C. L. Mowat, *Britain between the Wars 1918–1940*, London, 1955, pp. 438–40.

29 Pollard, op. cit., pp. 141–3.

30 Quoted by Pollard, op. cit., p. 145.

31 Mowat, op. cit., p. 256.

32 Pedley, op. cit., pp. 123–5.

33 Mowat, op. cit., pp. 252, 256–7; Howard Newby, *Country Life: a Social History of Rural England*, London, 1987, pp. 168–70.

34 Pedley, op. cit., pp. 48–50.

239

35 Ibid., pp. 143–7.
36 Ibid., pp. 152–5.
37 Ibid., pp. 155–62.
38 Ibid., pp. 113–19.
39 Ibid., pp. 119–22.
40 See, for example, Christopher Turnor, *Yeoman Calling*, London, 1939.
41 F. G. Thomas, *The Changing Village*, London, 1939.
42 Ibid., 18–19, 30, 69–70, 71–4.
43 *The Times*, 30 April 1931.

INDEX